A Doctor Reminisces

A Doctor Reminisces

Edwin Presley Hall, M.D.

THE STRODE PUBLISHERS, INC.
HUNTSVILLE, ALABAMA 35802

Dedicated to my wife
MILDRED

Table Of Contents

Introduction

A Doctor Reminisces is the true story of a career remarkable in its scope. Beginning with college days when fateful decisions are made, it reveals much about the lives of medical students, the exacting but stimulating training undergone and the pathos and comedy of eventful years in which thousands of patients, no two the same, were treated.

Experiences are related by the author, whose practice included that of physician for the District of Columbia Jail, ship's surgeon on Mediterranean cruises, doctor for a coal mine in West Virginia and for a forest camp in Alabama, medical officer in the army and physician in various kinds of hospitals.

This book tells of unforgettable people, places, things and incidents. All are real even though fictitious names are sometimes substituted. Happenings in greatly varied settings are disclosed. They bring the reader inside the hospitals for close-up looks, even into the operating rooms to watch operations over the surgeon's shoulder.

One chapter is devoted to my father, a general practitioner, or family doctor, who started his practice in a backwoods Alabama region prior to its "horse-and-buggy-doctor" era. There were only a few roads in the area and these were practically impassable at times. He went on horseback to see his patients.

Views of warfare and its results, as seen through the eyes of a surgeon in combat zones, are depicted. Some episodes in the lives of military people during peace and war are told.

Most of my memories are pleasant and these are appreciated more because of the less pleasant ones. Although busy with different activities and thinking of the future, I sometimes indulge in reminiscing and have been encouraged to record my recollections of certain events and personal observations that interested others. May you enjoy reading about them as much as I have enjoyed recalling them.

Doctor On Horseback

The rural Alabama air was still and the heat becoming oppressive at midday on April 24, 1908, when thunder, low and intense, broke the heavy silence. An ominous rumble persisted.

My mother and father were talking quietly at my bedside. Apparently it was time for a crisis in my childhood illness when there would be a turn for rapid improvement or for a worsening in my condition.

Looking out the window, Mama saw an unusual dark cloud in the southwest. "That's strange. Doctor, come and look at this bad cloud," she said to Papa, sounding worried. "It's big at the top and little at the bottom."

He studied it a moment. "It's shaped like a funnel, looks like there is wind in it and it seems to be getting closer."

They checked the doors and windows in preparation for the onslaught of wind and rain that surely would replace the stillness. Then they waited.

Mama called attention to the buggy, which had been standing in the driveway, rolling toward the gate, pushed by the wind. They talked in hushed tones, wondering what would happen when the full force of the storm struck.

Papa, watching and listening to its approach, must have had a premonition that all the knowledge and skill he had acquired as a doctor would be needed in the wake of the impending destruction. What education and experience he possessed had not been easily obtained. "Well, Wife, all we can do is wait and see," he said.

He had once read a book about a horse-and-buggy doctor, enjoyed reading of that doctor's experiences in a rural practice, and then said to me, "I came along before he did and was a doctor on horseback." That was before he moved to town.

When Papa first began the practice of medicine, there were not many roads in the area, few regarded as all-weather and none paved. Often, homes were not on a real road. He went to some places that could only be reached by horseback; anyway, he had no buggy then.

The way William Presley Hall, M.D., struggled to get an education can best be told in his own words written when he was about eighty years old:

"By the request of some of my children, I am making an attempt to give a short sketch of my business interests and how and when I obtained the way to get what education I received.

"First by the help of other members of my family I learned my letters at home, at about six to seven years of age. When eight years old I went to my first school which was taught in a pine pole house that was built by a community of new comers from Georgia for a church house and was named New Georgia.

"The school was taught by an old man by the name of Cap Hyde who could not hear good and knew just a little more than I did. The students were self controlled and were allowed to talk in the room during study hours if they chose, and spell out as loud as they could holler while studying their lessons. This is just a little of the way this school was managed and the mediator carrying on.

"After this I went short terms to the community schools in that locality, some better than others. I worked on the farm and attended school between the making and the gathering seasons of crops each year until I was nineteen years old, studying such primary branches as were taught in the schools of that locality at that time. At which time I learned of a school that was being taught in Dekalb County (Alabama), some three miles out from Collinsville, which was about forty-five or fifty miles from where we lived at Brooksville in Blount County.

"There were no buggies nor other ways of conveyance in the county at that time other than wagons. So I decided I would go and investigate the conditions up there. My parents were willing for me to go but were not able to finance me as we made our living at home, both rations and clothes.

"I had home made clothes and plenty of supplies such as meat, syrup, fruit and bread stuff. So I walked to where the school was, which was called Andrews Institute and was financed in part by the Methodist Conference supplemented by the people.

"After talking with the principal of the school I learned I could arrange to stay with him, as he was boarding some other boys who were going to school there, and pay my board by furnishing my rations, such as we had, and paying for the cooking of the same and furnishing my own bed. This I decided to do, after I found I could get work close by at a rock quarry to pay for my cooking and washing.

"Then I walked back home, loaded my stuff on a wagon and got a driver to carry it to the place. I entered school and stayed to the end of that term. By working evenings after school adjourned and getting up lessons at night and getting up at daylight and working until breakfast each morning and of Saturdays, I worked enough to pay for my washing, cooking and tuition.

"I went home in May and helped make the crop, went back at opening of next term, stayed two or three months, got sick and went home and helped make the crop that year. I stood an examination, obtained a third grade license and taught school in the summer after crops were laid by.

"That fall I was twenty-one years old. The next year I made a crop for myself. My father boarded me and charged me no rent. I worked his land and he gave me a good young mule.

"I sold my crop in the field, left my mule at my father's and entered school in Fowler's Cove Academy in Blount County between Blountsville and Bangor, stayed in school there two years. Prof. Addams was the teacher there. Each year while in school there, I sold books during the summer vacations, at which I made good.

"During the mean time I swapped the mule my father gave me for a smaller mule and got fifty dollars to boot, swapped that mule for a pretty young horse which I sold for one hundred dollars, made one hundred and fifty dollars for the first mule.

"Then next, after being in Fowler's Cove in school, I was an assistant teacher in school at Blountsville. At this time and place I got permission to have access to Dr. Whalie's office and books which I studied while assisting in teaching.

"I did this preparatory to entering Medical School, which I did that fall. I had no help or any money except what I had managed to get up myself, with what I made teaching, selling books and out of my crop I sold in the field and trading on the mule my father gave me. Besides I had traded and picked up, one way and another, a bunch of young cattle which I traded for 2 mule colts. I got one year's growth on them before I sold them and made pretty good.

"By the time I got the odds and ends all together I had enough to enter medical school, which I did in Atlanta, Ga. The school, then called Southern Medical College, was incorporated into Emory University.

"At that time there was no law to prohibit anyone from practicing medicine whom the people might risk and the rules and regulations of the medical schools were not like now. The students were allowed to graduate after taking two years, provided they could make the required grades.

"So with the two years of study in Dr. Whalie's office and two years in the medical school, I gave satisfaction on my examinations and got my diploma. But some students had to take four years before they could pass.

"One boy in my class the second year was making his third year and failed on the examination. He was a boy who had plenty of money and he spent too much time out of the class room. My money was so limited, I had to make each day count for all it was worth. That was one place I learned that too much money was not good for anyone.

"The students were not allowed to graduate for less time than two years full time in school, but at the end of my first year and examination, they gave me a certificate of qualification and I practiced between the sessions and did a good deal of work. So with what I made that summer in the practice with what I had on hand, I got through the whole time and only borrowed thirty dollars.

"When I came back I changed my boarding place. The year before I boarded with a farmer near to the brow of the mountain this side of Big Spring valley. He had a small grocery store which I used for an office and slept in his dwelling.

"When I moved I boarded with a man who ran a public cotton gin and had a small log house across the road from his dwelling where he sold groceries.

"I used the log house for an office and slept in it through the summer the first year but moved into the dwelling to sleep when the weather got cold. I stayed there two years and during the second year bought an improved tract of land and had a house built on it.

"This was 1887 and in the spring of 1888 I married and began housekeeping in said house and have never moved but one time since. Whatever financial success I have had since then I attribute it very largely to the faithful help and the management of our family and home economics to my wife who is still with me.

"We are keeping house now by ourselves and she is my boss and all the one I ever had. But she is kind and agreeable and sometimes lets me do as I choose about some things. Anyway she is taking very good care of me now.

"After I married I bought several places which were unimproved and one time had over thirteen hundred acres of land. So in connection with my practice I have had a good deal of land cleared, have operated saw mills, cotton gin and other machinery. I have had a lot of land cleared and put in cultivation, lumber sawed, shingles cut and houses built. I can recall thirty odd houses I have built or had built, some very cheap and some of them rather expensive, but never lived in but two, only moving one time since I married.

"Besides other things I have done, I have traded a good deal in live stock and merchandise in connection with the practice of medicine but I gave my first attention always to the interest of my patients and the spare time to other things.

"We had a rather large family but we never had any real trouble with any of our children except the parting with the ones that died.

"Just prior to the World War my assets all told were around one hundred thousand dollars, my liabilities practically nothing. Circumstances beyond our control consumed it.

"What we have is invested in our children of which we have living three daughters and two sons, also three granddaughters and two grandsons all of whom we are proud."

He continued the practice of medicine as long as he could, even seeing patients in his home and prescribing for them in his last year.

Papa was a general practitioner who began his medical career as a country doctor in the nineteenth century in an area where there were no hospitals and few pharmacies. He bought drugs and supplies from wholesale drug firms. In his office were shelves of big medicine bottles and gallon glass jugs of syrups for use as vehicles in formulations. There were boxes and bottles of pills and powders, as well as empty containers and glass bottles in various sizes under the counter. Narcotics were kept in a combination lock safe. The few surgical instruments and supplies were under covers.

He prepared, mixed and dispensed the medicines that he prescribed. In his medicine bag were rows of vials held in place with fasteners. When called to a home he would select the appropriate drug for the sickness. Sometimes a liquid would be poured into a clean, empty bottle that the family had saved and washed carefully.

When a particular powder seemed to be indicated, he might make little packets or charts in small paper squares. This was done by taking the powder out of the container on the point of a knife and placing it on the paper, which would then be folded. He would leave six or eight of these perhaps, with directions for use. Sometimes the powders were put in capsules.

There were few specific drugs for a particular disease or illness. There were sedatives, stimulants, analgesics, antipyretics and antiseptics. Calomel, castor oil and Epsom salts were commonly used as purgatives and paregoric for diarrhea. Some medicines were given as alteratives, as tonics and to aid digestion. Prescribing was, to a large extent, a matter of treating symptoms and for these there were many preparations from which to choose.

Medicines prescribed were commonly compounded or prepared for use either by the prescribing doctor or by a pharmacist where available. Patent medicines that a person could buy at a drug store or elsewhere were exceptions.

Medicines today generally come from the pharmaceutical houses ready for the patient to take when prescribed by the doctor. Most of them were not known early in this century, certainly not in the form now used.

Physical methods of treatment were also employed. The doctor sometimes resorted to cauterization by heat as well as by chemical means to control bleeding, to treat a tumor or lesion or for antisepsis. Hot soaks and poultices were used for swellings and inflammations.

Heat was applied for shock, cold and exposure and during chills. Hot-water bottles and blankets were commonly available. Ice caps, cold applications and bathing were used to reduce fever. This might be continued for hours when the fever was high and persistent. Prolonged rest in bed was commonly employed as a therapeutic measure when there was no treatment of choice.

"Give Mr. Nichols the medicine every four hours, just like I told you, and bathe him all over today," members of the sick man's family were instructed.

"We're afraid to give him a bath, Doctor," was the surprising response of one of them as if speaking of a drastic procedure. "He hasn't had one since he was a boy and went to the creek."

Patients were advised as to their diets and preparation of foods, consideration being given to the capabilities of the individual and of the kitchen in the home and the availability of certain kinds of food.

The instructions sometimes included a method of cooking such as, "Put the pieces of chicken in a fruit jar, put the jar in a pot of water, cover and boil the water until the chicken is done. This will save its juice that you need for nourishment." There would be a question and answer period.

Broken bones were set and splinted. Abscesses were lanced and simple operations were performed. For major surgery a patient would usually have to be sent to a city and even there the techniques often left much to be desired.

Wound infection was not uncommon. All things considered, surgery was generally the treatment of last resort. "Expectant treatment," or "masterful inactivity," or a "wait-and-see" method was often chosen and not much was done, certainly nothing drastic, in the hope that nature would take care of the condition.

The reason for waiting in many instances was to at least avoid harming the patient when intervention was considered risky and the results uncertain. Less conservative practitioners might regard this as neglect.

Pus was commonly seen in surgical incisions as well as in accidental wounds. There was a time when it was regarded as a normal part of healing and was called "laudable pus." If an individual had enough resistance to overcome the infection, healing would generally take place eventually, but more time would be required than in the case of an uninfected incision, and an ugly scar could be expected.

Peritonitis, inflammation of the lining of the cavity, often occurred in abdominal cases. No antibiotics or "miracle" drugs were available then. It was miraculous that doctors and nature

15

accomplished so much when effective means of treatment were so meager.

A dose of salts, magnesium sulphate, was sometimes taken for an attack of appendicitis in the early stage, an example of a practice which became outmoded. Purgation was not an uncommon method of treating gastrointestinal disorders in general, not just constipation.

Liquid diet and rest in bed with ice cap applied were commonly advised for pain and tenderness in the lower right side of the abdomen. The acute inflammation might subside if there were no perforation.

Papa often took me with him on house calls out in the country when I was a boy. In answer to one of these calls we went to a small farmhouse that was filled with a very offensive odor and found the farmer in bed with pus flowing from an opening in his navel. He gave a history of acute appendicitis followed by abdominal distension and tenderness.

Apparently the man's appendix had ruptured, and peritonitis resulted. Pus from the abscess that formed had managed to force an opening through a relatively weak spot in the abdominal wall. Fortunately there was natural drainage and he recovered.

Papa was amused when I made my exit for the porch and fresh air as he applied a large absorbent dressing to the patient's abdomen. Such smells would become familiar to me also in time.

Saddle bags were part of the equipment of the doctor on horseback. Medicine and supplies were carried in this pair of leather bags that had a broad strap between them which was placed across the horse's back next to the saddle, one bag hanging on each side. This was easier than riding with a conventional doctor's medicine bag.

Henry Jenkins came to the house one night on horseback to get Papa to go over some country roads to see his sick wife. The sickness was described.

"I'll wait and go back with you to show you the way. It's kind of hard to find if you don't know where it is," Henry said as Papa made preparations.

They soon left, Papa riding "Hogan," a big bay horse of which he was rather proud. He was gone for several hours. The next day he told Mama about an incident of the night trip. "On the way to the Jenkins' place we saw something laying by the side of the road. When we got close it looked like it might be a man, and I told Henry to get off his horse and look. It was a drunk man and he knew him."

"Why didn't you get off to see?" Mama asked.

"Because I was on the tallest horse," was his answer, a twinkle in his eye.

Some of my earliest remembrances of childhood are of being awakened by the phone ringing in the middle of cold nights and hearing Papa talking with people who called him to come and see the sick or injured.

"What is her complaint? How does she feel bad?" he would ask, then "Where does she hurt?" and "How long has she been sick? Why did you wait until tonight to call me?"

He already knew, of course, that the pain a person has had all day or longer seems worse in the night. Too, the sufferer and the family become more worried in the darkness of a long night and they then suspect the worst.

"Where do you live?" he would ask. After a few more questions and if he did not know the location of a home far out in the country, the caller was asked, "Can you tell me how to get to your place?" and, perhaps, "Could you have someone meet me where I turn off the High Point road and show me the way to your house?"

He would dress, get his medicine bag and leave as I, in my warm place in bed, went back to sleep. When older, I sometimes went with him, especially after learning to drive the Model-T Ford which in time replaced the horse.

If the night call was for an obstetrical case it might mean that we would spend the rest of the night there. In this event he would ask the people if they had a place for me to sleep while he attended the woman in labor. When the cry of the new member of the family changed the quietness of the night into a stir of activity, I knew that we would soon be on our way home.

All cases were treated in their homes as there was no hospital in the area. One night when I went with Papa to see Mrs. Mary Bowen near delivery time, she was found seriously ill and having exhausting convulsions with periods of unconsciousness. He told me that it was a case of eclampsia. In accordance with the accepted practice of the era, he tried to control the convulsions and shorten them with an anesthetic, chloroform. In this instance the results were dramatic.

When a convulsion started he would drop a few drops from

a can, with a wick, onto a gauze mask held over Mrs. Bowen's nose and mouth, not enough to completely anesthetize her. He found that the severity and duration of convulsions were reduced by this and reasoned that her waning strength was being conserved.

After a while it became necessary for him to give attention to other measures. For the first time I was to treat a patient. He showed me how to administer the anesthetic, which I did as he had done.

Standing there watching this woman, so desperately in need of help, through that fateful night, I had the satisfaction, not to be obtained in any other way, of seeing a seriously ill patient start on the road to recovery.

Before we got an automobile Papa used a horse and buggy, that is, after he moved into town and quit making calls by horseback. In cold weather he used a heavy laprobe and sometimes under it he had some covered hot bricks or other heating device so his feet would not get too cold. His favorite horse was the big, red, mischievous one called Sam.

The children were allowed to drive Maud, a gentle mare of mature age. She was of medium size, brown with white face. She knew the way home if we did not. If a peice of harness came loose, she would stop and stand still until we found and fastened it.

One day while Papa was hitching Sam to a post in front of the house, Mrs. Smith, age fifty-two, came walking down the sidewalk, hesitated, charted a course away from Sam and said, "Every time I come by that horse he runs at me and shows his teeth."

"That's his way of speaking to you. I don't think that he would hurt you," Papa replied.

"He's not funny. I think he's dangerous; anyway, you'd better see that he's tied good. I've been wanting to talk to you about something else. I'd like to have a baby. Is there something you could do?"

"You asked me too late. There is nothing I can do now. You should have come to me sooner," he answered with a grin as he came in and she went on her way laughing.

Papa came from a large pioneer family. His father was a farmer and preacher, not a slave owner. Where they lived would probably be classified today as marginal farmland.

All of his family had to work hard. Even so, they managed

to raise a few extra hogs each year to have plenty of meat for travelers who might tarry with them. There were not many hotels in that part of the country then.

Jesse Hall, one of Papa's older brothers, was a captain in the Confederate Army. He wrote a letter home just before he was killed at Chickamauga near Chattanooga, Tennessee, in the Battle Above the Clouds. His last words were "Follow me, men."

Papa told me that after he was graduated from the medical school in Atlanta, now called Emory, he thought that he would practice for a few years near his old home, save some money and go to Texas. His services were in demand in an area on Sand Mountain in North Alabama where there was no doctor at that time, and he quickly gained recognition after deciding to start there. He accepted almost anything in payment, such as chickens or calves, as there was not much money to be had during that period.

His reputation grew, with a busy practice over a large area in which he was the only doctor for a while and he began to accumulate property, land and livestock. With it all, he felt needed and tied down to that locality. An older brother who was physically powerful and adventurous did go to Texas and into a region where the West was still wild. He was shot and killed by a gunman.

The doctor on horseback made long trips in practicing his profession and became acquainted with people in the valleys as well as on the mountain. They took a personal interest in him.

Margaret Ann Young, a pretty girl living in Big Spring Valley, was also well and favorably known. "You should meet her," people often told him. They met at a party in the valley and the meeting seemed foreordained. He learned much later that her friends had been recommending him to her as a "good catch." The progress of the courtship was observed by both the mountain and valley people. Soon they were married and moved into the new house that had been built near his country office. This was on March 18, 1888. It would be many years before they would move to Albertville, Alabama, where there were a few other doctors.

They lived happily ever after but not without their share of striving, serving, sacrificing and sorrow. Neither the life of a frontier physician nor that of his wife was an easy one. While undergoing hardships and personal grief, they maintained dignity and allowed no lapse in service to those in need of such as they could provide.

My parents were always deeply devoted from the first but in playing their professional roles before each other and the public, each adopted a sort of formality in speaking of or to the other. She always called him "Doctor" and he called her "Wife."

She took telephone calls and talked with people who came to the house when he was not there. He was frequently away at night and she often slept with a loaded pistol under her pillow to be prepared for a possible intruder. Fortunately she never had to use it. Maybe outsiders suspected that the Department of Defense was ready.

They had ten children. Two died on the day of birth. Berna May, born May 23, 1890, died on June 30, 1891, of dysentery, an intestinal infection with persistent severe diarrhea that took the lives of many babies in that era but is now rarely a problem in this country.

Annie Vida died at the age of twelve with typhoid fever, a disease almost never seen in the United States in recent times. Burtis Olson, age fifteen, and Papa also had it but both recovered.

Papa thought that the well water might be contaminated. Typhoid was common then. He had another and deeper well bored in the front yard for drinking water and enclosed it in a small latticed building. The water from it was clear and cold, pleasing to the taste and evidently pure. There were no more cases of typhoid or other intestinal diseases in the family.

Water from the old well was used only for special purposes such as boiling clothes or putting out a fire. Once while drawing water from it, the windlass handle slipped out of my hand, flew back and struck a front tooth, knocking off a corner of it.

There was a third well on the home place. It was in the barnyard and used to water the stock. Fortunately water was plentiful and eventually we had a city water supply. The chore of drawing water and bringing it into the house in buckets became a thing of the past, a memory.

With purified water and inoculation to produce immunity from typhoid, the water-borne diseases are largely in the past in this country. The intestinal disorders of infants that were common during the summer months are now unusual when there is adequate refrigeration and better care of food and water.

As certain diseases prevalent early in this century have almost been eliminated, they have been replaced by other problems that cause worry. With medical advances, improvement in hygiene and health facilities and greater knowledge, people will still thoughtlessly or deliberately do things that are known to be harmful to the body and mind.

In those early days when there were few specialists, clinics or hospitals, the family doctor never knew what condition or emergency he would be called upon to treat. As a general practitioner he had to do the best he could.

"My brother Billy drowned in a post hole; Mama said to come quick!" a panting boy managed to utter between breaths.

"Come with me. Where do you live? What's your name?" Papa said, reaching for his medicine bag.

"Joe Martin—we live on the Boaz road," he answered while rushing to the buggy. Papa knew the family and where they lived beyond our home.

On the way while pushing his horse to the limit, he learned from Joe that the telephone company was digging holes for new telephone poles near their home. One had been left uncovered and was partly filled with water. While playing near it, his little brother had looked inside, lost his balance and fallen in while hunting for his ball.

Billy had been pulled out of the water and placed on the grass not far from the post hole. He was lying there prone, wet, not breathing, apparently lifeless.

"Stand back," Papa told the neighbors who had gathered around the boy. "Somebody get a blanket!"

He turned Billy over with face down and to the side, felt in his mouth, pulled his tongue out, stood over him—one foot on each side—raised his hips to get the water out of his lungs, and then did artificial respiration as the silent, somber crowd watched intently for any sign of life.

As time wore on the watchers became more pessimistic. Some said, "He's gone." Papa persisted. After what seemed an awful long time he thought that he felt a response in the boy, hesitated, looked, resumed. Then he saw the chest expand. Now there was no doubt. With little more assistance the youngster began to breathe unaided.

"He's alive!" several shouted. The parents cried for joy. Mr. and Mrs. Martin had their Billy back. "Thank God."

The boy's normal color gradually returned. Wrapped in

blankets and put in bed he soon was answering questions. "Yes, I feel good. Did anybody get my ball?"

Incidentally, the people of the telephone company were also relieved when Billy Martin recovered from near drowning. They were happy to pay the doctor a substantial fee for his part in making this possible.

Every day was eventful for a general practitioner in Albertville early in this century, but none was like that one mentioned earlier in April of 1908 when the dark funnel with a great cloud above it appeared.

As my parents watched it approach, the air became filled with whirling objects picked up by the wind. The house trembled. Some large trees nearby crashed down toward the northeast, adding to the noise of the storm.

It was evident that the main part of the cyclone or tornado, or whatever it might be called, was very close. Our house shook, seeming almost suspended. Would it hold together or be destroyed?

The cyclone was one of the worst ever suffered by Alabama and it left Albertville almost totally wrecked. Main Street lay in ruins and many homes and business buildings were destroyed. Our home was spared.

Many people, approximately thirty in and near town, were killed and over one hundred and fifty injured, many more than could be adequately treated by the few doctors in Albertville. There were no facilities for coping with such a catastrophe.

The Seventh District Agricultural School temporarily was turned into a hospital for the injured but help was needed to care for them. Suffering on such a scale had never been witnessed by the townspeople and many families were bereaved.

Ministers, undertakers, doctors, and all citizens did more and served more people in distress than they would have thought possible before the disaster struck. Stores of food and material of all kinds had been blown away or ruined. There was so much to be done and so few citizens were not seriously affected.

Doctors and nurses from Gadsden and other towns were brought in by special trains to assist the local doctors in treating the large number of patients who had been injured. Military supplies such as tents, blankets, clothing and food were sent in to provide for the needs of those left destitute.

After the cyclone many fantastic stories were told about

things done by it. Letters and papers from Albertville were found scattered over Tennessee. The wind's terrific force had driven pointed objects into tree trunks. Its power was appalling.

The cyclone picked up a huge kerosene storage tank, hurling it through the sky toward the eastern part of town over the wide path of destruction. An old woman looking heavenward and seeing it said in awe, "God help us, here comes the Lord in a balloon!"

My illness left with the storm, it seemed. Recovery was rapid and Papa took me with him in the buggy to see the devastated business area. Debris was everywhere, a scene of desolation such as I would not see again until World War II.

We, like many other families, had a storm pit dug soon after the cyclone. Ours, in the back yard, was covered with a low building, had steps leading down into it and was provided with benches to use in the event we sat out a windstorm there. Some storm pits in the area were dug into the earthen banks on roadsides near homes.

The main use we found for ours was for housing potted ferns and other ornamental plants that Mama liked to grow. In favorable weather the pots were arranged on the broad top of the balustrade around the front porch.

Unfortunately for its purpose, water rose in the pit. Eventually its cover was removed and the pit was refilled, but for years it was a reminder of the havoc witnessed in the spring of 1908. Among other reminders were the upturned roots of trees that had been felled.

Time marched on. Ways of living changed gradually. A doctor's son naturally acquired some knowledge of families in a community and their ailments. A teacher might appear to be in excellent health during the week, while busy and subject to the stresses of his profession, yet suffer with severe migraine headache on weekends when there is opportunity to relax. A patient may have worries and tensions that are not known to his or her family. Diseases and disorders have little respect for the social standing or position of people. A drug addict may be in a family that would be least suspected of harboring such an individual.

After having gone far enough in school to be considered reliable in recording items and amounts, I became a part-time bookkeeper in Papa's office, sitting on a high stool at a desk in a fenced area near the front entrance. This seemed curious to some men who came in. At that time and place adults were frequently seen who could not read or write. Attendance at school had not been compulsory.

The amounts charged for medical attention in the early part of this century seem very small compared to charges today. These entries copied from an actual account in a 1912 ledger are typical:

April 16	– To medicine	.25
June 6	– To visit	1.00
Aug. 10	– To prescription	.50
Sept. 8	– To prescription	.50
May 8	– To visit wife	1.00
May 8	– To 2nd visit night	1.50
May 9	– To prescription wife	.75
May 10	– To prescription & visit	1.75

It should be mentioned that a prescription included the medicine itself because the drugs were supplied by the doctor.

The charge for a visit or house call varied with the distance and time required. For many miles out of town as much as three dollars might have been charged. In an obstetrical case a charge of ten dollars for a delivery was not unusual.

For a proper comparison with today's prices, the purchasing power of the dollar then and now would have to be considered. Goods and services were comparatively cheap in the early part of the twentieth century. Too, one might want to give consideration to the quality of medical care in the two periods.

As a basis for comparison, a few more of the 1912 entries are copied:

April 15 – 1 gallon syrup	.60
Jan. 29 – 1 wagon	20.00
May 23 – 1 cow	30.00
May 26 – 7 gal. milk	.50
March 28 – 100 lb. flour	2.00
Jan. 13 – 1 hog	6.00
May 4 – 1 horse	100.00
June 8 – 15 lb. beef	.90

A suit of clothes could be bought for less than fifteen dollars, a pair of shoes for two, and a shirt for fifty cents.

It may be argued that the old-time family doctor compensated, to some extent at least, for his weakness in science by his proficiency in the art of practicing medicine. He is remembered as having more intimate knowledge of the individual patient, the family, the environment and the home.

The old family doctor is also remembered as having a better bedside manner, more time, patience, understanding and sympathy. Maybe he was no more kind or considerate or personally interested than the modern physician, but he gave the impression that he was.

Papa tried to keep abreast of the advances in medicine in the midst of all the distractions with which he had to contend. He read the literature as time permitted, attended the local medical meetings and participated in the discussions. He was interested in new drugs that were introduced and studied the so-called miracle drugs as soon as they appeared.

He never took vacations but went to the county fair one day and saw the sword swallower, the ossified man, the fire eater, etc. The most interesting thing he saw was a man exhibited in a sideshow as a freak. The man's esophagus was closed so food had to be put in his stomach through a fistula in his abdominal wall. Papa managed to sit and talk with him in the restaurant where he went to eat.

Automobiles brought new kinds of injuries. One that became common was a particular kind of bone fracture, the broken radius in the forearm due to the crank kicking back when a car was being cranked to start the motor. This was before the automatic electrical starters. The danger of getting such a fracture was minimized by holding the crank handle with the thumb and fingers on the same side. Cranking often required long and strenuous exertion. Although Papa did not always approve of the speed at which I drove, he was quite willing for me to do the driving.

Treatment results then, as well as many decades later, were not always precisely as desired or expected. Some were especially worrisome.

One day while far out in the country, Papa was asked to see a farmer living in an out-of-the-way place who had been injured and thought to have a broken arm.

The man was found to have a fracture, a complete break, of the upper end of the humerus near the shoulder joint, a difficult one to treat. The fracture was reduced by replacing the fragments into their normal positions and splinted as well as possible under the circumstances.

This man was to come to the office in town for further attention but did not and, incidentally, did not pay for what had been done. Afterwards he fell off his front porch and injured the arm again but did not report this to Papa. Instead, he sued him for a large sum when he learned that the bone alignment was imperfect after it had healed.

Papa worried over both the medical and legal aspects of the case. Although the court decided in his favor, the whole matter was a lengthy, unpleasant experience. Remembrances of such could make a doctor hesitant in giving emergency treatment in certain situations.

The responsibilities shouldered by a general practitioner in that area and era were heavy. Strong shoulders, actually as well as figuratively, were needed.

A hired hand, looking at Papa's broad back as he bent over a piece of equipment, remarked, "You used to be a powerful man with a back like that." Looking around at the man, he asked, "What do you mean by 'used to be'?"

My parents shared a rich life for nearly fifty-three years after their marriage in 1888. Perhaps one reason why Mama always called Papa "Doctor" was because he was her doctor, even for pregnancies and deliveries, and was the doctor for her children, contrary to the custom established for valid reasons which decrees that one physician should ask another to treat members of his own family.

At the time and place they established their home, he was the only doctor and did what he thought best under the circumstances. So he treated us, calling on some other doctor when in his opinion it was indicated.

One Sunday after church he took me to the office of a friend for minor surgery, assisted with the operation and, after we returned home in the buggy, gave me a drink for pain when the local anesthetic was no longer effective. On another occasion he treated me himself.

Cutting off the tops of cornstalks to use as cow feed, I had held the stalk in my left hand, back toward me, striking the stalk below with a long, sharp butcher knife. I must have become absentminded thinking of pretty girls seen the day before.

The knife struck the knuckle of my left index finger, cutting the tendon used in extending the finger. Papa seemed as sorry as I did that this had happened. A splint had to be worn until it healed. The good results that were obtained, with no limitation of motion or function, included the valuable lessons that I had learned.

I do not recall having any more mishaps or illnesses until having influenza during the widespread epidemic of 1918 when thousands died with a particularly virulent type of the disease. Not much is remembered about the effects in my case except for turning red, generalized soreness, becoming rather weak and being visited by the preacher.

Burtis, my brother, was much older than I. When he was grown and even before, many people called him "Doc." Before entering medical school he taught in the public school which I attended. He believed that I could finish two grades in one year, tested me on the subjects in the grade ahead of mine and got me promoted. The wisdom of this may be questioned as I was generally younger than my classmates thereafter. He, however, thought it best for me.

He taught me many things and in general did as is expected of a big brother. The first time I ever shot a gun he showed me how to load it, how to sight, take aim, hold the stock against my shoulder while standing properly and squeeze the trigger.

Graduating from Vanderbilt University in 1917, he began practice by treating the employees of the construction company that was building Camp Gordon in Georgia for training World War I soldiers. After that he returned to Albertville and entered private practice in partnership with another doctor.

He considered this as temporary, expecting to be called for army duty soon, and spoke of "when I get back from the war." His practice was general and became very active and there were many house calls to make at irregular times.

Once when I went with him far out in the country, we took our lunches with us. At noon we found a pleasant roadside place to eat and opened the food bags which contained sandwiches and cake. Ordinarily, if bought at a country store, it would have been cheese or sardines and crackers and a bottle of soda water.

He ate his piece of cake before anything else and I asked him why. "You never know what might happen," he said. "I didn't want to miss eating that."

His office was in the business section of Albertville on

Main Street. He had married a hometown girl while in medical school and they had a baby girl. When we were together he talked about his plans for the future, about decorating the home he had bought on East Main Street. "Big Brother" did not have the connotation of evil that has been associated with the term in recent years.

When the influenza epidemic came it was the worst ever known. There was hardly a family without sickness, and this during a great war. Burtis, out of medical school only a little over a year, was busy at all hours of the day and night.

His throat became sore in the second week of October and he did not feel very well but continued to make calls. One night his car became overheated and he had to get water from a creek to put in the radiator. Afterwards his temperature became elevated and it was apparent that he was suffering from the contagious disease that so many of his patients had.

Acute bronchitis, then bronchopneumonia, complicated the influenza. A young doctor with excellent reputation and cheerful confidence came from Boaz to see him but there was no effective medicine. His condition rapidly became worse.

We were permitted to see him, wearing gauze masks as protection, and stood by his bed. He looked up at us and in an attempt at levity said, "You look like a bunch of night riders." That was the last time. He lived only five days after being confined to bed.

Often we ponder over what might have been if drugs and treatment methods presently in use had been available in times past. No doubt future generations will have like thoughts concerning the present one.

After 1918 my world was not quite the same. The following year I went away to school and thereafter was on the mountaintop only during vacations and on visits to Albertville.

Changes taking place had been accelerated by the world war. Modernization does not always mean improvement but it is doubtful if many would like to return to the good old days in all ways.

Tuscaloosa, The University Of Alabama, And Virginia

Tuscaloosa, Alabama, and the Black Warrior River flowing by this university city are named for the gigantic, courageous Indian chief Tuskalusa who fought DeSoto in 1540. His name came from two ancient Choctaw words, tuska ("warrior") and lusa ("black").

This city was the capital of Alabama from 1826 to 1846 and some old residences date from that time. One of these is the Governor's Mansion, which still stands proudly off University Avenue. Magnificent oaks line the wide streets and Tuscaloosa has been referred to as "The Druid City."

The University of Alabama, founded in 1831, was burned by the Union Army during the Civil War, only a few structures being left standing. Enormous trees contribute to the beauty of the campus. The Gorgas Oak was named to honor a family intimately associated with the university, in front of whose home it stood.

General William Crawford Gorgas played a prominent role in the control of yellow fever which made possible the building of the Panama Canal and changed the Canal Zone from an unhealthy, unsafe place to one with conditions excellent for health. The Gorgas Institute in Panama is another living memorial to this great man.

Principal colleges of the university, including Arts and Sciences, Law, Engineering and Education, are on the main campus together with the library, gymnasium, stadium, student union and numerous other buildings. The university's medical school is in Birmingham and other branches of the university are located in various cities of the state.

Bryce State Hospital for the Insane and Partlow State School are just north of the campus and beyond them is the Veterans Hospital. The main part of the city is to the south. Mound State Monument, not far away, contains thirty-four Indian mounds on a tract of land preserved in cooperation with the National Park Service.

My introduction to Tuscaloosa and "The Capstone," as the institution at the top of the state's educational system was called, was at summer school in the period after World War I. Upon graduation from high school, I took a review course at the university in preparation for the state examination for teachers.

The university and Bryce Hospital had approximately the same enrollment. The latter was jokingly referred to as the Postgraduate School. At that time the Veterans Hospital had not been established.

That summer I roomed in Manley Hall, one of the large dormitories facing the central quadrangle of the campus. Many of those taking courses were teachers complying with requirements for continued employment or pursuing subjects that interested them personally.

Hazing, as practiced then, became known to me firsthand soon after my arrival in the dormitory. The most common method was the vigorous application of a bed slat across the freshman's buttocks while he bent over grasping his ankles without bending the knees.

After summer school I took the examinations and as a result was awarded first-, second- and third-type teachers' certificates that fulfilled the educational requirements for teaching in the public schools of the state. Instead of teaching, however, I returned to the university in the fall as a premedical student with chemistry as my major subject. For this session three other boys and I rented a room over a drug store and ate our meals in the same building. We had two double-decker beds, two tables, and four chairs, but not much else in the room. Power of concentration was a requirement for study.

A big poker game was in progress one Saturday night when an excited student rushed in to report that the blue coats were coming. Thinking that a police raid had begun, some of the boys went out by way of the rear second-story windows, dropping to the ground below. The only casualty was a minor ankle sprain.

Hazing, other than corporal, was done in various ways. On

one occasion I directed traffic at a street intersection on University Avenue. Some jokers would drive directly toward me, only to deviate at the last moment.

The night of the first freshman class meeting, about six of us were walking to it when intercepted by a group of upperclassmen, including a varsity baseball player who later played in a major league but at the time was enjoying a reputation as a breaker of bed slats.

The group detoured us to a hill back of the campus and told us to wait there while they went after slats. As soon as they left we ran down the hill in the dark, not knowing what was at the bottom of it.

Suddenly we went off a high creek bank, through the air and tangled blackberry vines into water, losing our little green "rat" caps temporarily. After noisily splashing around in the water we got out of the creek on the other side and decided to return to our rooms by a railroad track nearby.

The Southern, the Gulf, Mobile and Ohio and the Louisville and Nashville railroads served Tuscaloosa. We did not know on whose track we were walking but knew that it went in the direction we wanted to go.

We came to a trestle over a ravine and walked over it wondering what we would do should a train come across at that time. If we had seen its height and distance, as I did one day much later, we would have been more worried, but we got back to the campus without incident.

Joe Sewell, brother of Toxie Sewell, who was the athletic coach and one of my teachers in high school, played shortstop for Cleveland in the World Series his first year out of college. Another brother, Luke, became catcher on the Cleveland team and they were joined by Riggs Stephenson. So one-third of the lineup of the World Champions that year could be from the same Alabama team I watched play.

At the first football game, the freshmen were supposed to do a snake dance on the field before the game, running in single file and criss-crossing the gridiron several times. In climbing the fence between the stadium and playing field, the seat of my pants was torn by a nail. I retired to the gym, where the man in charge of uniforms made sufficient repairs with needle and thread for me to get back to my room. Thus began my career in spectator sports in college. There was not much time for participation in sports as I took four years of work in three.

Some Albertville athletes were induced to come to the university. At that time a promising star might be offered work to help in meeting his expenses. A friend of mine worked his way through college by sweeping the "A Club" room about once a week. Paul (Bear) Bryant, Lee Roy Jordan, Scott Hunter, Richard Todd, Ken Stabler, Bart Starr, Harry Gilmer, Don Hutson, and Joe Namath, to name only a few, played football here. A host of others became professional players. Coaches in many colleges over the country are former 'Bama players.

Many students were enabled to attend the university by having part-time jobs. Most of the mess hall, kitchen and power plant employees were students. Some of them who qualified were given teaching fellowships.

John Sparkman, for example, fired the university's coal-burning boilers and had a fellowship. He graduated with honors and became a successful lawyer and a United States Senator for many terms.

Reserve Officer Training was required of all men students except ones physically unfit, so I was a member of the Corps in the Coast Artillery. We wore the uniform for drill and classroom instruction.

Summer training for six weeks was taken twice at Fortress Monroe, Virginia, which is near Norfolk, Portsmouth, Newport News and Hampton Roads, in an area rich in early American history. It was here that Jefferson Davis, president of the Confederate States, was imprisoned for two years after the Civil War and where heavy shackles were riveted to his ankles but removed because of northern indignation.

Davis was subjected to indignities such as the continuous tramping of two guards by his cell and a lamp burning all night at his bedside. He was released on $100,000 bail after his health was shattered, vouched for by Greely, August Belmont of New York and other prominent northerners. He was never brought to trial and the treason charge was finally dismissed.

Fortress Monroe faced the sea and a moat was around the other sides, with a drawbridge originally at the entrance, like a medieval castle. The thick walls were mellowed with age but surmounting them were the emplacements for the artillery intended to defend the coast.

The huge guns, pointing eastward, would recoil after being fired and disappear in their pits behind the wall. A gun crew consisting of about a dozen men would bring the projectile into position on a carriage and shove it into the barrel with a long rod at the command, "Home Ram!" Then behind it were placed the powder bags and the breech was closed.

A long lanyard was pulled to fire the gun. The detonation sometimes broke glass in homes in the vicinity of the fort. The projectile or shell could often be seen striking the water in the bay, then ricocheting and skipping over the water with several glancing rebounds before exploding and sending a jet of water high into the air.

Behind the guns, in the plotting room, calculations were made using various figures, including those for the tide and wind direction and velocity, or miles per hour. The period allowed for plotting and stating the results so that the gun could be directed in the proper direction was brief.

One day some of us were on the boat which was pulling the target, a small, red, tent-like structure on a raft, on a long rope behind. We watched to see where the projectiles hit the water in respect to the target and estimated the length of the miss by use of an instrument, which was divided into spaces, through which we looked.

The big shells sent on their courses by R.O.T.C. students having their first experience with live artillery ammunition sometimes seemed to come as close to us as they did to the target. This information was sent to the gun crews so that corrections could be made. Improvement was noted.

We spent the time fishing while not busy with our duties. I never caught so many fish in one day as once when we were in a big school of flounder for about an hour. They bit as fast as the bait was offered. A big fish—dog shark, I think—broke my line when it dived under the boat. The boat crew accepted my catch as I could not use the fish.

One week of the training was at Langley Field, Virginia, where the railway guns were located. Outriggers were placed before the guns were fired. The noise seemed to reverberate even more than that of the emplaced coast guns. A few boys were almost blown from the trees which they had climbed to get a good view. An outstanding remembrance of Langley was the unpleasant taste of the mineral water there.

While at summer camp we went sightseeing on Saturdays to places of historical interest, usually taken in army trucks. Jamestown, Virginia, site of the first permanent English settlement in America and founded in 1607 by the Virginia Company of London, was one of the spots visited. It was the capital of Virginia until 1698, when the seat of government was moved to Williamsburg. Captain John Smith, governor for two years, was captured by the Indians but saved from execution by Pocahontas, Chief Powhatan's daughter.

Williamsburg was seen as it was before being restored. It was the political, educational and social center of Virginia for almost a century. Here was founded the second oldest college in the United States, the College of William and Mary. The building where the Phi Beta Kappa scholastic honorary society was founded is there.

We visited Yorktown, where Cornwallis surrendered to General Washington to end the Revolutionary War and bring independence to the colonies, and visualized the position of the French fleet at that time. A cannon ball remaining in the wall of one of the buildings was seen where it lodged.

Newport News, Virginia, on the James River has an excellent harbor accessible to Hampton Roads and is where many of the largest naval and marine ships are built. We went through the shipbuilding yards and were allowed to see a large battleship under construction. When the noon whistle blew for lunch, we saw thousands of workmen in motion.

In the R.O.T.C. barracks at Fort Monroe were students from various colleges across the country. An opportunity was provided for them to learn something about the people and customs of sections with which they had had no previous contacts.

The information dispensed was not always accurate, however. For instance, boys from Alabama were heard telling tall tales about life in the South in answer to questions of Pennsylvania or Minnesota boys when it was learned that they knew so little about the southern states. The northern boys easily believed that the South was something like life on plantations as pictured before the Civil War and that the typical southerner spent most of his time sipping mint juleps under a magnolia tree.

"What do you do with rapists?" was one of the questions asked the southerners.

"Oh, you see them hanging on telephone poles along the roads," Joe Dean answered, as if serious. He had never seen such a thing or anyone who had.

The boys from Minnesota were perhaps only polite and no more credulous than we were when hearing of the feats of Paul

Bunyan, the mythical lumberjack of the northland.

In one way the boys from the North seemed less polite. They, as well as we, noticed the differences in our pronunciation and speech but they were the ones who, assuming that their manner of speaking was proper, expressed amusement at ours.

The expression "you all," which we used to include everyone in a group as a matter of courtesy, they erroneously thought was said in addressing one person. No amount of explanation sufficed to change their notion of this expression. Maybe they thought it funnier to say "you all" to an individual rather than using it in the plural as we did.

While walking on a path inside the fort I met a young officer with his wife. He looked familiar and smiled as I hesitated. "Well, why don't you salute?" he asked. I then saw that it was Capt. Eric Strickland, who was reared on a farm between Albertville and Boaz. He and a younger brother who had been in my class in high school were West Point graduates and in the regular army.

The daily training schedule of rifle drills, marksmanship, marching, close-order drilling, calisthenics, etc., included an hour of instructions in swimming. The evenings, after retreat ceremonies, were generally free until taps, when the lights went out.

It was amazing to see how young the children of the fort were when they began saluting the flag and standing still and quietly for the playing of the National Anthem. Seeing these little tots standing at attention with right arms raised and tips of extended fingers touching the brow contributed to the emotions one felt on these occasions.

Walking down the beach to the Chamberlain Hotel at Old Point Comfort and watching the promenading there was a favorite pastime in the late afternoon after the day's duties were over. One day we found a large cannon ball in the sand almost too heavy to lift. An officer riding by on horseback said, "Why don't you take it home for a souvenir?"

Buckroe Beach was another popular place for evening diversion. It was here that I had the thrill of riding on a roller coaster for the first time but it did not have as great a physiological effect on me as on my companion. As soon as we alighted he quickly expressed a desire for relief, if what he said may be so politely interpreted.

R.O.T.C. training time was cut short one summer for lack of funds. Some of us went to Baltimore for a day or two and also had a week for seeing the sights of Washington, D.C.

In Baltimore we saw many streets with blocks of old solid-front red brick row houses with gleaming white marble steps leading onto the sidewalk. Many ships were in the harbor and overlooking it was Fort McHenry, preserved as a national monument. It was here that Francis Scott Key wrote *The Star-Spangled Banner* while on a ship during the bombardment of the fort by the British in 1814.

The Johns Hopkins University Medical School was of special interest to me. I took a long walk to see it and go through some of its laboratories.

We went to Annapolis, saw the Maryland capitol, the U.S. Naval Academy, and the boats used in training the midshipmen. We enjoyed the Chesapeake Bay seafood.

There were so many things to be seen in Washington that I tried to see the ones more important to me first, such as Mount Vernon, the Capitol and White House. I did not know then that the city would become familiar some years later, so I made the most of the time on that first visit. Several of the main tourist attractions of today had not been built then.

In the Government Printing Office we saw publications in various stages and, in the Bureau of Printing and Engraving, stacks of new paper currency.

We quickly climbed the Washington Monument and were amused on noting that some climbers stopped to rest on the way up. The view was worth the climb.

We gazed upon the paintings of famous artists in the art galleries. When we reached the Smithsonian Institution, Steve Manson, one of the fellows in our group, spied a couch and in the voice of a tired traveler with aching feet said, "I'll wait here while you all go through." Another one, Jack Friedman, managed to meet President Harding and had a short talk with him about our R.O.T.C. training at Fortress Monroe.

Night walks in downtown Washington were pleasurable and carefree. Strolling in the vicinity of The Mall and Capitol Hill area were people enjoying the coolness of summer evenings. Nearly all the park benches were occupied by romantic couples, some in the light of the moon, others in the shadows, all apparently free of any worries.

I attended one summer session at the University of Virginia and took a course in English literature taught by an elderly gentleman who liked to sit on the lawn and talk to those who stopped to hear his words of wisdom. One bit of advice he gave was, "Don't marry a girl in a college town; you're apt to get a pipe that has already been smoked."

My room at the university was on one of the lawns. Edgar Allan Poe's old room, kept locked, was not far from it. On Thomas Jefferson's tomb I read the epitaph that he composed himself: "Author of the Declaration of Independence; of the Statute of Religious Liberty in Virginia, and Founder of the University of Virginia." One afternoon, with a few other students from the university, I hiked the ascending road to Monticello, Jefferson's home. At that time there were not many visitors and we talked to the caretaker for a while. He told us, "When I was a boy many would walk up here from Charlottesville but this is not done much any more."

The amphitheater in a natural setting on the campus provided entertainment under the stars on the pleasant summer evenings. A pipe organ in it was said to be one of the best in the country.

A feature of the University of Virginia campus which provided a means of entertaining budding astronomers was the observatory, which was acquired when only a few institutions of higher learning had such.

"We can go up there at night," a student of astronomy confided, "turn the telescope toward buildings several blocks away and get close-up looks at girls through the windows." I was so advised of the educational advantages available at Virginia.

The summer was filled with activity in various localities. Time had been found to attend a student Y.M.C.A. conference in Blue Ridge, North Carolina. This was in the mountains near Mount Mitchell, the highest mountain in the eastern part of the continent, in the midst of beautiful scenery. The nearest city was Asheville.

Meetings were held outdoors on sunny days. At one of these a speaker from a school of divinity tried to interest the students in entering the ministry. The president of Tuskegee Institute spoke at one meeting.

Provision was made for athletics during the week. Swimming was done in a pool, the icy water of which was furnished by a mountain stream. It was so cold that one did not stay in it long but remembered how it felt for years.

That fall I returned to Tuscaloosa and the University of Alabama and did more exploring. There were navigation locks on the Black Warrior River in which the water could be raised or lowered to permit the passage of a boat or barge up or down stream. Up the river was a recreation area and beyond that a big sawmill. There was a long water chute down which logs sped to the river. Across the river was the town of Northport that could be reached by walking across the bridge.

Back on the campus in Smith Hall, where the Geological Survey Museum occupied most of the space, there was a very large relief map of the state. In the northeastern part of the map was an extensive elevation labeled "Sand or Raccoon Mountain." I never heard it called by the latter name by anyone. The exhibits included examples of various kinds of stones and the mineral wealth of the state. They showed that in the Birmingham area especially there were extensive deposits of limestone, iron and coal, side by side, making it especially favored for making steel.

While Ralph Lester and I were taking a walk, we met an old man who tipped his hat to us as students often did when meeting a professor. This polite man was black. The greeting was not expected but we responded and Ralph told me of an incident in his boyhood. "I was riding in a wagon with my father. We passed a colored man and he tipped his hat to us but I didn't speak." As we walked along he continued, "The next tree we passed under my father stopped the team, cut a switch, gave me a whipping and said, 'The next time somebody tips his hat to you, tip yours to him. You can be as polite as he is.'"

Students liked to swim in the Black Warrior River near the dam and locks. One that I knew, Ed Davis, was too near the area where there was strong suction. He was drawn under the water and drowned. The river, it was said, claimed a victim each year.

There was a boat excursion on the river on a special holiday. Most of the passengers were school children, about fifty of them, enjoying an outing that was unusual for them. They rushed to one side of the boat in childish excitement to see something that attracted their attention.

The boat overturned and was filled with water. Some of the children were trapped inside, many others could not swim to shore or be reached in time to save them and over half of

38

them drowned. It was a sorrowful sight, seeing them being removed from the capsized boat and placed on the grassy river bank.

One day a wizened old man seated on a low wall near the campus book store was telling us of his experiences as a slave on a large plantation. "I was big and strong," he said, "and was the stud. Eighty-three of the children there took after me and made good workers." He seemed to enjoy recounting events of those times.

During my second and third years I roomed in Manley Hall and ate in the large mess hall just across the quadrangle in Woods Hall. The food was placed on the tables, family style. Just before meal time we gathered before the door which was barred inside until the appointed time, when the bar was removed for the big rush. We had regular places to eat at the long tables and reached them without delay. We ate with more enthusiasm than etiquette, in common with many other young men blessed with healthy appetites. On a few occasions when the meat was unusually tough a piece of it might be seen sailing through the air.

Early in the morning on the first day of April we looked across at Woods Hall and could hardly believe our eyes. There on top of this three-story building, across the center peak, was a big farm wagon. Where it came from or how it got there was a secret but it took a crew of workmen most of the day to get it down.

The cause that most college boys in that era seemed to espouse, other than finding the means of going to college and making the grades that would enable them to stay there, was having fun. This included dancing most of the night during certain periods of the year. Certain socialites would sometimes come to morning classes still in evening dress.

A pep meeting around a bonfire was sometimes started the night before an important football game. Tuscaloosa officials complained one time when one of these was held on the street; it was not good for the asphalt. The young ladies of a college across town did not make a complaint when once a snake dance went through their dormitory.

The time Bert Shawn's pet monkey got loose, there was excitement in the usually orderly book store. On an exploring expedition the animal reverted to the wild state. He ran across the shelves and knocked contents to the counters and floor until collared by an unknown hero as agile as the monkey.

When not studying, there was always something for the students to see on the quadrangle, in one corner of which was the post office. A classmate, Tom Burns, got a letter, tore the envelope open, took the letter and threw it away without reading it.

"Why did you throw it away before you read it?" I asked him.

"There was no check in it. They always say the same thing."

A sporadic diversion was dropping a paper bag filled with water from a stoop or porch onto the head of someone on the ground below. Once only, one dropped on the commanding officer of the R.O.T.C. Apparently he felt that this was conduct not in accord with West Point tradition. Water-cooled but red-faced, he bounded up the steps brandishing his swagger stick on a mission, the objective of which was to neutralize the source of the offensive action. But he could not locate or establish the identity of the irreverent trainee. The next training period, however, included an unusual amount of double-time drill.

The pursuers of education in that era thought that there was a time and place for all things but the men's dormitories were just dormitories. If the denizen of one of them had been so rash as to have a female in his room, the terminology used for the purpose of the visit would not have been "entertain."

Every nook and cranny of the state was represented at the university. All of the students did not pronounce words the same, the pronunciation of those from the Mobile area, for example, being different from that to which I was accustomed.

My roommate, Bruce Lanier, was from Talladega and had attended Auburn before coming to the university to start a premedical course. He often spoke of Auburn's "Wah Eagle" football yell. Years later I learned that it was "War Eagle."

Comparative anatomy was one of the premedical subjects. The anatomy which we compared to that of human beings was usually a cat's. Many of these felines were needed so there was a market for them. Several enterprising young businessmen, students by day and prowlers by night, undertook to supply this need, motivated less by altruism than the desire for spending money. A number of homes in the vicinity of the campus reported the mysterious disappearance of pets. This became such a problem that other methods of acquiring laboratory animals

40

had to be instituted.

The professor who taught my class in French often made cutting remarks when mistakes were made. "To make a mistake like that is the same as going out through the window instead of the door when class is dismissed," he remarked after an incorrect translation. "You say that you made only five mistakes. That is like an engineer who had wrecked a train saying, 'I killed only five,'" he told an unprepared student.

"Jacques quit school and returned home to work in the store of his father," according to the story we were translating when our teacher became so exasperated with our versions that he exclaimed, "That is what most of you should do—stop school and go to work in the stores of your fathers."

Another teacher of French used another technique to secure motivation. He talked of his experiences in France, the people and their customs, and showed pictures to stimulate interest in the country and the language spoken there. In different years I was in the class of each of these men. The reader may guess in which order.

The lectures in one chemistry course did not vary much from year to year, it seemed. There were some sets of notes available that even included the jokes which were told to illustrate certain chemical reactions. This simplified to some extent the preparation for class on any day's subject.

A course in quantitative analysis given in the summer session consisted of a stated number of experiments. The instructor advised that the completion of these, together with reports and summation at the end of the course, would fulfill the requirements for credit. We had permission to start as soon as the regular session ended. My laboratory partners and I worked evenings, Saturdays, Sundays and holidays. We were about through with the experiments by the time the summer session was scheduled to start. When he saw how quickly we had done the assignment, the instructor decided that another experiment should be completed.

Analyses could be done faster when there were not too many students in the laboratory. At an irregular quiet hour, I was performing an experiment which involved the generation of hydrogen sulphide, a flammable poisonous gas which has a disagreeable odor, over a Bunsen burner.

The last that I remembered before losing consciousness was becoming suddenly ill and unsteady and trying to set down

41

the flask. The noxious gas, which has been fatal in some instances, had been escaping from a leak in the apparatus and had overcome me insidiously. There was a period of time, the number of minutes not known, during which I was not aware of what happened.

When conscious again, I was lying in the open air near the laboratory door with Bill McKissack by me. He had been the only other one in the building, saw me drop to the floor and pulled me outside. As soon as revived, I vomited profusely and was momentarily dizzy. Slight nausea and weakness which persisted the remainder of the day disappeared with light diet and bed rest. I noticed a vague uneasiness for years after the episode, however, whenever I smelled hydrogen sulphide.

This happening illustrates the importance of provisions for the elimination of harmful gases from the environment, especially chemical laboratories. It also suggests the need for adequate supervision of personnel or students as indicated.

Premedical students in small groups were sometimes conducted through the wards and recreation grounds of the Bryce State Hospital for the Insane. Examples of various types and degrees of mental diseases and deficiencies were shown. Many appeared sad. Some seemed contented but seeing thousands of these patients together was rather depressing.

Those able to exercise outside and to work seemed happier than the patients who had to be confined. We went to see a dance given for the inmates and here they seemed the most cheerful of all. Visiting a young man there that I had known for many years was a moving experience. He improved rapidly under treatment, soon returned home and was able to lead a normal type of life.

Hospital staff members invited us to accompany them in walking through the grounds where patients were enjoying the fresh air, sunshine and gardens. A woman who was disturbed mentally but in exuberant health otherwide ran to us from behind and jumped onto my back. She held onto me tightly. A doctor and three nurses were required to disengage her. The doctor said that I had served as a substitute for the one she craved, so maybe she was afforded a moment of pleasure. I hope so.

Judge DeGraffenreid taught the University Men's Sunday School Class that many students attended. The president of this class was also president of the student body, and later became a U.S. Senator. The superintendent became governor of Alabama.

The DeGraffenreid family had left their ancestral home, which was a castle at Bern, Switzerland, and founded New Bern, North Carolina. They contributed much to the New World. Many years after my sojourn in Tuscaloosa, I visited the castle with my brother-in-law, who was Air Force attache at our embassy in Bern. The lady of the castle at the time took us on a tour of all parts of it. She showed us an old painting of a nobleman. "Visitors from the United States have pointed to it," she told us, "and say that the DeGraffenreid nose shows in the painting. I don't have the heart to tell them that this particular painting is of a King Louis of France."

I was standing at the rail on the stoop in front of my room watching the ever-changing quadrangle scene when my classmate, Ted Hewitt, came to me with a look of horror. "Ernie has shot himself," he said in a low voice. "Where is he?" I asked. "In his room just over yours."

We went there quickly. He was seated in front of his small desk, facing the door, body drooped, chin on chest, motionless. A little red, round hole was in the center of his forehead and from it a small stream of blood trickled down his face. A pistol lay near his feet beneath a limp hand.

Other students soon appeared and a doctor made the pronouncement. All were stunned, not only by the sudden death in our midst but by the thoughts of one of our number being so unhappy as to take his own life.

Ernest Saunders, so far as we knew, had been an average student. Physically he was above average, large and muscular, and a member of the freshman football team which had played Georgia Tech's freshmen the day before in Atlanta. He had not been known as a complainer and was ordinarily quiet and studious. Someone said that because of comments made by him, it seemed that he was worried over conditions at home, but we did not know if this had resulted in the tragedy.

The preacher of the church that many of us attended referred to the tragic event in his sermon the following Sunday. Among other comments, he said, "A kind word from a fellow student might have prevented this sad happening." The inference seemed to be that it may have been our fault or perhaps he was using it for an object lesson as to the value of kindness.

How serious a friend's worry is to him may not be realized. In a particular case, even a specialist in the science which treats of the mind could have difficulty in determining its importance to the individual.

The cultural activities of Tuscaloosa were those of a university community. There was a theater for moving pictures and one for stage shows at which visiting companies performed. Musical comedies of that period were popular. Various university organizations sponsored programs and social clubs brought prominent dance bands to the campus for special occasions. This was early in the great band era.

When the First Presbyterian Church acquired an excellent new pipe organ, the company which installed it sponsored an exceptional concert by a talented organist. Although the event was not anticipated with much enthusiasm, it was not forgotten by those who went to hear something different from the ordinary music. The program had evidently been arranged to employ to the fullest the whole range of the fine instrument. It included selections from Rossini's last opera, *William Tell*. The part recreating the great storm was rendered so realistically, the roaring reverberating sounds so natural, that many in the audience shuddered. Incidentally, even though that opera is now performed only rarely, its brilliant overture is one of the most famous and in more recent times thrilled millions watching exploits of "The Lone Ranger" in a television serial popular with the young.

During a summer session the university engaged a male singer to lead in singing at certain periods in the Morgan Hall auditorium. He taught some songs, including a few that he referred to as the lilt type. The words of one were like this:

> Row, row, row your boat,
> Gently down the stream,
> Merrily, merrily, merrily, merrily,
> Life is but a dream.

We thought that it was a new one but when Mama heard it she said, "We used to sing that when I was a girl." This was another illustration of a phenomenon; the older I got, the more knowledge my parents seemed to have.

A message came from Papa that Mama was seriously ill and I should return home. The next train toward home left Tuscaloosa at about three o'clock in the morning so I had to be awake at two. My roommate said, "You won't need an alarm clock; I'll get you up. I can be awake anytime you say."

I awoke at two, dressed quietly and left him still asleep. The time was more important to me because of the importance of the reason for leaving so I had not slept soundly. On the train there were many worrisome thoughts to occupy the time.

The infection which had caused Mama's illness and Papa's concern subsided soon after my arrival and she recovered quickly. My absence from the university would be brief.

Mama stood on the back porch looking intently at something, apparently in the distance. I saw only green trees, the garden and spring flowers and asked, "What do you see?"

"I was just looking at how pretty the world is," she answered, a touch of awe in her voice.

Medicine was my tentative first choice of the careers considered on graduation from high school, but I wanted more time and experience in college study before making the decision final. During my last year in Tuscaloosa I decided that I wanted to be a doctor and could do whatever was necessary to reach my goal.

Vanderbilt, Tulane and the University of Alabama medical schools accepted me. They were the only ones to which I had applied. Tulane, among other considerations, had an abundance of clinical material in the New Orleans hospitals and, besides, the city appealed to me. Papa had gone to Atlanta to study medicine, Burtis to Nashville. Alabama's medical school at that time had only the first two years of study and these were on the Tuscaloosa campus. Some years later the school was expanded to four years and moved to Birmingham.

The profession that I had chosen would introduce me to people in practically all walks of life. I would treat patients representing many callings, vocations, trades, and some occupations of which I had never heard. Disease and injury not respecting status or position, I would come to know people literally inside and out at all levels of society as well as at all body levels. I would find that the quality of medical care one received did not necessarily depend upon the price paid for it.

Spring comes early in Tuscaloosa. It was and, no doubt, still is a time to cram for final examinations, to look forward to graduation, summer vacations or work.

The activities at the end of a school year and the anticipation of events soon to come that would change our lives made concentration on studies difficult. Many who were weary of looking in books and at the four walls of their dormitory rooms were loafing on the quadrangle grounds one day.

A senior who was valedictorian for his law class appeared at the rail of the top stoop of his dormitory in an exhilarated state and in stentorian tones began to orate. In his distinguished voice that could be heard by all dormitory dwellers, he gave the splendid oration that was to be heard a week later at graduation.

The baccalaureate sermon was delivered by a noted bishop. He began by saying, "It is a pleasure for me to be here with you at Emory," but plunged on to give advice and inspiration to the University of Alabama graduates in traditional and scholarly fashion. Some points he made are still remembered, such as those in reference to the meaning of commencement and the reconciliation of science and religion. "Some call it evolution, some call it God," was one line of a poem that he read.

The joy of graduation was tinged with sadness. Commencement would be the beginning of a new life pattern, leaving familiar scenes. Most of the friends of the past few years would not be seen again. The teachings of the professors and instructors would be heard no more. Many of these educators would not be forgotten, however.

Dr. Denny, then university president, had a remarkable memory and could retain for years individual information on thousands of students and call them by name. It surprised me to learn, at a chance meeting, that he not only knew me but also what courses I was taking. "I think that medicine is a fine profession for you," he said.

Dr. Graham, professor of biology and graduate of a famous German university, was one of my teachers who encouraged me to be a writer. He taught a subject important in my preparation for the study of medicine.

Another professor, or his automobile, is vivid in my memory. He drove a Stutz Bearcat, an advanced sports car that was a contemporary contribution to prestige. Incidentally, he was brilliant in his field of science.

One who pursues an education through two or more colleges is apt to be most impressed by the first attended. There are so many memories of my first one that only a relatively few of them could be told in this writing.

The hour for graduation had finally arrived. We had donned our caps and gowns. The tassel was dangling on the proper side of the mortarboard. Seated in the auditorium, we were awaiting the time for our names to be called. In a few minutes I would have a diploma signifying that I was a graduate with a Bachelor of Science degree. A horrible thought struck me. During the last three years I had been taking more subject hours than recommended. Suppose credit would not be allowed for the extra subjects taken and my name did not appear on the list now being read?

Names starting with the letter "G" were being called and then I heard "Hall" loud and clear and knew that for me an important milestone had been reached.

The words to our Alma Mater, as remembered, were:

Alabama, listen, mother,
To our vows of love;
To thyself and to each other
Faithful friends we'll prove.

Chorus

Faithful, loyal, firm and true,
Heart bound to heart will beat,
Year by year the ages through,
Until in heav'n we'll meet.

College days are swiftly fleeting,
Soon we'll leave thy halls,
Ne'er to join another meeting
'Neath thy hallowed walls.

So farewell, dear Alma Mater,
May thy name we pray,
Be reverenced ever pure and stainless,
As it is today.

Medical School, Tulane, And New Orleans

Medical school began in the gross anatomy dissecting room which extended half the length of the Richard Memorial building on the uptown campus of Tulane University. In this room were two rows of long tables, high stools around them, and the air was laden with the strong, penetrating odor of formaldehyde.

A human body, the subject for dissection just removed from a vat containing the preservative and disinfectant preparation, lay on each table, face up. Most of the bodies were white but there were several black ones. All this was sensed with smarting eyes and nose.

Each budding anatomist was assigned to a certain table and a particular part of the body. Generally there were four to a table, one on each side of one end and one on each side of the other end, rotating during the course. Everyone did his own dissection, aided by the instructor and sometimes by his partner on the opposite side of the table.

The first assignment might have been the head and neck or the abdomen or one of the extremities, for example, but before the dissecting instruments were used, the greasy material covering the subject (called "stiff") had to be removed. Before the end of the year every part of the body would be dissected by each student who remained in medical school.

A few freshmen concluded that they and medicine were not compatible soon after the introduction, looked toward other careers and dropped quietly out of sight. Those who stayed gradually became accustomed to their new environment and before long felt at home, even among the "stiffs," and it was not unusual to see someone eating a candy bar at the dissecting table.

The man who took care of this laboratory and the bodies told me that it was difficult to find help and more difficult to keep them. "They come and take the job, find out what it is like, see the corpses and the next morning don't show up."

He had been there for many years and had become an expert in cutting the thin sections from anatomical specimens, then dyeing and mounting them on glass slides for examination with a microscope. So part of his time was devoted to preparing slides for the class in microscopic anatomy. In that class each student had to supply his own microscope to study the slides and other material.

The instructors in the laboratories went from table to table to advise, answer questions, show the proper way to dissect, and to observe and assist in locating muscles, blood vessels, nerves and structures that might be difficult for a student to identify. A few comments or occasionally an anecdote helped a weary dissector and encouraged him to greater effort.

"Do you know at what period in the month more women menstruate than at any other time?" Dr. Cummins asked us when he came to our table, where we were studying tissues of organs in the female reproductive system, the ovaries and uterus.

"No, when?" we asked, not sure of how serious he was but interested. His smile was barely perceptible. "When the moon is full, according to some statistics," he answered and none of us was in possession of facts with which to contradict him.

After the soft structures in one part of the body had been identified and dissected the student advanced to another part. Along with this, bare bones were also studied and the names of the projections and depressions fixed in memory, until all 206 distinct bones of the skeleton had been learned.

At a quiz the professor, Dr. Smith, in his long white coat, would walk into the room where the members of the class had assembled and were seated in tiers, pitch a bone to one of them and say, "Describe it." The name of the bone would be given, its parts identified and the marks for muscle insertions, tendons, vessels and nerves located on it.

Memorizing occupied much of our study time. Just learning and using the anatomical terms increased the vocabulary ordinarily used by approximately one hundred percent. Most of

49

the newly acquired words were of Greek or Latin origin.

Various rhymes, using words the first letters of which were the same as the first letters of certain anatomical terms in a group, helped in remembering the names of structures in the body such as, for example, the cranial nerves starting with "On Old Olympus' Towering Top—." Doctors will recall this one and others.

Organic chemistry, physiology, bacteriology and pathology were some of the basic or medical science courses other than anatomy and embryology. Medicine, surgery, pharmacology and therapeutics, materia medica and prescription writing and the specialties would follow.

When I was a Tulane medical student, the first two, or pre-clinical, years were taught on the main campus uptown off St. Charles Avenue, and the last two downtown on Canal Street. After completion of the new building on Tulane Avenue next to Charity Hospital, all four years were taught downtown.

During my first two years in New Orleans, I roomed in a dormitory on the main campus in the residential area of the city opposite Audubon Park. Many fine homes with lush, subtropical shrubbery and palm-lined streets were all around. A zoo was in the park, where leisure time could be spent watching the alligators, snakes, birds, monkeys and other mammals. Some of the latter were very pretty, inspiring songs such as "Way Down Yonder In New Orleans."

The dormitory was strictly for men only, no femininity being allowed. One man who brought a girl to his room one night was not only expelled but lost all of his credits.

A roomer returned from an evening walk with the knuckles of his right hand skinned. "How did you do that?" we asked him. "A jaw came in contact with my fist," he explained.

Dormitories on the campus of the Sophie Newcomb College for women, a part of Tulane University, a few blocks away had social halls on the first floors where the residents could have visitors at certain hours. Henry Perry, my laboratory partner from Texas of Irish and Indian ancestry, lost his visiting privileges after appearing too exuberant one evening while living better through chemistry.

This was during the period of national prohibition, which conflicted with the habits of a few followers of Hippocrates even in New Orleans, "the city that care forgot." The typical chronic, impecunious state of students generally and of these few in particular was a major factor. It was demonstrated that pure alcohol was even worse than "white lightning," but once one of them was so desperate as to utilize that which was in a jar containing an anatomical specimen.

My classmates came from a large number of states but many of them were Louisianians of French ancestry and often their language bespoke this. On occasion one of them felt called upon to explain to an outsider, "In Louisiana a Cajun is a person of Acadian French descent. A Creole is a white person descended from the French or Spanish settlers." I had read Longfellow's "Evangeline" and had visited St. Martinville, St. Martin Parish, the region made famous by the poem. So I was glad to hear the story again from those whose ancestors were driven from their homes in Nova Scotia (Acadia). I would visit Nova Scotia later.

The Loyola University campus on St. Charles Avenue adjoined that of Tulane. Some of those in my dormitory attended mass there. Paul Marchand, one of the more devout ones, had prepared for a special observance at the church by abstinence, by having only pious thoughts and by solitary meditation in his room for hours. Then he went to bed with his alarm clock set to awaken him in time. A practical joker, not so reverent and knowing of the preparations of his friend, quietly locked him in his room while he was asleep. Paul, awakened by the alarm, dressed while engrossed in holy thoughts and then found his door locked. The spell was broken.

The language that Paul used was certainly not in keeping with the mood he had developed, but he climbed out the window and went on to church anyway. If he had known who locked his door, he probably would have been guilty of more than using the name of the Lord in vain.

My room for one year was in a boarding house on Canal Street, a street originally a canal but now the main business thoroughfare and one of the widest in the United States. I often walked on this street for relaxation and exercise, but it was not always the same and could be provocative. It extended from the Mississippi River at one end to the cemetery, a distance of five miles, so going to the end in each direction made a ten-mile walk.

The cemeteries in New Orleans are rows of marble vaults as burials are above ground because the water level is reached not far below the surface, parts of the city being below sea level.

51

For the same reason, homes were built without cellars or basements. Before erecting a large building, piles—long timbers like telephone poles—were driven into the mud to provide a foundation upon which to build.

Two of my classmates roomed at the same place I did, but did not care for walking or outdoor exercise and joked, "Do you hear voices that make you take those long walks?" The answer was that I did hear the city voices and other sounds and see the sights of New Orleans, which were so different from those of my boyhood. "It might help you lazy bums to listen and go too," I would invite, and they would laugh.

Whether the walks influenced my health was uncertain but certainly they were enjoyed after hours of study. I saw the mighty Mississippi, "Ol' Man River"; ships; passed the Custom's House; small shops of all kinds; Maison Blanche and other big department stores; theaters; hotels; homes; and people.

One of my classmates had to quit his internship because of tuberculosis, and another died with this disease a few years after graduation.

High levees protected the city from the river. Made of earth and covered with grass, they sloped upward toward the river and had the appearance of hillsides. Cows grazed on some of them. As one looked toward the levee, a passing ship could sometimes be seen at a higher level than the amazed spectator.

Docks and warehouses stretched for many miles along the waterfront. Here cargo vessels from ports throughout the world brought exotic products from far places and loaded cotton, grain, foods, goods and materials in such volume as to make New Orleans the nation's second largest port. When walking along the wharves those days and seeing ships with strange names, curious cargoes, foreign crews, and stevedores; smelling coffee and the spicy odors brought from places like Brazil, Ceylon and Zanzibar and the banana and other fruity odors of Central America added to the characteristic aromas of the river; and hearing the creaking sounds of machinery, the rattling of chains, thuds, hoarse steamboat whistles and other tones, the walker was always conscious of the sensations this distinctive and essential part of New Orleans produced.

Fastened transversely around each hawser, the thick Manila mooring rope, was a large, metal disc between each ship and the wharf. It was to prevent a rat that might be on a ship from reaching shore and would also keep wharf rats off the ship. This protective measure was routine but intended primarily to keep out rats that might bring bubonic plague from countries in which this disease was endemic or occurred occasionally. It is one of the precautions taken by ports to prevent the spread of disease.

The son of the landlady in the house on Canal Street where I roomed on the second floor had a dance band that practiced on the first floor. They played at a night club in the French Quarter. When practicing, they repeated certain parts over and over, rarely playing completely through a piece without stopping, until finally each musician got the correct sounds from his instrument in the proper time. Concentrating on my studies was not always easy during a band practice session and the frequent interruptions of a pleasing tune to improve a certain passage were rather disconcerting, especially when the first rendition sounded perfect to me.

One year I roomed on Claiborne Avenue, named for the first territorial governor of Louisiana in the American period, bordering the Vieux Carre, the old French Quarter. It was only a few blocks from the medical school.

A funeral procession accompanied by a brass band, the members of which were black musicians, would sometimes come by the place where I lived. On the way to the funeral the band would play a slow dirge. On the way back they played lively jazz tunes or a version of "When the Saints Go Marching In."

Curt Blake, a friend who also found exploring a pleasure, and I decided upon a plan to explore every block in the French Quarter. To be sure not to miss one, we systematically walked the length of all streets in each direction in the eight-by-fourteen-block area over a period of months. Afterwards we returned to those that interested us as often as time permitted.

Theresa and Suzanne Runyon invited us to their Metairie Ridge home for the Thanksgiving holiday and dinner. The girls were dressed in the flapper fashion that was in style then. They were excellent dancers in a period when dancing was a popular form of entertainment and people usually took pride in learning and executing the movements and their personal variations of them.

Waltzes, the foxtrot and one-step were common; then came the Charleston. The girls had us roll up the rugs in their living room and proceeded to teach us nearly a dozen of the latest steps of the basic Charleston, the less intricate ones. This was the prelude to a few games of tennis, the big turkey dinner and a walk around Metairie afterwards.

One of the streetcars that we had to dodge on the narrow streets was the one named "Desire." Whenever we heard the street to which it went mentioned, the French pronunciation was used, the final letter being accented as well as the first two syllables.

Some parts of New Orleans such as Jackson Square were visited many times. There in the center stood the equestrian statue of Andrew Jackson whose men, with the help of Jean Lafitte's pirates, defeated the British in the Battle of New Orleans in 1814, after the treaty of peace had been signed. News traveled slowly then. The heroic general always appeared gallant on his charger, his hat doffed.

The buildings on two sides of the square, built in 1849 by Baroness Pontalba, were some of the first apartment houses to be built in the country and still in use. St. Louis Cathedral, named for the patron saint of New Orleans and probably the oldest religious institution in the Mississippi Valley, facing another side of the square, always seemed as if newly discovered by me. It was founded in 1718 and had been rebuilt twice, the last time in 1794.

The Cabildo, the Spanish colonial headquarters built in 1795 and the site where the Louisiana Purchase was signed in 1803, standing on one side of the cathedral, was visited many times to view the old building and its exhibits. On the other side was the Presbytere, which was intended for church use when built in 1793 but housed government offices until made into a museum.

At the French Market near the square, we sometimes drank chicory-flavored coffee and ate square, airy doughnuts or beignets with powdered sugar on them after a night out. Students did not eat in the famous restaurants such as Antoine's, Arnaud's, Brennan's, or Galatoire's very often. I usually ate breakfast and dinner at the boarding house. Lunch was a sandwich and drink at school.

The dining room at one of our boarding places was affectionately called "The Greasy Spoon. ' Each morning without fail we had two fried eggs and at night some kind of meat and vegetables or jambalaya served family style. The conversation at the table was generally light, the meal being a time of respite from the day's tensions. For Sunday dinner there was always fried chicken.

Seafood was plentiful with the gulf, river, lakes and bayous nearby. Gumbo or a dozen oysters on the half shell, with a hot sauce, served by a fast shucker at an oyster bar was a rare treat.

Hot tamales, wrapped in cornshucks, from a street vendor with a cart near our boarding house were frequently a gourmet item when we were famished after studying late. In spite of the way in which the lives of medical students may have been depicted in some quarters, most of our nights had to be devoted to serious study.

"I'm going to be in the opera!" Jess Craigor informed me. He was tall, slender, and studious, without any musical talent that I had heard of.

"What part are you taking?" I inquired, skeptical but asking a straight question.

"A bunch of us went down and tried out for soldier parts. They took the tallest ones. We will wear costumes, carry spears and yell. At rehearsal we'll learn when to go on stage, where to stand and so on. It will be fun, I think."

Students were sometimes hired as extras and instructed in the essentials of their parts in shows. When there was a convention such as that of the Daughters of the Confederacy or Daughters of the American Revolution attended by large numbers, some students might be asked to volunteer to serve as escorts for the visiting women.

Musical shows or light opera, such as Gilbert and Sullivan's *Mikado*, could be seen for fifty cents in a theater from the top balcony that we called "The Pit." *Blossom Time*, based on Schubert's life and melodies, was popular. *The Student Prince*, a musical version of *Old Heidelberg*, was a favorite. Many years later I would visit Germany and the University of Heidelberg.

Late-evening entertainment was obtainable without cost at the night court. Those arrested were brought before a judge, who advised them and asked how they wished to plead. Many of them were charged with minor offenses such as being drunk and disorderly or urinating on the sidewalk in front of Godchaux's Department Store, for example.

One night about twenty men were in a line before the judge, who told them that they could plead guilty to the charge of gambling (a common pastime, especially in Jefferson Parish on Lake Pontchartrain just outside the city) and have him set the penalty or, if preferred, be tried in court later. The latter procedure required an affidavit. He asked each man, in turn, to state his preference. One man pleaded guilty. All the others asked for an affidavit. The one pleading guilty was freed and the others were returned to jail after a brief lecture by the judge.

Prostitutes frequently appeared before the night court judge. When a fine was imposed on one or several, there always seemed to be a man waiting with the money to pay it and they left with him. Perhaps it was counted as a business expense.

Why some who practiced this "oldest profession" were arrested and charges made was not clear to us as there was a large red-light district then. We assumed that they were brought into court for not observing the rules.

If a man walked on certain streets at night he heard greetings and salutations from many windows and doorways that opened onto the sidewalks, which were often overhung by balconies with wrought-iron railings.

Dick Boyd, a lanky, big-boned fellow, was not really reckless; neither was he an ascetic. When he wanted to cross a crowded street he would hold his hand high and stop the traffic. He came in after a late-evening excursion, tossed his hat on a hook and interrupted our studying long enough to tell us, "I was looking at a girl who was hissing to me from across the street, where I went for a stroll, when another one grabbed my hat just as I went by a low balcony and said, "You'll have to come inside, honey, to get it."

All the pros did not confine their endeavors to the district. Some used automobiles to solicit business, stopping at the curb, perhaps, to hail a pedestrian prospect.

Another night Dick told us, "A hooker spoke to me on Canal Street. I used to see her driving a Cadillac; then she drove a Ford for a while. Tonight she was walking."

The people of New Orleans, as I may have intimated, are generally friendly and warmhearted. Many living in the northern part of our country think that it is always warm this far south, but actually the weather can be uncomfortably cold at times. In the spring and summer sudden, brief showers often send shoppers scurrying for shelter but many do not seem to mind a little dampness.

Occasionally, when conditions were favorable for mosquitoes, winds blowing over swamps toward the city would bring them in large numbers. At such times many people on a business street could be seen waving their hands around their ears in response to the high-pitched singing of the little pests. Besides the annoyance of the itching caused by their stings, there was the possibility that the mosquitoes might transmit malaria, a disease characterized by recurrent paroxysms of chills, fever, sweating and progressive anemia if not properly treated. Large doses of quinine for many weeks was the treatment then in use.

Often when riding streetcars, I noticed that most of the men tipped their hats whenever we passed a Catholic church. Citizens seemed to be able to recognize college students. This puzzled me when I was one but not when, more mature, I returned to the scene of our crimes.

Fraternities provided some extracurricular activities, not all fun and horseplay. There were regular meetings and occasional social affairs. Older members could sometimes help their "brothers" in preparing for tests.

Initiation of new members in a hall where boisterous play would be tolerated was a high point of the year. Part of this could conceivably consist of the initiate feeling, smelling, tasting or otherwise sensing certain objects such as spaghetti or an oyster while blindfolded and under the power of suggestion being made to believe, in some cases at least, that they were other things. Before the evening was over, the new brother was given the secrets, handshake and password. On Mother's Day each year, the members of our fraternity attended a church service together at a place and hour we agreed upon.

The annual class banquet was in one of the famous New Orleans restaurants. At the affair a prominent medical figure spoke. There was no absenteeism on these occasions.

Mardi Gras was the big event of the year in New Orleans, the climax of the social season just before Lent when many carnival organizations gave parties and balls. For several days there were parades of spectacular floats, each led by the one on which the royal couple and attendants of the sponsoring club rode, with many marching bands, military units and funmakers in fanciful and colorful costumes. The costumes of the king, queen and members of their court were elaborate and rich in materials and ornamentation. Masks were worn.

Each parade had a theme such as, for example, a period in history, mythology or Mother Goose rhymes. Trinkets were thrown to the thousands of spectators in the stands, streets and balconies along the way, many of whom also wore masks and costumes during the day.

What one wore was limited only by his or her imagination and might consist of yards of cloth, skins, feathers, decorations or almost nothing, representing birds, animals, pirates, demons, or anything fancied. The mother, father and children of a family often were dressed in similar outfits. Little Red Riding Hood could be seen having fun with the wolf, a convict with a ball and chain, knights, clowns, stilt walkers, Robin Hood—everything imaginable.

Musical groups of many or only a few musicians, playing whatever instruments they had or could devise, roamed or rode around the streets contributing their sounds to those of the large, organized bands. There always seemed to be music in the air, heard faintly in the distance or distinctly and getting louder as the source drew near.

Street dancers, personifying the carnival spirit, danced to parade music, uninhibited, prancing, twisting, strutting, vibrating ecstatically, doing the cakewalk or any other movement that came naturally. They seemed to exhibit their feelings and have more fun than any others among the jubilant thousands crowding the streets.

Attendance at the Mardi Gras balls was by invitation. My roommate, Roger Brookfield, who was an amateur socialite, and I were invited to some of them. For the first part of the evening, guests sat in the balconies and watched the grand march, court ceremonies and several dances of the royalty and club members before being asked to join in the dancing.

A girl who resembled one of the movie stars at that time was a few rows of seats from me in the balcony, which was filled with those who had received invitations to one of the most brilliant balls of the season. Every time I glanced her way she was gazing in my direction but spoke only with her eyes. She must be looking beyond me, I decided.

The next day Roger said, "The Dupreys are having a party at home tonight for their friends from Birmingham. Marie asked me to come and bring another. How about it?"

I did not know them but agreed to go along with him, and he told me something about the family, their shipping interests, connections with the port and other items while I was trying to study.

Their stately home was impressive even in an area of magnificent residences in this old city of half a million people and varied architecture. It reminded me of my boarding house, because it was so different. We rang, soon the door was open, and we were inside. The girl standing there and I looked at each other in amazement. We had seen each other across a crowded balcony the night before.

"First," she said, "I want to apologize for staring at you last night. You looked like someone I knew." As for me, I was willing to be someone she knew, so the following night I went dancing with her on the Mississippi River excursion boat called *City of St. Louis.*

All the events of this evening and others experienced in periods of escape from studies cannot be related within the limits of this account of "College Daze."

Saturdays during the football season were exciting times. Home games were played in the Tulane Stadium, which later would be referred to as the "Sugar Bowl," Louisiana being a leading producer of cane sugar.

The Louisiana State University games were the big ones and alternated between New Orleans and Baton Rouge, the state capital and location of L.S.U.'s Tiger Stadium. Special trains would be run, a late one following the Saturday night dance after a game.

During the Christmas holidays a classmate and I were sent as delegates to an international meeting sponsored by the Y.M.C.A., which was held in Indianapolis, Indiana, and attended by thousands of students from many colleges and universities. In contrast to the mild winter we left in New Orleans was the heavy snow which greeted us in the northern city.

Those from Canada that we met, having a different viewpoint, seemed to be enjoying the Hoosier climate, saying, "This seems like a nice spring day to us." I think that we enjoyed the convention and wintry days spent in Indiana's capital city fully as much as our Canadian friends.

The girl seated by me at one of the meetings was Harriet Fairington from a college for girls in Atlanta. Her home was in Little Rock, Arkansas, where she taught dancing when not in college. We exchanged addresses and corresponded after the convention.

I visited her at home the next Christmas vacation, going by train from New Orleans. The Mississippi had overflowed its banks, the flood spreading over wide areas, including the railroad. At some points the muddy water extended as far as I could see.

The water was in many houses and lapped at the roofs of some homes. Pieces of furniture, boxes, logs and other objects could be seen floating around partially submerged buildings and trees. The engineer went very slowly through flooded stretches with water up to the steps of the train, the passengers uncertain that we would reach our destinations.

This was a scene of utter desolation, but eventually the polluted water would recede and people would return to their homes, clean out the mud, make repairs and resume their ways of living. Floods were a part of life along the great river and those who loved it returned to its banks and fertile valley just as families living at the base of Vesuvius in Italy came back to it after an eruption of the volcano.

In Little Rock, I watched Harriet teach classical dancing, noting that she frequently reminded the pupils to smile, and later saw her perform the adagio on the stage of the local theater. Her muscular but graceful partner was an accomplished young man who had been a subject in Ripley's "Believe It or Not" column because of the astonishing strength of his fingers, two of which could support the weight of his body with his feet in the air. I could not accomplish this feat using all my fingers and thumbs.

The friend of Harriet's sister was a star player on the University of Arkansas football team, the famed Razorbacks. Whatever athletic ability resided in me, I was no football hero. Neither did I swim the deepest river at the next vacation and learned that, in some cases, absence makes the heart grow fonder of someone else.

During the summer after my third year in medical school, I did social service work at the Bowery Y.M.C.A. on the teeming lower east side of New York City at No. 8 on East Third Street. Students engaged in the program came from various universities over the country. Many of them were from Ivy League schools. With me at the "Y" was a friend from the University of Alabama, Homer Robertson.

Because of my medical training, I was designated as "House Doctor" to do whatever was possible for the men applying to the institution for help who did not require treatment at Bellevue Hospital. Many of them were in the state that society sometimes regards as "human wrecks."

Each man who came in was given a physical examination

which included a search for communicable diseases or for vermin such as lice. While being examined, his clothes were washed and cleaned. He was given a bed and tickets for meals served in the building, which were charged to his account.

If the man was able to work, a job was found for him. From his earnings he paid the small costs for incidentals, lodging, food and other essentials provided. He could buy a few items such as toilet articles at the desk in the lobby.

"Here is your office," I was told, "and you will sleep here in this room next to it." A few minutes later there was a commotion outside and a boy who had been cut on the back of his neck was before me. "This boy was hurt in a street fight. Will you take care of him?" was the request made of me.

I looked through the supplies on hand. There were no suitable needles or suture material. Examination showed an incised wound of the skin. I cleaned it thoroughly, approximated the skin edges and applied zinc oxide adhesive plaster. Examined subsequently, the wound was found well healed.

The first night, I was awakened by a knock and voices at the door saying excitedly, "A man in the dormitory is having a fit!" I went to the man at once and found him on the floor surrounded by a score of anxious men who shared the large room with him and had been aroused from their sleep.

These men, reputed to be tough, were revealed as having capacity for compassion and wanted to assist their fallen comrade. I tried to keep the man from injuring himself or being injured by attempts to aid him. Fortunately the convulsions were brief and all concerned returned to their beds.

Part of the time, especially on weekends when some of the regular staff were away, I worked at the reception desk in the lobby. One of the duties consisted of making telephone connections at the switchboard. It seemed that there were more calls when there were the most men in line at the desk making requests. Then the board would light up with the red signals of callers.

Occasionally an angry man would become troublesome if he did not get what he wanted or if what he wanted was not immediately available. A policeman's club was kept in a convenient place under the counter for protection in case of emergency. I managed to get through some provoking confrontations without using it.

Most Bowery men who came for help seemed to appreciate

whatever was done for them. In common with people elsewhere, drinking made some of them friendly and talkative, often too much so, but some were made belligerent. Many in the Bowery became stuporous, then staggered, stopped and often slept wherever overcome. One, for example, who came inside and was at the desk, trying to be insulting, made sarcastic remarks concerning southern accents but he was exceptional.

The languages and accents that I heard represented many lands beyond the seas. Most of the people where I had been reared spoke with the expressions, words and sounds brought from the British Isles several generations before. In some areas of the South, speech had been influenced by those from various European countries and Africa.

A dumb man who was staying in the "Y" building communicated by writing on a pad of paper that he carried with him. On it he would write his requests and answers to questions asked him. One day he became angry when someone tried to get his place in a line of men and cursed the offender fluently.

Near the Bowery were a variety of communities, each peopled largely by recent immigrants from a particular country. Chinatown was not far away. In one section of the city nearly all were Germans, in another Italians, in another Irish, and so on.

Exploration occupied most of my spare time. One day I went to Ellis Island, where immigrants were received following their voyage across the ocean and soon after they saw the Statue of Liberty for the first time. Many of them were met by members of their families, relatives or friends who had come to this country earlier and then had sent for them. The meetings were usually marked by evidence of deep emotion, joy, warm embraces, fervent kisses and tears. Some had brought very little with them from the old country, often only the odd clothes they wore, the contents of a battered valise and perhaps a cloth-covered bundle they held.

Seeing the relief, hope and anticipation of a new life showing in the faces of these new arrivals and the glow of happiness in those who met them was enough to make one born in America more appreciative of the citizenship that had been taken for granted and the opportunities that this country offers. Then I returned to the Bowery, where so many with all these opportunities had gravitated.

To the Bowery had come citizens from various walks of

life and from many different states to join the natives. Some had landed there by chance, by train, ship or highway. Many had voluntarily come to the big city from the country, villages and towns across the nation seeking the easy money that they had heard was there. There were those who had lost their jobs and preferred drifting to working at something else and had gradually reached their level with other drifters, diurnal drinkers and defectives.

The same pattern did not fit all Bowery dwellers. Many of them, however, found there the conditions or climate most compatible for them, where in time they felt more at home than anywhere else and stayed there by choice. These generally were considered dregs by citizens living in better circumstances, especially those in the froth of society. Often the chief difference between the dregs and froth was based on the amount of money people in these levels had. Differences in character and intrinsic worth or value to society as a whole, between the froth and dregs, were frequently not apparent, but perhaps such criteria are considered unimportant by much of our society.

In our earlier years, not much was heard concerning classes in our democracy or republic. The industrious, law-abiding, not rich or poor but self-supporting people of the United States of America that detractors sneeringly call "The Middle Class" were not blamed for all the evils of this and other countries.

As people became tagged with class names by some other people, so have parts of cities become tagged, depending on how those living in a particular part during a certain period maintained, changed, improved or abused it, not on how it had been before or would be later.

A city district comprising thickly populated streets or alleys marked by squalor or wretched living conditions which commentators and writers of a particular persuasion label a "ghetto" (loosely using a term that had been applied to restricted areas in European cities) was called a slum in those days.

The character of the Bowery, however, was different from any other area. The name goes back to Dutch colonial days when it was an Indian trail called Bowery Lane joining Peter Stuyvesant's farm or bouwerij with New Amsterdam. The area included a street of the same name extending from Chatham Square to Astor Place and was said to have been the theatrical center of New York at one period in the last century. It became a notorious section which somehow seemed to glory in its notoriety.

Along the street were many small, shabby hotels known as "flop houses" where a man could get a bed, such as it was, for less than a dollar. Among the other establishments were cheap restaurants and barrooms or saloons. Over the Bowery were the tracks of the roaring elevated trains which darkened the street, shading the sidewalk and doorways where usually dirty men, drunkened by cheap alcoholic concoctions, could be seen sleeping. Men such as these, often referred to as "Bowery bums," composed most of the clientele of the "Y" where I worked. From such men, who had been reclaimed, had been recruited some of the regular staff employed there.

One of the workers had been a noted safecracker. He showed old newspaper clippings to me which told of his skill in robbing safes before being reformed. After his reformation he wanted to devote his life to helping others and decided that here, where so many needed help of the kind that he could give, he would serve. "My experience is an example of what salvation can do" was included in his message to the men.

Another member of the permanent staff was a graduate of the Harvard Law School but he had never practiced law. Upon graduation he, with a group of friends, took a yacht trip to celebrate. "After the cruise I continued the drinking started while celebrating and eventually landed in a Bowery gutter. The 'Y' rescued me and I have been here ever since," he told me. He had been conducting religious services, among other duties there, for many years when I knew him.

The student volunteers working at the different institutions in New York during the summer met together weekly at one of the large Manhattan churches for a swim in the pool, lunch and discussions. Some of them spoke of "liberal clubs" to which they belonged in the colleges they represented and the moderator mentioned "socialistic programs in which our government is already engaged." This was long before "The New Deal" of President Franklin Roosevelt. We had a chance to learn the viewpoints of young men with backgrounds different from our own.

A serious, sedate student told me of the burlesque show that he had just seen, his first. "It was a sort of caricature of life today," he said, amused. "There were some comedians and singers and a lot of dancing girls who got into all sorts of positions and there were some funny skits with courtroom scenes, different things, some of them pretty good," was his description of it.

There was greater variety in such shows then, it seems, and the entertainers apparently tried harder to please and this by proficiency rather than just by exposure of intimate anatomy. Perhaps the attitude of audiences changed, too.

Homer, my fellow missionary to the Bowery for the summer, envisioned a program of sports and team play for the children in the neighborhood, using the "Y" equipment.

"I'd like to have some games for the kids out here in the street if we can get it roped off. The boys could play ball together and it would give them a chance to learn sportsmanship, too. Maybe the parents would come out and we could get acquainted with them," he said while making plans.

The Police Department was cooperative, as were the "Y" officials and, when requested, diverted the traffic away from Third Street at each end of the block. A goodly crowd arrived to see what would take place.

Many youngsters in the vicinity were motivated to participate in the proposed games, but it appeared that they were more accustomed to individual rather than team effort except when amusing themselves with a few buddies. Many children were being killed by cars and trucks every month in the streets of New York and other cities.

Homer had some surprises. "At first when a ball game was started some boy would grab the ball and run away with it, dart into an alley and not come back," he told me. "But after a while they learned that it was more fun to stay and play ball with the others. The older people enjoyed it, too." Discouraged in the beginning, he felt that something for the better had been accomplished by the summer's end.

We were pleased to see at least temporary improvement in the conditions of those from the Bowery who had entered the "Y." Many who had arrived unsteady, malnourished, malodorous and dirty, with bloodshot, bleary eyes, had become clean, returned to work and with renewed strength could again stand erect and look at the world with clear eyes.

The summer had also been enjoyable as well as educational for all of us who had used our vacations at work that we hoped would give a little help where needed. We knew that at least the "Y" had done more for men who came there than the flophouses on the Bowery and that we had assisted in providing an opportunity that might result in rehabilitation for some of them.

That fall I returned to New Orleans for my final year of medical school, which would include practical application of the basic sciences, theories and the art of medicine that we had been studying. There were still lectures to attend, but much of the time we would be watching demonstrations and operations and seeing patients in the hospitals.

We had to be present for the delivery of a certain number of babies. Some of the obstetrical cases were seen by the students in the homes, accompanied by a doctor. The procedures used for normal cases and for complications were observed.

Mrs. Delaney was very talkative during delivery. While under partial anesthesia to ease her pains, she was speaking of somebody named Joe. "Don't say anything against Joe," she pleaded. "He is all right. He gave me things when my own husband wouldn't. Joe is all right. Don't say anything against him."

Most of the patients we saw were in the wards of the Louisiana State Charity Hospital, where there were nearly two thousand injured and sick people with almost all kinds of ordinary and exotic diseases imaginable. Because of the seaport, these came from various countries as well as from Louisiana. Because of proximity to the tropics, there were many cases of tropical diseases, especially from the Latin American countries to the south. Ailing and suffering men, women and children were also seen in Touro Infirmary, Hotel Dieu and other hospitals and a few in their homes.

Leprosy or Hansen's disease cases were visited at Carville, Louisiana, where there were a few hundred under treatment in the leprosarium, the only one of its kind in the country. We stayed a day with the patients, having lunch served by them in their dining room. Old ideas concerning lepers and the chronic disease afflicting them which caused them to be considered "unclean" and to be avoided had to be adjusted here.

Cases were seen representing different aspects or stages of the disease, which was known even in biblical times but not given much medical attention until this century. Patients that we saw apparently were not suffering pain but many with destructive types of the disease were pitiable. In some advanced cases parts of feet, hands or the face were missing and large open sores present. Even so, most of them seemed cheerful.

Treatment consisted primarily of a medication, chaulmoogra oil, given regularly in capsules; local treatment of the lesions; and physical measures. The results were not very satisfactory but the medicine seemed to slow or arrest progression of the disease and to reverse it in some instances. A few were able to leave the institution.

The search for a cure for leprosy was a continuing one and eventually a remedy would be found. Some of the nurses were Sisters of Charity who had worked there patiently for many years. One of them whom we had known at Charity Hospital was asked, "Would you rather be here or back in New Orleans?" She smiled and said, "That is not a fair question."

Although leprosy had been associated with revulsion and fear through the ages, the doctors at Carville told us that often only one case was found in a family and that they had seen no case of transmission of the disease there. We saw it in a new light after that.

Our class in surgery visited the Delgado Trade School to watch the procedures being taught in carpentry, plumbing, mechanics and other classes. We found that the principles employed were applicable, under different methods, to a great many surgical operations. A purpose of the visit was to teach us that use might be found for any such knowledge acquired, from whatever source, and to avoid closing our minds to that obtainable outside ivy-covered walls and ivory towers.

In the surgical amphitheaters, operative techniques were observed and the pathological specimens were examined. Patients' histories, physical examination findings, radiograms and laboratory reports were correlated with the disclosures of the operations.

At examinations of bodies after death, information was obtained concerning the various tissues, organs and systems not revealed by all of the previous means of study. Mistakes and missed diagnoses were often uncovered that might increase understanding and be of aid in other cases. Too, we found that the practice of medicine was a never-ending quest for more learning.

During the last year, under the eyes of staff doctors, we did the things that we had learned to do through reading, watching and other ways, such as assisting. My first assignment in one division involved irrigation of the stomach of a woman. We had practiced passing stomach tubes on each other in class so I found that passage of the tube and irrigation of the stomach was not difficult in this instance. The patient was cooperative in undergoing an unpleasant few minutes in the hope for

67

relief.

What one does for the first time may be remembered while the numerous times the same thing is done afterwards are forgotten. Another occasion, however, in which a stomach washing was necessary will be mentioned later.

Toward the end of the year the realization came that the association with teachers and classmates that I had known for four years would soon end. Approximately half of those who started in my freshman class at Tulane would survive the four years and graduate.

The apparent reasons why certain ones fell by the wayside were recalled. One who was interested in local politics became too involved and attended so many meetings that his studies were neglected. Another devoted so much attention to girls and superficial anatomy that he failed in gross and microscopic anatomy. One classmate did not pass the final examinations of a year that he was repeating. His family was reputed to be very wealthy, his father treasurer of another country at one time. It was understood that he had not chosen medicine as a career but that his family wanted him to be a doctor.

An Egyptian in our class was frequently called "sheik," instead of Ismail, by fellow students and when so addressed would patiently explain, "It is my uncle, not I, who is the sheik. A sheik is a religious man." The word had acquired a different meaning in this country.

Archaeologists exploring on Ismail's land discovered an important tomb. Interest in it was increased by the significant findings in that of King Tutankhamen earlier. His studies were interrupted by the personal attention his affairs required after the discovery, the reports of which we read in the papers. That he did not graduate with us was understandable.

A few students found that they were more interested in vocations other than medicine. For example, one enjoyed singing more than dissecting and took more pride in appearing on the stage than in an operating room, so he departed. Fortunately for their potential patients of the future, such students dropped out to enter other fields. Too, the courses were more difficult than some had anticipated.

One discouraged classmate decided to quit school and was at the railroad station waiting for the train to return home when seen by one of his teachers, who persuaded him to try a little longer. He tried a little harder also, was graduated and became a successful physician.

In the years to come many of our several hundred medical school teachers would be remembered. A few of these will be mentioned, rather than attempting to list the faculty. Charles Cassedy Bass, the dean, was also professor of experimental medicine and director of the Laboratory of Clinical Medicine. Important contributions that he made included his investigations into the etiology and treatment of malaria, the disease that was causing more deaths than any other in the world. Yellow fever and malaria together, according to estimates, have accounted for one-half of all human deaths in history.

Rudolph Matas, professor of surgery, had won an international reputation as a pioneer in vascular surgery and originated an operation for aneurysms. Some of the operations required several hours, and then at night he would sometimes remain at the bedside of a charity patient. "The more experienced a surgeon becomes, the more he respects one drop of blood," he told us. Dr. Matas, a renowned surgeon, had a wide knowledge of history, literature and art that flavored his lectures and technical demonstrations in surgery. In discussing a certain abnormality, to stimulate interest in the subject he might mention a famous person who had had the same condition either congenitally or acquired. Presidency of the American College of Surgeons was among the honors he achieved. Our Senior Class presented a portrait of him to the school and he gave the farewell address to us on Ivy Day. One of his parting thoughts was of our need for enough ego, without egotism.

Urban Maes, professor of clinical surgery, was the chief surgeon in many of the operations we watched. The last time that I talked with him was in a surgical clinic in Philadelphia, which he visited while I was a postgraduate student there.

Isidore Cohn, another professor of clinical surgery, was chief of surgery at Touro Infirmary, one of the institutions in which we received instruction. He used selected cases for object lessons.

Charles Warren Duval, professor of pathology and bacteriology, did early research on the causation of diarrhea in babies and identified the bacteria causing one of the main types of the disease that had resulted in the death of thousands of infants. He was a noted authority and recognized the fact. To his students who respected his high position he was known as "King Duval."

Irving Hardesty, professor of anatomy and a distinguished anatomist, particularly in respect to the nervous system, was one of the authors of the textbook on human anatomy that we studied.

Wilbur Cleveland Smith, professor of gross anatomy, was considered hard but fair. Once, for example, after a heavy rain he flipped a coin to see if he or a student who was also looking at flooded Willow Street would carry the other across; he lost. The student rode on his back and reached the other side with dry feet.

Oscar Walter Bethea, professor of clinical therapeutics, was also author of our textbook, *Materia Medica and Prescription Writing*. Prescriptions were written in Latin words and abbreviations. It was just as well that the layman did not know what he was taking. The poor handwriting of physicians is not taught; it just comes naturally.

John Herr Musser, professor of medicine, was transplanted from Philadelphia, where Mussers had been physicians for several generations, and he maintained a proud tradition.

Willey Denis, professor of biochemistry, one of our few women teachers, came to us from Harvard. Mary Byrd Dees was assistant professor of anatomy. There were three women in our class of approximately one hundred would-be doctors.

Aldo Castellani, professor of tropical medicine, author and internationally famous, came from the London School of Tropical Medicine but his pronunciation was more Italian than British. After a lecture he would go by taxi to the hotel where he lived then, which was about a block away across Canal Street. Perhaps long residence in the tropics taught him to avoid exertion under a hot sun.

Harold Cummins was assistant professor of anatomy and friend of students struggling with the mysteries of anatomy as shown by the microscope—the cells, chromosomes, mitotic figures, cytoplasm, nuclei, all the minute structures made visible by magnification of minute slices of tissues which could be identified in this way. By telling facts in an interesting way, he relaxed those tensions that could interfere with learning processes.

The weeks before final examinations witnessed the intensive study called "cramming" by those facing the ordeal, although their fates had largely been determined by then. The more confident ones would try to find relaxation the night be-

70

fore a test with some outside diversion and on returning sometimes found a roommate grimly holding a book and drinking coffee but without much more knowledge acquired. At such a critical period each had to decide what was best to do in order to be prepared.

An examination of a class in another school in the university indicated that there had been some cheating and the evidence pointed to a certain few. Several others, innocent but wishing to help these and believing that in unity there is strength, circulated a petition which, among other things, stated that all were equally guilty of the apparent irregularity.

Everyone in that class signed the paper, many without reading it carefully. The outcome of all this was that the whole class was expelled and there was no graduation in that school the year in which they otherwise would have graduated. It was an expensive lesson for all the individuals affected by the unfortunate affair.

We were naturally rather tense the night of the meeting called to notify each senior whether he or she would graduate. The written notification was given individually in an envelope, which was opened with trepidation. If it contained one message I would have a Doctor of Medicine degree within a week, but another would mean that the degree would be delayed at least until after summer school or possibly would never be awarded.

My notice directed me to be present for graduation, giving the time and place for the ceremony. It was one of the most satisfying sights in my experience, making all the work it represented seem worthwhile. Otherwise it would have been one of my greatest disappointments.

We learned that a few classmates failed to meet the requirements and could not be graduated with those friends with whom they had shared adversities, as well as basked in the sunshine of rosy-hued success, for four years. Incidentally, Roger, my friend who had not neglected his social life, was one of those who had this misfortune, but perhaps he had consolation prizes.

The list of those graduating included the three women, Miss Adelaide Mary Zoeller, Miss Suzanne Sophie Schaefer and Mrs. Julia Johnson Nelson, whose marriage gave her the title of "Mrs." before she acquired that of M.D.

Commencement morning, on the way to the Shriner's Mosque where the graduation exercises took place that year, I stopped in a "Pressing Done While You Wait" place to get my suit pressed. The proprietor directed me to a booth, where I removed my suit. He took it away and I waited. As the suit was not returned within the time expected, I called to the man who had disappeared with it and asked, "Hey, Mister! Is it ready? I have to get to the commencement by ten o'clock."

"We don't do any pressing here; it has not been returned yet but should be back soon" was his surprising reply. There was not much time left before what promised to be the memorable ceremony in the Mosque would start, and this follower of Hippocrates and subscriber to his oath was elsewhere, without even a toga. Luckily, the pressed suit was retrieved quickly enough for me to get dressed and to the Mosque on time with a sharp crease in my trousers.

The program was followed without deviation, as if a rehearsed play, but with dignity and solemnity. Before we realized that the momentous moment had arrived, our names were being called.

"Archinard, Barber, Baumhauer, Bayon, Beavers, Bell, Beven, Billeaudeau, Blakeney, Brown, Bullock.

"Childers, Christman, Clements, Clyde, Collier, Conwill, Cunningham, Eckford, Edgar, Efron, Falletta, Feingold, Floyd, Fuselier.

"Geddie, Gill, Goode, Granberry, Graves, Grayson, Gueymard, Hale, Hall—," and we were recognized as doctors.

Internships would follow and soon these new doctors would be scattered to the various hospitals over the country which had accepted them for expected mutual benefit. Many would remain in New Orleans to serve and to gain experience in hospitals they knew.

Hearing of the advantages in the Louisiana State Charity Hospital in Shreveport, I had a conference with its superintendent, applied for an internship there and was accepted. I took the Louisiana State Board examinations and obtained a license to practice medicine in the state. I was embarked on a career that would take me to a variety of hospitals and from isolated areas to towns and the great cities and to countries beyond the seas.

Training And Internships

"The girl who was just brought in tried to commit suicide. She took bichloride of mercury," the emergency room nurse at Shreveport Charity Hospital told me.

I had just been assigned to this service, my first in the rotating internship starting that morning. This girl was my first patient. Whether she lived or died would depend upon what we did for her.

The day before, I had arrived and was shown through the hospital by Steve Nealon, an outgoing intern. He also sold me his uniforms, which were in fair condition. He said, "The operating rooms are on the top floor" but did not go there. "You'll see them plenty," he added. "We get an awful lot of injury cases from car accidents, fights, shootings and such," Steve said. "You'll be treating knife cuts, gunshot wounds, head injuries, burns, everything else. You'll see more blood, pus and corruption than you care to."

We went through some of the wards on the various services. "The others are about the same; there's no use going to all of them now," he said.

"There is a medical and a surgical resident. Each has an assistant. You will find out what they are like. I won't prejudice you. They don't bother you much if you do your work.

"Most of those on the visiting staff are all right. In surgery they will let you do some little things after you've been there a while. Dr. Murchison, the eye surgeon, does not even want the intern in the room with him when he is operating."

"Does he tell them to stay out?" I asked.

"Not exactly, but you get the idea. Dr. Caldwell, the or-

73

thopod, is one of the best. He will try to help you get started."

"Are you always crowded like this?" I asked. We were on the white male medical ward. All the beds on it were occupied and there was a row of makeshift beds of sheet-covered mattresses on each side of the hall. There were nearly as many patients lying on the floor as in the regular beds.

"Nearly always. Sometimes it's worse. This is a busy hospital. We get patients from all over North Louisiana and emergencies from other places," he said.

He introduced me to a few of the ward nurses, showed me how the records were kept, the various forms such as history sheets and temperature charts and the way laboratory requests were made.

"The laboratory and X-ray are overloaded just now and we have been asked not to make unnecessary requests. Urinalyses, complete blood counts and Wassermanns are routine. X-rays are done on chest cases and suspected fractures, of course. There are no objections to reasonable requests," Steve advised me.

At the outpatient department all seats were taken and there were lines of patients waiting to see the doctor, to get treatment or a prescription filled. Some wore casts or splints and many had bandages in need of changing. Most were waiting quietly but a few appeared as if their time were more valuable than that of the others.

"Sometimes you see people drive up in a Cadillac and come in here for free treatment. Maybe some of them think that the treatment given here is better than what they get outside. Too, occasionally one of them may expect to see a certain doctor," Steve said.

The hospital was an old red brick building which, viewed from the street, had a sort of dowager appearance. Inside it looked as if brawlers had lived in it for a long time. Actually the effects of wear and tear were everywhere. On the walls were the marks of wheelchairs, rolling stretchers, cleaning tools and human beings.

Equipment showed signs of use as it should since most of it was used to capacity daily. Frills and luxuries were absent. Cleanliness, however, was almost an obsession in this institution of hard-working staffs.

The day the new interns arrived there was a meeting in the staff room at which the superintendent, Dr. Griffin, addressed us.

74

"First, I want to welcome you to Shreveport Charity Hospital," he began. "I am pleased to see you again and I hope that you like what you have seen here. You can see that there is plenty of work for all of you. What you have been learning the past four years can be put to good use in the hospital and you will have an opportunity to get the experience you want.

"Your pay will be ten dollars per month, as you know. You will get room and board, of course. Two will be in each room. Each intern must buy his uniforms but the hospital will launder them. I do not need to tell you that you are expected to be clean at all times.

"This is called a charity hospital, but so far as you are concerned each person under treatment is a paying patient and is to be treated accordingly. You are to treat them as if they were your private patients.

"I want you to use whatever is necessary but remember that our funds are limited and we cannot afford to be wasteful. Let us know of any special needs and we will consider them.

"You will be on duty twenty-four hours of the day but naturally you are not expected to work all of them. Your primary responsibility will be to the patients, on the services to which you will be assigned. And you will relieve on the others whenever this is required to keep all wards fully covered. The residents will see to this," he said.

After these preliminary remarks he proceeded to inform us concerning the hospital, organization, divisions, services, visiting staff, patient eligibility and to advise us regarding our work. He ended his talk by saying, "I am sure that if you all do all your assignments to the best of your ability, you will have nothing to worry about, the patients will get good treatment and you will benefit from your internship."

Jim Babcock, who was graduated from the University of Tennessee in Memphis, shared my room in the hospital. He was tall, lanky, and deliberate in his work. But he was quick to get a number of girls' names, addresses and phone numbers in the little book he carried.

Our room was not much different from those to which I had become accustomed in dormitories and boarding houses and so was not disappointing. The furniture was simple and just adequate. Sounds that first night were novel but I slept well. Many nights in the future I would be awakened to see patients with complications, pain or changes for the worse.

A call in the quietness of the night would mean bad news or a message of discomfort or weakness. The doctor does not expect to be aroused from sleep to hear glad tidings.

Steve Nealon and the others who had finished their internship had departed to start practice or to get more training in other hospitals. The beginners must now do what they could for the unending stream of suffering humanity passing through the hospital. Each of us had a beginning of his own.

Fate ordered that I should begin with Jean Dole, a girl less than eighteen, who had been so unhappy that she did not want to live and attempted to take her own life just at the threshold of adulthood. But there was not time for me to think about this.

Only a little while had elapsed since the girl had swallowed the poison, so its removal by gastric irrigation seemed feasible. She had been so distraught that realization of the consequences of the act came to her only after she felt the corrosive material descending. Then, wanting to live, she made known what she had done and was soon on the emergency room table where I now saw her, a beautiful young girl in distress.

I passed a lubricated stomach tube without delay and removed all the stomach's contents at once with copious irrigations, administered an antidote and admitted her for further treatment and observation. Fortunately this was not my first time to insert such a tube. It was also fortunate that she had changed her mind so quickly.

People attempting suicide, in many cases, I learned, asked for emergency treatment soon after the attempt. In some instances we wondered if they really wanted to die or if what was done was to influence or punish another person. A few of these had numerous cuts on the wrist, none deep enough to bleed much.

The girl recovered without any organic effects. She told us what had happened. "My father ordered my boy friend away from our home and told him to never come back. He said that I could not see him again. That's why I did it but now I want to get well."

A few days after the girl's admission, her father was admitted. In anguish over what had occurred, he, too, had taken poison in large amounts but delayed so long in asking for help that treatment could only make his last misery easier.

On the medical wards were some heart cases with the condition called "cardiac decompensation." The heads of their beds were elevated and many of them were being given digitalis regularly.

There were several patients with cirrhosis of the liver to the extent that large quantities of fluid accumulated in the abdomen, which had to be drained at intervals of a few weeks. This was done with the patient sitting so that the fluid would gravitate to the lower part of the abdomen.

Under local anesthesia, a small skin incision was made in the mid-line between the umbilicus and pubis and through it a trocar and cannula were inserted into the abdominal cavity. On removal of the trocar, the fluid flowed through the cannula and was caught in a pail. The patient could then breathe more easily. This was one of the earlier minor surgical procedures performed by the interns.

The diabetic cases were given enough insulin to take care of the controlled amounts of carbohydrates that they were receiving in their diets prepared by the dietician. A search of the beds of these patients would sometimes reveal sweets such as candy bars that they had concealed to satisfy a later craving. Occasionally one of these patients would become unconscious, either in insulin shock or diabetic coma, and would be given a solution of glucose intravenously with sufficient insulin to provide for its metabolization as determined by calculation with the use of a formula. The quick response was dramatic. To see a comatose person become conscious, alert, look at you and talk with you again was one of the intern's many rewards.

Pellagra accounted for the overflow of medical wards at times. In a mild form it was a common, chronic skin disease of that part of the country in that period but occasionally became a major medical problem. For example, when the Mississippi flooded hundreds of people from their lowland homes into refugee camps, many of them who were eating a faulty diet became ill with this disease.

Dermatitis of the exposed skin and diarrhea were the first manifestations of pellagra. Dementia eventually followed in some of the more severe, long-untreated cases, and a few of these did not survive. Treatment consisted of correcting the dietary deficiencies and giving vitamins, medication and general care. Results were generally good but minimal skin symptoms of the disease often persisted.

The first major operation for which I scrubbed was on the

orthopedic service. It was an open reduction and fixation of a hip fracture. I assisted Dr. Guy A. Caldwell, a distinguished orthopedist. My assistance consisted mainly in holding the retractors so that he could see and have room to work.

My first operation as the surgeon was an appendectomy. I had done operations on dogs and had assisted in many on our patients, but this was different. The man with appendicitis was on my ward. I had taken his history, examined, prepared and posted him for the operation.

After putting on an operating suit, cap and mask, I had scrubbed my hands and arms to the elbows with brush, soap and water for ten minutes and dipped them in the antiseptic solution. With sterile gown and rubber gloves on, I took my place as usual on the anesthetized patient's left side to assist with the operation. The surgeon, Dr. Campbell, came around the table and said, "You work on the other side this time."

This was what I had been slaving and waiting for. My walk to the patient's right was a short one, but to me it seemed that I had come a long way.

The sterile sheets had been draped over the patient and towels placed around the operative site, the lower right abdomen. I took the scalpel and drew it across the skin over the appendix. To avoid cutting too deeply, I had not pressed the blade down firmly enough. I repeated the movement and this time incised the subcutaneous fat to the fascia.

I had made the incision; now to clamp and tie the bleeders. After that, the muscle was divided, the peritoneum grasped and then opened while held up by me and my assistant.

The appendix was not readily located. Sometimes from the other side of the table I had seen appendices in the incisions, once even crawling out like a worm, but not this time.

"Let me take a feel," Dr. Campbell offered. He felt inside, seemed puzzled for a minute or two, then delivered the appendix into view.

"It was in an unusual position, behind," he said, perhaps to console me. The next time I would know how it felt.

When watching operations as a student, I generally could not see what was being done very clearly, often only the backs of the surgeons. Even when assisting as an intern I was not in as favorable a position for seeing inside the incision as now while I was operating.

I did the rest of the operation, following the steps seen

many times, but it did not seem the same as when I had watched others. The mesoappendix was clamped, cut and ligated; the appendix was ligated at the base, cut and the stump treated with phenol and alcohol; then, on the second try, it was inverted with a purse-string suture that had been placed before cutting the appendix. After a final inspection the abdomen was closed in layers.

Knife cuts, stab wounds and assorted other injuries made Saturday nights exciting in the emergency room, and in the operating room these cases often meant hours of suturing and repairing the damages. Fights accounted for many of the injuries, which were often multiple.

"How did you get so many cuts?" I asked one patient, with nearly a dozen gashes that I was suturing.

"The fellow with the knife walked around me," he said with a grin.

"Who was he?"

"Just a friend."

"Why did your friend cut you up like this?"

"Oh, we just had a friendly little argument."

As usual in such cases, he would not tell who had attacked him or why. When pressed for information, patients frequently said, "I don't know who he was or what made him do it."

Policeman brought many of these cases to the hospital, sometimes more than one at the same time, and when this occurred the receiving doctor had to decide the order in which to attend them. The policeman could sometimes give useful information but did not always agree with the doctor's priorities. They, as well as patients and members of their families, apparently did not in every instance regard interns as "real doctors."

Ministers, priests and a rabbi were available for the patients' religious needs and the services that they could provide. Those critically ill were generally given special attention. When a transfusion or an infusion of saline or glucose was started on a patient, it was a common thing to see a chaplain soon appear at the bedside without any other invitation.

Lack of the appearance that much of the public associates with experience was considered a handicap in their public relations by some of the interns. According to Jim, "Every doctor should have gray hair and hemorrhoids—the gray hairs to give a look of maturity and dignity, the hemorrhoids a look of concern." He thought that these attributes would contribute to the

79

effectiveness of his bedside manner.

Hemorrhoidectomies were among the operations that interns were permitted to do under the proctologist's supervision after sufficient experience in assisting. Circumcisions were common on the genitourinary ward. They provided the beginners in surgery a chance to practice.

Tonsillectomies were done in large numbers, so we had the opportunity to develop skill in removing tonsils. On certain days school children who had been found to need the operation were brought to the hospital in big groups. One day eighty pairs of tonsils were removed, including those of a little boy who had accompanied his sister and was sitting with her on one of the benches reserved for the ones waiting to be operated upon, but he was not there for an operation.

Another small boy was brought to the hospital by his parents for a tonsillectomy and while under the anesthetic had a circumcision done at the parents' request. When he regained consciousness he was puzzled, not being able to understand why taking his tonsils out made his penis sore.

The hospital pet was a little black boy, Jerry Adams, with tuberculosis of the spine, who had been there for many months and was known by almost everyone. Doctors, nurses and attendants were fond of him and did whatever they could for him. He was in traction but was able to sing, which he often did in a small voice.

Jerry was good natured and always cheerful in spite of the circumstances under which he lived. His attitude inspired those around him whose troubles were minor by comparison. "Mister Doctor, will you give me a drink of water?" or a similar request he would confidently make of me if the nurse was not near.

Syphilis was usually treated in the outpatient department. Neoarsphenamin given intravenously weekly was the treatment of choice then. There was always a long line of patients waiting for treatment at the times injections were given. We became proficient in inserting a needle in an obscure vein, which could be difficult, especially in a fat arm.

The obstetrical service was a busy one. The welcome cry of a newborn baby was a familiar sound. Perhaps a birth was not thought of as miraculous because it was such a common occurrence.

Money for operating the hospital was obtained from

appropriations by the state legislature. Some of the more important positions in our hospital were filled by individuals who were acceptable to the elected state officials. On election day some of the employees waited to see which way the election was going before they went to vote.

One night the superintendent of the hospital asked me to go in an ambulance with the chief nurse and some orderlies to meet Adrien Cartwright, who was arriving by train. Young Mr. Cartwright's leg had been severely injured in a football game, I was informed.

We were unable to get Adrien's stretcher through the narrow door of the passenger car of the train, so we lifted him carefully through the window, got him safely into the ambulance and reached our destination without any mishap and apparently without causing him any pain.

He was a personable, cooperative young man and seemed to appreciate our help at a trying time. I felt flattered that the superintendent had selected me for this mission upon learning later from Lucien Lecours, the resident in surgery, that "the amounts of money appropriated for our hospital are determined largely by Adrien's father in the legislature."

Shreveport is not far from the Texas line in North Louisiana. To the west are Marshall, Longview, Kilgore, Tyler, Dallas, and Fort Worth. Located on the Red River near the Caddo oil field, there were numerous oil wells in the vicinity and much industry, the fuel for which was furnished by natural gas.

El Dorado, Arkansas, was northeast in an oil-field area. In that direction was "Boom Town," spawned by the atmosphere created by the discovery of numerous new wells. The flow of "black gold" and promise of wealth to come attracted all kinds of men and women, some of them itinerants whose activities did not relate directly to the petroleum industry.

An oil company was seeking a doctor, preferably one who could treat injuries of employees as well as the usual sicknesses. Their representative talked with me concerning a position with the company and offered a salary that seemed enormous when I was making only ten dollars a month. When my time was not occupied with doctoring, I would be expected to do oil research. I had majored in chemistry in getting my Bachelor of Science degree. I considered the offer, for five minutes at least. The prospect of immediate big pay was tempting but I decided to continue my internship.

The Louisiana State Fair was held in October and the hospital maintained a first-aid station on the fairgrounds to treat minor injuries and emergency cases. When on duty there we were at a fair but not for pleasure. It was a change, however. A few of the visitors who came in took advantage of what they considered an opportunity to get professional advice concerning chronic ailments.

"Doc, I think I've walked a blister on my heel. Could you put something on it?" one man asked.

"Sure. Sit down here and I'll take a look."

"My back has been hurting low down, 'specially when I first get up. What do you suppose is wrong?"

"I would have to know more about you and maybe get X-rays and examine you to find out what the trouble is."

"What do you think would be good for it? Could you suggest something? It's bothered me a long time."

"There, I've taken care of your heel. You can put your shoes back on. Don't walk any more than necessary today. You had better see your own doctor for your back complaint. We can only give first aid here."

"Okay, Doc, just thought I'd ask. I can see that you're right busy now."

The public amusements in Shreveport were rather limited compared to New Orleans. We went to a movie occasionally; Jim liked westerns. There were a few plays staged by traveling troupes. In one of these, the rugged hero, in reference to exploits in the wild and wooly West, came to the script line which mentioned Texas. The part of Texas best known to Shreveport people was very much like the Louisiana they knew, so the actor changed the locale of the heroic action to "West Texas." The obvious switch did not lessen the humor of the comical drama.

Volleyball games were fun the way we played them and provided exercise nearly every day when enough of us could get together. This often was during the noon hour. Sometimes we walked downtown if free in the evening.

There was a man living in Shreveport at that time who had made a reputation as a mind reader. It was said that whenever a stranger went to see him, he could call the stranger by name and give details of his past. What he could tell about a person that he had never seen before was amazing, we had been told.

We decided to test the man's powers. One Sunday night

several of us went to his home unannounced, thinking that in this way he would be unable to get any information about us beforehand. He would not see us, however, saying, "I don't work on Sunday." We guessed that the accounts of his unusual gifts of perception had been exaggerated.

"I've rented a car for tonight," Jim told me one day. "I have a date with Helen. Why don't you ask her friend Trudy? She likes you. All you'd have to do is push her over if you wanted to."

"I don't know. I might not be able to get away and besides, Trudy may not want to go."

"Well, find out. We can share the cost and neither one of us will be out much."

We went, the four of us. The main event, as envisioned by Jim, was to be a romance in the country. It was a beautiful moonlit night. He stopped at a grassy knoll and hinted that Trudy and I should get lost. "Would you two like to take a little walk?" he suggested, and we did.

We sat on the grass in the moonlight, saw some shooting stars and talked, but Trudy did not seem romantically inclined and she was not the most attractive girl I knew, even in the light of the moon. We were away from the hospital sights, sounds, odors and feelings for a little while and enjoyed the difference.

Jim called to me before very long and we returned to the car. "We're going back," he said rather abruptly. Helen did not look too pleased either. Not much more was said.

It was evident that the excursion had not been as Jim had contemplated. He was quiet and drove as if in a hurry to end it. Since no one seemed inclined to communicate their thoughts and as it had been a busy day for me, I reclined on the back seat and did not see the car leave the road.

The first thing I knew, we were bumping noisily and the car was tilting. It landed with a crash on its top with the four of us under it. I was the only one who could crawl out but managed to pull out the other three. Luckily, perhaps, I was reclining at the time of the accident. The terrible moment of anxiety when the conditions of the others were uncertain was followed by relief. We were fortunate. None of us was seriously injured.

We were at the bottom of a high embankment, which we climbed after a check indicated that no bones were broken. A man seeing the wreckage below the road stopped his car to look. Amazed to see that we had survived, he brought us back to town, sadder but wiser, I hope, than when we left.

A patient on my ward was scheduled for an eye operation to be done by Dr. Murchison. I did not want to miss being present although Jim told me, "I never went in the room when he was operating. He likes to work alone."

"I'm going in anyway and hear how he will ask me to leave."

As customary when patients from my wards had operations, I went to surgery, scrubbed to assist if permitted and entered the operating room. To my surprise, Dr. Murchison seemed pleased to see me. He prepared the patient for the operation, an enucleation (removal of the eyeball), then asked me, "Would you like to do it? I'll help you." He did.

Dr. Murchison directed me in the various procedures and the operation was completed. "That was all right," he said. "I'm glad that at least one of the interns is interested in eye surgery." The socket healed well and was fitted with a glass eye before the patient was discharged.

One of the advantages of being an intern was in being able to follow the course of patients after medical treatment or surgery. For example, before when I had seen an operation I did not generally know the outcome of it. Whereas previously I often knew only what was learned in the operating room concerning a surgical case, I now took the patients' histories and examined them before and after the operation and could follow the patients at least until discharged. Specimens removed could be examined and in the event of a fatality, the findings at autopsy could be seen when permission was given by the family or by the medical examiner under certain circumstances.

Friends and members of the family could visit patients at a certain hour in the evening. Sometimes they wanted to see the doctor, too. One visiting girl, Hope Hilton, that I had seen in the hospital a few times was friendly, had pleasing features and once when I saw her gave me the impression that she would not object to my company. "I'll be seeing you," I said.

Jim, with his conditioned reflexes, would probably have asked her for a date the first time they met if he had been so impressed. I thought that I might the next time as something indefinable made me hesitate.

A few days later I was in the venereal disease clinic giving intravenous injections to a long line of patients with syphilis. The graceful arm of a young female was presented. With syringe and needle poised, I glanced up at the patient. It was the girl, abashed. The way she looked that last time I saw her is an unhappy memory, although I tried not to hurt her more than the one quick thrust of the needle.

Another thing that Jim enjoyed was golf. We bought a set of clubs together, both of us using the same set whenever we played. I even went to the links with him on the rare occasions when it snowed, which made finding the balls even more difficult. At first, I was in the rough much of the time. The course on which we played was not the best in the world but fine for us. At the end of the year we matched and I won the clubs.

"I'm having a spinal puncture done today," Jim told me one morning.

"What for?" I asked, noticing that he appeared to be somewhat worried. He had not complained.

"Wassermann," he said. "I think something is wrong with me and I'm trying to find out what."

"Why not a blood test?"

"I've had four already and they were all negative, but I want to be sure."

Why he thought that he might have acquired a spirochetal infection he did not say. But he had the spinal tap, after which he had severe headache and had to stay in bed two days with the foot of the bed elevated. I had seen patients with headache after withdrawal of spinal fluid, believed to be due to change in pressure. Why his persisted so long might have been due to leakage temporarily at the puncture site.

Jim's favorite dessert was chocolate pudding. This was on one of the trays brought to our room for him. He did not even feel like eating that. I knew that he must really be suffering when he said, "You can have this chocolate pudding."

The headache was completely gone in a few days and the rest in bed seemed to have revitalized him. A negative report on the spinal fluid elevated his spirits and he soon resumed his usual activities inside and outside the hospital.

Perhaps the reason that Jim was afraid that he might have syphilis was the tendency of many medical students and recent graduates to imagine that they have the disease under study at the time, matching their real or imaginary symptoms with those stated in the textbook. In time, they learn that their subjective feelings or signs of abnormality are usually unrelated to the disease in question unless there is corroborative evidence.

Young doctors find that diseases do not always precisely fit the textbook description of them. What the book states serves as a guide, but in the individual case a disease or abnormality may be atypical. Too, the doctor learns that he does not always get the results with medicines that the book leads him to expect. The dosage or drug may have to be changed or a combination of measures may often be required. Even then the results are ineffective in certain instances. Fortunately many illnesses and discomforts are self-limited or healed by nature. Patients may recover because of the treatment or in spite of it.

A few of our interns were induced to leave the state charity hospital to continue their internships in a private hospital in the city, where their living conditions were more pleasant and the work was not so hard. Their quarters were nicer and in the dining room they had a choice of food, but they did not boast of the training they were getting in that hospital. In that private hospital were the paying patients of the doctors who hospitalized them and there was very little chance for an intern to do much actual surgery. They did have an opportunity to see what private practice was like.

In our hospital we made a study of the attending staff, that is, the doctors from the outside, as well as the residents and the patients on the service where we were at a particular period during the year. In this way we learned the characteristics of the various surgeons and which were best to work with and which gave the most encouragement to the intern, in order to improve by doing as well as watching. Too, we learned which ones were best for a patient.

We had some control over which surgeon did an operation by a bit of manipulation and timing. A patient had to be admitted to a service and to a certain ward. Normally a history was taken, examination done and laboratory reports obtained. In some cases a consultation was indicated, particularly if both medical and surgical problems were involved.

As a rule, the surgeon saw a patient scheduled for a morning operation on the day or night before. He might also look around the ward to see what other cases were there.

Generally the hospital administrative machinery worked rather smoothly. Differences in opinion sometimes arose when a person admitted was neither definitely medical nor definitely surgical. Which service would get the patient? The question became more complicated if the patient had a condition such as gastric ulcer, diseased kidney, gall bladder or ulcerated leg, for example, that could be classed as surgical but would not be operated on immediately, perhaps never.

The risk involved in a contemplated operation was one consideration. What medical measures were indicated before surgery was another. An elective operation on a diabetic or cardiac case made cooperation between the services essential in the best interests of the patient. When the diagnosis was uncertain, a decision had to be made as to the proper ward. If transfer from one ward or service to another were indicated, it was done through mutual consent and understanding. This promoted orderliness and generally prevented flaring of tempers and intemperate language.

Preoperative care and medication were usually given on the surgical ward to which the patient was admitted. This often included an enema, as well as shaving of the abdomen or other area, which was done on the ward or in the preparation room.

Morphine, grain one-fourth P.R.N. q. 4 hrs., was frequently ordered for postoperative relief, which meant that it could be given for pain as often as every four hours. Other drugs were substituted as soon as feasible to avoid addiction. This was a factor that had to be considered in long-term patients complaining of considerable discomfort. I know of none who became addicted while hospitalized.

Hemorrhage was one of the more troublesome complications with which we had to deal, especially when it happened in the middle of the night. Sometimes it occurred after a relatively minor operation such as a tonsillectomy or a hemorrhoidectomy. If the latter, the pressure of a pack might control it or perhaps a clamp on a bleeding point. In some instances of preoperative or postoperative bleeding, the patient had to be taken to the operating room to give every advantage, including a transfusion if necessary.

A fatality resulted from hemorrhage in a case of nephrectomy (excision of a kidney) that we had seen performed elsewhere by a renowned surgeon. The bleeding was coming from the aorta, we were informed later. A surgeon does not like to reopen a wound, but occasionally it was necessary. If internal bleeding was suspected, a decision had to be made as to which was a greater risk—further observation or immediate intervention, taking into account the patient's general condition.

When to operate and when not to was found to be one of the most important problems facing the surgeon. Judgment had to be developed with experience and presumably this improved along with operating skill and technical knowledge. I would find that some surgeons were proficient in operating but lacked discretion.

We were nearing the end of our year of rotating internship. I had served in the various subdivisions of the medical and surgical services, had taken my turns on ambulance runs, in the emergency room and outpatient service. I was sure that I wanted more training before beginning private practice but was not certain regarding specialization.

A young doctor who was in my medical fraternity at Tulane but had graduated before I did opened an office for general practice in Shreveport after interning for one year. I saw him from time to time, once or twice at a downtown church, and he told me that the number of patients he treated was growing. His income seemed large to me then, yet I did not follow his example.

That year Charles A. Lindbergh won the nickname "Lone Eagle" and many honors when he made the first solo flight across the Atlantic Ocean in the *Spirit of St. Louis*, landing near Paris. The event thrilled everyone and at the time seemed as newsworthy as the flights to the moon in the future. Some years later he worked with his friend, the medical scientist Alexis Carrel, in developing a "mechanical heart."

"How would you like interning in Washington next year?" Jim asked me. "Gallinger Municipal Hospital wants interns. I think that they might take us as we have already had one year. What do you say?"

"We could apply and decide when we see their answer and what they offer if they accept. In the meantime we can do some more checking."

The idea of working in a large city hospital appealed to me, especially when considering that the city was the nation's capital. I had spent a week there but had not seen the hospital.

Jim's enthusiasm for Gallinger was contagious and several of the interns became interested. It appeared that some of my friends planned to go there so all would not be strangers. Henry Snodgrass and Ralph Locke, both from North Carolina, Jim and I applied. All four of us were accepted.

Oddly, Jim was the only one who did not go. I bade him, and Louisiana, farewell as, for some reason, he changed his mind and took another position. But destiny decreed that our paths would cross again.

Resident Clinical Director

"So this is Gallinger Municipal Hospital in the nation's capital," said Henry Snodgrass, shaking his head incredulously.

We were looking at a row of old low, wooden buildings that had the appearance of some oversized former residences that had been painted white. Beyond them to our left was a two-story red brick structure that evidently had stood there for a long time, which we soon learned was the nurses' home.

Two newer brick buildings, with a covered driveway between, were further back from the street to our right. The windows were securely covered with heavy steel screens. We found out that this was where the psychiatric patients were hospitalized.

"I don't know about you guys, but I'm ready to hunt for another hospital," Ralph Locke said.

"We had better check in first now that we are here," I suggested.

Our first view of Gallinger after arriving from Shreveport was disappointing. Washington, D.C., being the capital did not mean that it was the country's medical center, but we three had expected to find a more impressive general hospital there. It was located at Nineteenth and C Streets in the southeastern part of the city near the Anacostia River.

We made our presence known in the office of the superintendent, Dr. Blalock; received information, assignments and instructions briefly; and were directed to our quarters in a two-story wooden building conveniently located back of the medical and surgical wards. The building had a kitchen, dining room and a small lounge space. Our bedrooms were just that, not remarkable.

The interns were paid thirty dollars per month, three times as much as we had been making. A wealthy woman offered to increase our pay, we heard, but her generous offer was not accepted by whoever made the decision, although we were allowed to keep the radio-record player that she donated.

A recreation room in the nurses' home provided a place where we could visit in the early evening hours when the girls were hospitable. There were tennis courts nearby which, under the circumstances, encouraged us to get needed exercise.

Next to the tennis courts was the enclosed yard of the big District of Columbia Jail, the inside of which I would come to know well. The jail and hospital were closely associated.

When going into the center of the city toward the Library of Congress and the Capitol, we walked over to the south end of the streetcar line on Pennsylvania Avenue. On the way we passed the District Morgue and the Congressional Cemetery, walking on Seventeenth Street and Potomac Avenue, past the end of Kentucky Avenue.

The medical school faculties of Georgetown and George Washington universities staffed Gallinger Hospital. The hospital was used for the instruction of the medical students of these two schools, so we had the opportunity of being exposed to the teachings of the outstanding medical men of the city. The wards supplied a great variety of cases, particularly in the field of psychiatry and neurology.

Soon after we arrived, Dr. Argyll, the visiting physician who was a professor of medicine, was showing us through the medical wards. A patient in one of the beds had red, rough, dry, thick skin of the face, neck, hands and exposed parts of the arms.

"There is a pellagra case," Ralph Locke remarked quietly in passing, as if stating what was obvious.

Dr. Argyll overheard him and said, "So that is what it is," as if relieved of a burden. "We have been trying to make a diagnosis ever since he was admitted."

"We saw many cases like that in Louisiana," I said, "some much worse."

"Will you give a lecture on pellagra to my class next week?" he asked me.

"Sure, I'll be glad to tell them what I know."

On the wards were several cases of tuberculosis. "These

will be transferred to the sanatorium when the diagnoses are confirmed with another positive sputum," Dr. Argyll said.

There were two cases of liver abscess; a few chest empyema cases; one patient with draining peritonitis; several chronic cardiac cases; and a number of patients with swollen, ulcerated legs, elevated on rubber-covered pillows, some with heat cabinets over them. There was the usual assortment of common diseases.

Soon we were settled down to the work of doing the things necessary for the treatment of sick and suffering individuals. They could not be treated routinely, but certain procedures were carried out for each patient. All had to have a medical history, a diet, laboratory tests, medicine as indicated, and findings on physical examinations recorded.

On the surgical wards were a few gastric ulcer cases who had had gastroenterostomies, two thyroidectomies, a head injury, a number of orthopedic cases, many obstetrical patients, several tonsillectomies, hysterectomies, appendectomies, hernia repairs and other cases awaiting surgery. However, they were not in numbers as large as we had been accustomed to admitting in the hospital from which I had come.

One part of the skin preparation for surgery was different from that in any other hospital where I had served. Tincture of iodine was applied by drawing a gauze sponge saturated with the tincture across one side of the operative site. This sponge was discarded and another one wet with the tincture was drawn across in line with the first iodine path, slightly overlapping it. The second was discarded and the procedure repeated until the whole area was covered. It was a tedious process, but the chief of the surgical staff, Dr. John Cannon, thought it was justified to minimize the spread of any possible contaminant on the skin.

A treatment for syphilis used at Gallinger that I had not seen employed elsewhere was inunctions of mercurial ointment. Patients selected for treatment by this method were rubbed with the ointment for approximately half an hour at regular times.

After operations, patients were confined to bed for long periods of time, often for several weeks, particularly after hernia repairs. It was believed that this would favor wound healing. This theory was generally discarded eventually and patients were encouraged to get out of bed as soon as possible, on the same day as the operation in many instances. Obstetrical patients stayed in bed for ten days after delivery.

Some of the interns had not previously come in contact with psychotic patients and were somewhat apprehensive when near them. Sidney Green, especially, was concerned when duty on the psychiatric service was being discussed in a "bull session" in front of the interns' house.

"I don't feel easy around them. You never know what one of them might do," Sidney said.

"You shouldn't ever let one get behind you," Henry advised. "In a round room they can't hem you in very well but don't let them get you into a corner. Keep your eyes on them at all times."

Sidney departed from Gallinger the day after being assigned to serve in the psychiatric department and we never saw him again. We heard that he was accepted as an intern in a hospital in Massachusetts.

Interns were in the United States Civil Service and the hospital depended upon appropriations for its support. In common with other teaching hospitals and hospitals in general, the amount of money available for the hospital's needs was not excessive. One of the places where economy was noticeable was in the meals in our dining room, although they were adequate.

Dinner dessert always consisted of cherries, the yellow, canned kind, except that they came in drums. They must have been cheaper that way. Since we had them week after week we assumed that they had been purchased wholesale, a carload lot perhaps. Marzinski, however, liked them so well that he would get an extra handful of them as he passed the pantry on the way out.

One touch of color and refinement we often had was the presence of flowers. When there was a party or reception in the White House at which large quantities of flowers were used, they would be sent to the hospital after the event and distributed to the wards.

The United States Marine Band favored us with an orchestra for some of our dances. The bandsmen, in their colorful uniforms and evincing pride in their organization, were welcomed. They were excellent musicians, gave "class" to our affairs and were appreciated, but some of the dancers considered their music a bit conservative for their swing tastes.

Each state, it seemed, had a club organized by the people from that state living in Washington at the time. These clubs gave elaborate balls which were attended by its members and invited guests. This gave them an opportunity to enjoy an evening of music and dancing and perhaps take a close look at famous people of whom they had read or seen only at a distance before.

The congressional delegation and office holders were usually at the state's ball. Current gossip could be heard along with the orchestral sounds.

"My brother is assigned to the President's yacht," my dancing partner at one of these balls informed me.

"It must be a nice place to be and should be interesting when the President is on board."

"He said that President Coolidge never talks to anybody, not even those who come with him."

The girl who invited me to the Ohio State Ball was anxious to meet the senior senator from Ohio, who was sitting in one of the special boxes by the dance floor.

"I will introduce you to him," I volunteered.

"Are you acquainted with him?"

"No, but that does not matter. Come with me."

As anticipated, the senator was pleased and very gracious. He happened to be alone and invited us to sit with him.

At one ball, the girl I was with was the daughter of an influential congressman who had the reputation of exhibiting a fiery temper when provoked. The newspapers had recently reported that he had thrown an inkwell at another congressman who had angered him in a dispute in the Congress. The subject came up during our conversation.

"Aren't you afraid of him?" I asked teasingly.

"No. At home he is nice and gentle," she said with a smile and in a tone that indicated love and esteem for her father. It was evident that her view of him was different from his public image. Anyway, his daughter was nice.

In addition to my duties in Gallinger Hospital, I also served as visiting doctor for the District Jail next door for a while. When I went there for the first time it seemed even larger and its walls more massive than seen previously from the street. The great front door was unlocked by a uniformed guard to let me inside, where I saw many men at desks, as in a business office. I learned later that these men were trusties.

Tom Manson was the inmate who took care of the medicines and supplies and helped me give attention to those who needed it or had complaints for the doctor to hear. He guided me through the cell blocks, bringing along a big wire basket containing dressing materials and common drugs that might be indicated. We made rounds through the jail, including death row.

Sicknesses and injuries treated were generally minor, but some constituted problems and a few required hospitalization outside of the jail. In this event the constant presence of a policeman on the ward might be necessary. Rarely was a patient handcuffed to his bed and then under unusual circumstances which involved crime of a serious nature.

"I was with the Department of Justice," Tom confided one day. "Our division dealt with the custodianship of alien or foreign-owned property that had been seized in this country. Some of these assets were mishandled. An investigation was made and it was decided that there should be a conviction. They made me the goat, so here I am."

At least he had more freedom of movement and could spend his time easier than most convicts. He liked to talk and told of his life and experiences in better days.

Sometimes when I had to examine a man, a guard would lock me in the cell with him. This was not always necessary as some needed only a simple medication such as a laxative or headache medicine.

The most trying part of my efforts for the prisoners was when I was with the unhappy men who were under sentence of death and awaiting execution. They were in a row of cells in a section of the jail secured from the rest. A common request was for medicine to help them sleep.

One man, Harry Mann, whose execution had been set for the next Friday, asked me for sleeping medicine each day I went to see him and I gave him a dose sufficient to enable him to sleep through the dreaded long night. On Monday Harry had said, "Doctor, could you give me something to make me sleep?" On Tuesday, Wednesday and Thursday it was the same, except for the depth of anxiety we felt with time running out as the fatal day approached.

Thursday was the last day I could see Harry. Early Friday morning when they came for him he could not be aroused and virtually had to be carried to the electric chair between two guards, I was told. Apparently he had managed to save enough medicine for the final dose to prolong the sleep of his last night through the execution.

The doctors in Gallinger were the main source of medical attention for the prisoners in the District Jail as there was no full-time jail physician then. Ailments and complaints were generally made to Tom Manson, who reported them to the visiting doctor. The prisoner patients were then able to make their complaints known to the doctor directly and he would evaluate them, being aware of the possibility that a prisoner might try to get transferred to the hospital by malingering.

A new electric chair was installed in the jail that year. The first time it was used was for the execution of a criminal who had received the death sentence near the time of the new interns' arrival at Gallinger. The hospital's chief medical officer, Dr. Howery, was asked to be present to pronounce the man dead after the heavy voltage of electricity had passed through him. This method of execution was instituted as an improvement over hanging, an advantage being its quickness. It was not believed to cause pain.

Dr. Howery described it to us later that day. "There were not many of us who saw it," he said. "Besides those who had to be present, there were a few reporters. A priest was with him when he came into the death chamber. The ones watching stood over by the wall. I was closer to him then.

"He was strapped into the heavy electric chair. Electrodes, metal plates, were attached to the top of his head and the calf of one of his legs. The switch was turned on to pass the current from one electrode to another through his body. He lost consciousness but was still alive when I examined him.

"One shock was supposed to do it, but this was the first time that the chair had been used and something must have been wrong. They tried it again with more voltage. Again I could still get a heartbeat with my stethoscope."

"What was the matter; wasn't there enough juice?" one of the interns asked Howery.

"There should have been. It was set for over two thousand volts. Anyway, they increased it but I could detect a faint heartbeat after the third and fourth times. Only after the fifth time were all signs of life gone and I pronounced him dead."

Many accident and drunken cases were brought to Gallinger. Often a patient was both injured and drunk. The doctor on admissions had to take this into consideration in disposing of a case. A man who was only under the influence of alcohol might be left in the custody of the policeman who arrested him for disturbing the peace, but one who was "dead drunk" might also have a broken back.

In one instance a man was brought to the hospital in an ambulance, where he was seen by a doctor who found him in a deep sleep and reeking of alcohol. The doctor, seeing no signs of injury, left him on the ambulance in charge of the police, who took him away. Later it was found that the man had been seriously injured while on a spree. The newspapers were very critical of the doctor and the hospital.

Roy Sapphi had contrived to get a medical degree that would be awarded after the successful completion of a year's internship and it seemed to be mainly for this that he was at Gallinger. His thinking was more along legal lines than medical. While many young doctors gave one the impression that underneath their armor they were idealistic, Roy appeared cynical and without much sense of morality or ethics.

Too often the sole criterion for admission to medical school and for graduation is the individual's ability to get acceptable grades, regardless of how they were acquired. A person of poor judgment and a weakling in many ways may be proficient in memorizing what is in a book.

One night the nurse on duty in obstetrics called Roy to awaken him and notify him that Mrs. Culver was in the delivery room and was presenting. Annoyed by having his sleep disturbed, he told her in a disagreeable voice, "Ah, stick your foot in it." The nurse reported him and this brought to light grievances of other nurses regarding his conduct. A hearing was called with the chief nurse and chief of the medical staff and witnesses present.

Roy told some of us what happened at the investigation. "It was like I was on trial," he said. "Dr. Cannon acted like he was president of the court-martial. They were all there when I went in. A funny thing, all the nurses got up, as if on the ward, for me, the accused.

"Dr. Cannon said, 'What did you do when you were notified that Mrs. Culver was in the last stage; did you understand that it was urgent?' I said that yes, I did understand, that I had seen her earlier and after examination, thought that there would be a foot presentation. When Miss Nelson called me I told her to put the foot in. By that I meant for her to use pressure to slow delivery until I could dress and get there. She must have misunderstood. I went over as soon as ready.

"That stopped them and the subject was dropped for a while. Dr. Cannon then said, 'Some of the nurses complained that you have been obnoxious on the wards sometimes. What do you have to say concerning that charge?' I wasn't sure which nurses had said what, but thought it must have been about the way I talked to one or two who wouldn't go out with me.

"I said that the word 'obnoxious' by definition meant 'of foul odor' I thought and that I took a shower every day. If I had been offensive, it was regretted, I said. Then I threw this at them, 'One or two ward nurses have not carried out orders properly and neglected patients on a few occasions. Rather than report them, I bawled them out and am sorry if they found me objectionable.'

"After that they seemed to want the matter to lie and dropped the subject. I don't think Dr. Cannon was satisfied but soon excused me, said that what had been brought out at the hearing would be considered and that I would be informed of any decision made. I'm not too worried except that I need to stay a year to get my degree."

We heard later that, in effect, he was reprimanded for acting improperly. Although permitted to continue his internship, he was to consider himself as being on probation.

This crisis in Roy's internship had passed but it was not his nature to lead a tranquil life. It was inevitable that he would be a key figure in another unpleasant affair that also involved grounds for a hearing.

Dr. Carl Watkins replaced Dr. Howery, who resigned to enter practice in partnership with a prominent physician. Dr. Watkins was somewhat older than the average hospital resident and came from the Midwest. It was his first time in the East, having driven from his hometown to Washington.

"I got onto one of those circles on an avenue during rush hour and went around about a dozen times before I could find a chance to get off on the right street," he told us, laughing.

He enjoyed seeing a city new to him and serving in a hospital different from those to which he was accustomed. He took his duties seriously and made an effort to see that all the patients received proper treatment.

"I'm not going to bring my family to Washington until I find out if I'm staying and locate a place to live," Dr. Watkins told us. He had been looking at houses in the southeast area convenient to the hospital.

The interns continued on their same assignments, a new chief making no significant change in their work. Dr. Watkins exercised normal supervision but gave no indication of being domineering. He had not been there long, however, until Roy complained to the others, "Watkins is riding me. I don't need him to tell me what to do. He's just a G. P."

The ill feeling that Roy had toward the chief seemed to increase as time passed although Watkins did not act as if aware of it. We were astounded when the word spread that Roy had reported to Dr. Blalock that Watkins was a homosexual.

"Why did you accuse him of that?" we asked Roy. Apparently he had nothing definite upon which to base the accusation.

"When we were all in the lounge the other night telling the big yarns, after most of you left he asked me if I would like to come up to his room. What else? I didn't go."

Watkins told us later, "There is nothing to it. Roy resents me and my checking on his work. He wants me out and is using this way to try to get me fired. He is without principle. It's too bad that medical schools have no tests for character, integrity, decency or fairness when they are evaluating applicants for admission."

"What are you going to do about the charge?" someone in the group asked him.

"There is not much I can do except deny it. Then it would be his word against mine. If I try to defend myself, his accusation will only be advertised. I'm damned if I do and damned if I don't. Rather than being subjected to the indignity of being tried and possibly drummed out, with all the publicity, I think it best just to leave quietly, go back where I came from, where the people know me." He did.

I had been at Gallinger nearly two months when informed that the position of resident clinical director was open. The salary was many times that of an intern and the hours were generally more regular. Too, it offered an opportunity to obtain some training in psychiatry. The psychiatric department was the largest department and had the most modern buildings at that time. Since I was not definitely committed to a specialty, I concluded that the job was the best available in the hospital, at least temporarily. I applied for it and was accepted.

Dr. Henning, head of the Department of Psychiatry, was also the District of Columbia alienist. An alienist, I understood, was an expert in the treatment of insanity. At that time to me he appeared elderly but was quite active. He was a large man, enjoyed ice cream cones, and was rather gruff, the type of whom people say, "His bark is worse than his bite."

A full-time doctor for the District Jail was employed at about the same date I became resident clinical director at Gallinger. Who should it be but my old roommate at Shreveport, Jim Babcock. Evidently he had not given up the idea of living in Washington. I went over to see him.

An office in the jail had been equipped for the new doctor. He was informed that he could order more equipment and supplies as needed. Too, one of Gallinger's best nurses, Mary Marsch, was transferring from the hospital to the jail and after her initial hesitation looked forward to it as an enjoyable challenge.

Jim seemed to be enjoying his position as jail physician. It had been a bit confining at first but he had adjusted very well and made friends of some of the inmates. He found an unused space in top of the jail, set up a boxing ring and sometimes boxed with prisoners who had some skill in the sport.

Tom Manson, my old associate in the prisoners' health care, lost most of his duties to Mary Marsch when she began her work in the jail. This fact was reported in a prominent nationally syndicated newspaper column that was popular in that era.

Cranks from all over the country flock to Washington intent on seeing the President, the Secretary of Defense, a certain senator or some other official concerning schemes for solving the nation's problems. Some of them exhibiting obviously abnormal mentality were escorted to Gallinger for observation and care. These required attention and disposition along with numerous alcoholics and addicts.

Each morning there was a lineup of questionable cases, accompanied by policemen, in the office of Dr. Henning. If one happened to be a simple drunk and disorderly case, now sober and without an injury requiring hospitalization, he might be released to the police. If a complete examination or further observation was needed, he would be admitted to the hospital. A patient suspected of being mentally incompetent, for example, could be held for ten days. A patient admitted for mental observation would be released at the end of this period if he wished to leave and sufficient evidence for confinement had not been found. Those requiring commitment to an institution would be transferred to St. Elizabeth's Hospital under specified legal procedure involving expert testimony. They might be taken there by ambulance with a doctor and a nurse accompanying them.

A delirium tremens patient who had been hospitalized after prolonged and excessive use of alcohol would show signs of mental disturbance and hallucinations. Sometimes one would point to the ceiling or a wall in various directions and if asked, "What do you see?" would answer, "Snakes!" or perhaps name a wild animal.

Addicts were generally treated by gradual withdrawal of the drug to which addicted, reducing the dose and increasing the interval of time between doses, or by substituting another drug for a varying period or by a third method under which the drug was discontinued entirely at once. The last method, called "cold turkey" by many, was rather drastic and supportive measures were often indicated. Close watch was instituted when this means of "cure" was employed and the suffering of these patients was not pleasant to see.

One psychiatric ward was occupied mostly by incorrigible teen-age girls sent by a reformatory that was unable to cope with them. One night a few of them succeeded in loosening the heavy protective screen over one window and ran away, but they were returned in a day or two. Generally they were cooperative, even amicable on occasion, as when one big girl asked loudly, "Dr. Hall, would you like to mess around with me?"

On the ward for women, the one who used the most foul language was a former choir singer and considered very religious. One was very artistic, spending much of her time drawing pictures. She said that she had drawn one of me and then showed it, an excellent representation of a large tomcat.

Once when I came on this ward, a frenzied patient had three loudly protesting female attendants on the floor, holding them by the hair, handfuls of it, thereby creating much excitement. Apparently she was aggressive only toward other women because she released the three when I ordered her quietly to "let them go."

A man with delusions of grandeur thought that he was in control of the whole world. During a period when he was feeling benevolent and wishing to show confidence in his doctor, he made me the biggest offer I had ever received, "I'm going to put you in charge of South America."

One method of treatment for an excited patient was the use of a continuous bath. The patient was suspended in a tub of water maintained at a comfortably warm temperature and kept there for an hour or more or until tranquilized by the soothing water, with an attendant constantly present.

A committee representing Congress once visited the hospital and was shown through all parts of it by Dr. Blalock. When they saw patients in continuous baths, the members of the committee looked from them to the superintendent questioningly. He became the most eloquent I ever heard him.

"Nothing has been found that soothes excited patients as well as continuous, gently flowing water at a pleasant temperature," he assured them. "They become quiet, comfortable and often sleep. It is a most helpful means of treatment."

The visitors walked out quietly to see other parts of the department. At least the baths must have been an improvement over strait jackets which were available but rarely used, never on my orders. Sometimes a violent patient was placed in a padded cell so that he would not injure himself.

Dr. Alfred Fried, an Austrian from Vienna, who had been a student of Sigmund Freud, to whom he often referred, was a psychiatrist at Gallinger. He was dark and stocky. A bundle of energy, he usually walked rapidly. He also talked as rapidly as his proficiency in English would permit.

As the patient load per doctor at Gallinger was not as heavy as at Shreveport, there was more time for recreation. Some of the interns took advantage of the nearby Anacostia River to go swimming on hot days. "I was sitting on the bank dangling my feet in the water, felt something sliding by my leg, looked down and it was a snake," one reported.

A friendly citizen took the nurses and interns for a ride in his yacht on the Potomac River one day. At a favorable spot we stopped for swimming. Pollution of the river was not such a cause for concern then.

One night we had an outing by a cornfield near the Anacostia or Eastern Branch. The main picnic food item was corn on the cob, boiled in big borrowed pots, buttered and salted. The supply was plentiful.

The biggest party of the year was at the Christmas season, when there were more refreshments, decorations and festivity than usual. Gifts exchanged were mostly of the funny kind and the notes with them, written in similar vein, were usually read aloud. For example, the intern who was most vehement in condemnation of smoking and complained if anyone smoked near him was given a pipe in a pretty package with a note saying, "May you enjoy many happy hours."

It was rumored that a few couples used the old cemetery near the hospital grounds as a trysting place. One night Herb Ruffin, bent on romance, took a walk in the moonlight with a pretty girl of the athletic type. They went into the cemetery and were strolling along the walks when they saw two ghostly objects at a sepulcher. Without investigating, they left the cemetery faster than they had entered. Turning toward the hospital on reaching the sidewalk, they ran into the "ghosts," a couple of their friends, and all could then laugh together.

Herb, who was from Atlantic City, was driving his old Franklin home for a long weekend and asked me to go with him. He was one of the few interns who had cars, an indication of affluence in those days. Only those who could afford a car were expected to have them. An intern's salary did not allow such a luxury.

We had not gone very far when I discovered that his brakes were not very efficient, but that was not all. While going down a hill on a residential street in Baltimore, we got a jolt when the right rear wheel came off. It came rolling by, went into a front yard, crushed the downspout from the house roof and spun around on the small lawn, doing a fairly good job of demolishing the grass. Fortunately the homeowners were understanding.

Going down another long hill in the countryside, we saw a number of automobiles standing in line at the bottom of the hill. Herb drove on and around them without waiting to see why they had stopped and then we saw. A fast train appeared in front of us, its whistle adding to the noises that only a train can make. It was crossing the road as we sped downhill toward the tracks.

Our feeble brakes could not be trusted. Herb was working them but not able to slow down. I opened the door on my side, getting ready to jump out before we struck the train. But at the last moment Herb swerved to the right, driving between the train and the automobile standing first in line, parallel to the train, until he succeeded in stopping the Franklin.

Back on the road once more, we got behind a Chevrolet, the driver of which did not drive as fast as Herb wished to, but he would not give us a chance to pass. When there was an opportunity to go around him he would increase his speed. Herb's exasperation grew with each mile. We were going through a small New Jersey town and the road widened so that Herb could get beside the offender. To teach him a lesson, he knocked off one of the Chevrolet's hubcaps when he passed it and went ahead.

I looked behind after we had gone a short distance and saw a police car. We were signaled to stop. "What's the matter, officer, am I getting a flat tire?" Herb asked.

"A man back there said that your car hit his," the officer said.

The man came walking up with the evidence, a hubcap in his hands. "Let me see your driver's license," said the officer. The name "Ruffin" on it apparently meant something to him.

"Do you know Mr. McClure, our chief of police in Atlantic City?" Herb asked him.

"Yes, I've met him. Do you know J. R. Ruffin, the mayor?"

"Yes, he is my uncle. My other uncle is speaker in the legislature. My father is in the real estate business."

"Well, if you and this gentleman want to settle this between you....," the officer replied.

"You can get your car fixed and send me the bill," Herb offered the gentleman, who agreed and took his address.

We resumed our trip and before long Herb said, "Smell that salt air! That's what I've been missing." Our arrival after dark had been so delayed that his parents were relieved when at last he appeared, complaining that he needed a faster car. Being in a luxurious home for a few days was a welcome diversion for me.

Bad news awaited us in Washington. Jim had had a pulmonary hemorrhage as a result of tuberculosis. It had happened while boxing with a prisoner in the jail. So that must have been his illness in Louisiana when he was worried over the possibility of a blood disease.

Often it is the doctor who is inadequately treated. Once in the doctors' dressing room of the surgical suite, a surgeon mentioned that the large, irregular, ugly scar on the right side of his abdomen had resulted from an inflamed appendix, which, undiagnosed, had ruptured while he was taking a postgraduate course in surgery at a famous clinic. He had neglected to get an examination and blood count.

Jim believed that a warm, dry climate offered the best chance for his recovery and decided to go to Arizona. Arrangements were made for going west and he did not wait long to make the move, which he felt confident was on the road to health.

The interns worked together in harmony, peaceably at least, with few exceptions. Once during a heated argument in an office, one intern called another a name which was intended as a gross insult. The offended intern hit him in the eye in the brief fight. A black eye resulted.

A few days later in the quarters, the injured intern brought a liquid in a bottle with a dropper to me and said, "Will you put a drop of this in my eye?" There was still some redness of the conjunctiva.

"What is it?" I asked, not wanting to put something unknown in his eye.

"Belladonna," he said with assurance and tilted his head back. Its use seemed logical under the circumstances. I let a drop fall between his lids onto the eye. He put his hand over his eye, fell onto the bed, groaned loudly and then said, "Let me see that bottle again." Looking at it with the other eye, he said in a terror-stricken voice, "I got the wrong bottle; that is silver nitrate!"

Interns in other rooms heard and rushed in. One called the ophthalmologist. The albumin of a raw egg from our kitchen was put in his eye. The eye specialist soon arrived and started treatment, which lasted for several days. The intern was kept in a dark room for two days before we learned with relief that his eye was out of danger. "It got well without a scar or any loss of vision," he was able to tell us when, clear-eyed again, he returned to duty.

The Psychiatric Department functioned as a sorting center as well as for treatment of mental disorders. Consultants in neuropsychiatry assisted us. The social service ladies were very helpful, especially in making contacts with patients' families and providing for needs beyond those strictly medical.

St. Elizabeth's Hospital, with its thousands of beds and provisions for treating the mentally ill, took most of our patients who required prolonged care. Some needed aid to get back to the states from where they had come. Some were in need of immediate medical or surgical treatment aside from, or as part of, the attention required for their neurological or mental conditions.

The attendants as well as the nurses were important in

handling the psychiatric patients, especially the excited or violent ones, for example, a paranoid case. Resistance or combativeness might be encountered.

"Be sure you have plenty of help to control a patient, if necessary, whenever you enter his room," Dr. Henning warned. "Otherwise the outcome might be disastrous."

We had a number of strong male attendants who were experienced and adept in managing aggressive individuals without injury to them. Their presence often sufficed.

No two people being exactly alike, physically or mentally, each patient constituted a problem different from all others. Each had to be given a mental as well as a physical examination. On these wards the mental examination took the most time. In a few instances a diagnosis might soon appear obvious while others required considerable study and observation over a period of many days.

Washington does not ordinarily get much snow during the winter but occasionally there is a heavy snowfall, as there was one day the winter I was at Gallinger. It was also windy and the snow drifted. That was a good night for me to stay in my room, but this was not to be. I had a phone call. It was from Dr. Henning.

"A man tried to rob the Harrison Jewelery store tonight and shot up the place. The police arrested him but think that he might be crazy, the way he acted. They say that he is from Nevada. I would like for you to go over to the jail and, after you have seen him, call me back and let me know what you think."

So I went tramping through the deep snow over to the jail. At one point there was a drift almost up to my hips. In the jail I was conducted through the corridors under the gaze of the prisoners in the rows of barred cells, a series of iron doors being unlocked for me along the way, until we were at Nevada's cell. The jailer locked me in with him. "You can call me when you're through," he said.

Nevada was slim, sinewy and rough, with steely eyes, high cheekbones and sandy, tangled hair over a high forehead. The most remarkable thing about his appearance was his bruised, bloody forehead and the fact that he was manacled.

"He was beating his head on the wall," the guard told me.

I talked with the prisoner for over an hour. He was not very communicative, seeming to understand that I was a doctor but volunteering no information. When asked where he was he said, "In a hospital, I guess." He was not oriented as to time. Getting answers from him was a rather tedious process but I heard enough to convince me that he was deranged. A diagnosis would require more study. I called for the jailer and he let me out.

The senseless way in which the prisoner had attempted the holdup, or so it seemed to me, reinforced my opinion of him. From what I could learn, he had entered the jewelry store and emptied his pistol, shooting at random without accomplishing anything except scaring everyone. They thought that he must be crazy, reported the policemen who had brought him to jail.

I telephoned Dr. Henning and told him, "I have seen the gunman and think that he is insane."

"Don't tell anybody what you think," he said.

The next morning when I walked into his office he greeted me with, "Why in the hell did you say that you thought that man was insane? Don't you know that every criminal in jail tries to make you think that he is insane and that all the insane people in the hospital try to convince you that they are sane?"

I advised him as to the man's appearance, his irrationality, disorientation, attitude and the way he impressed me during the hour I was alone with him in his cell. "What I told you was my opinion based upon what I saw and heard last night. For a definitive diagnosis, more than this is advised, but I do not believe that he is sane."

At a hearing before a judge about a week later, Dr. Henning testified that the gunman from out west was insane. He was recommended for treatment in St. Elizabeth's Hospital and, on the basis of the testimony, was committed to that federal institution.

We had books, guides, tests and criteria by which to determine a patient's mental state and arrive at a conclusion as to his sanity. Dr. Henning did not expect me to say, "My intuition tells me," or "I had a feeling," or "It struck me that the man is insane." A scientific evaluation was expected in each case. In making a decision, however, the examiner may be influenced by intangibles that cannot be measured such as the patient's expression, the way he looks at the examiner or does not look, the lack of spark or light, the unawareness of stimuli to which a normal person is responsive or excessive response.

Melancholia, mania, negativism, incoherence, catalepsy and dementia were the kinds of descriptive terms used in writing reports of mental examinations. Aside from findings to which such terminology would apply, there were less definable symptoms that could not be given acceptable names. Sometimes when trying to communicate with an incomprehensive patient, it seemed as if the lines of communication had been cut or that there was a frustrating, saddening power failure in the mechanism of reception, like a battery going dead.

A quiet patient sitting alone in the men's ward was so introverted that he took no notice of the activities all around him. Another was walking rapidly, waving his arms and talking loudly and excitedly. Still another, when you placed his hand on top of his head he left it there until you came back and removed it. Others, with more comprehension, had the appearance of having been placed in the wrong section of the hospital on initial inspection. They even helped in the care of other patients, a heartening thing to see.

An individual's traits not particularly noticed by the general public may be significant to a psychiatrist and might also be meaningful to a psychologist who is not a medical doctor. With experience, these signs or signals are more easily detected and become clearer to the trained professional. When these traits appear unusual or pronounced in a certain individual, untrained people make comments such as, "He's a screwball," "He's off his rocker," "His front porch light has gone out," "He is off the beam," "We are not on the same wavelength," or "He's nuts." Too, some individuals that give one the impression of being brilliant, especially when seen only once, may in fact be psychotic.

Dr. Ryan, a consultant, told us of an experiment he made with a group of nonmedical scientists in the National Bureau of Standards. These were outstanding men in various fields of science and discernment in them might be expected to be well developed. They were of the government agency that deals with the standards of accuracy, quality and precision in respect to products. They set standards for weights and measures for the country and did basic research in physics, chemistry, mathematics and engineering.

A girl that Dr. Ryan brought before the group was attractive, well dressed, vivacious and bright in appearance. She conversed in a pleasant, witty way in light conversation on common subjects but nevertheless was a psychotic patient. After she left, Dr. Ryan asked the scientists their opinion of her mentality. Without exception, they thought that she was normal or perhaps of above-average intelligence.

The attention received by psychiatric patients in Gallinger was not characterized by a wealthy, worried individual reclining on a comfortable couch in an expensive office telling his or her troubles to a listless listener, each with an eye on the clock. It is unlikely that any of our patients ever talked with their society friends about "my psychiatrist."

One of the things I learned during the year there was that I did not want to specialize in psychiatry. Some doctors say that the reason certain of their brethren like the specialty is because "birds of a feather flock together."

While in Washington, I applied for and was granted a license to practice medicine and surgery in Maryland by reciprocity with Louisiana, where I was licensed. I had appeared before the board in Baltimore and presented my credentials, which were found acceptable. Although I could not then foresee when, if ever, the license would be used, it was found useful before I anticipated.

I decided to specialize in general surgery, sent an application to the Graduate School of Medicine of the University of Pennsylvania for admission to the two-year course leading to a Master of Medical Science degree in surgery, and was accepted. Dr. Blalock was informed of this. His decision was that at the end of my year, which was the end of June when personnel changes were usually made, I would be replaced by a doctor whose interest was in psychiatry.

It was for me to find an answer to the question of what to do until the course in surgery started that fall. Before receiving the certificate stating that I had "faithfully and satisfactorily filled the position of Resident Clinical Director," I found another position that was completely different. A remarkable summer was before me.

Coal Mine Doctor

A doctor was needed in a coal-mining town on the border of Maryland and West Virginia. The address was Kempton, West Virginia, as the little post office was on that side of the line. In one room of my house I could be in one state and could go into the room across the hall and be in another state.

Kempton is in the Allegheny Mountains of the Appalachian range, southwest of Cumberland, Maryland. Morgantown, West Virginia, where the state university is located, is to the northwest, Clarksburg is west and Elkins south.

The coal mine at one end of the main street of Kempton was marked by the elevator tower over the shaft, a utility structure, car-loading apparatus and huge piles of shale and waste. At the other end was the company store and a few other buildings, the post office and superintendent's home. The schoolhouse was near the middle of town.

The miners' homes, all wooden and of similar construction, were on this main street and paralleled streets on the mountainside terraces above. Wooden steps at intervals led to the upper levels. Differences in the appearance of homes were due to the care given by those who lived in them.

All the homes in sight were of a uniform dull color. The lots on which they stood were of approximately the same size. Flowers and shrubbery made some almost attractive and others less drab. Miners lived in nearly all of the homes, but the pride they took in them varied, as pride that people in general have in their families varies, and various strata of society were apparent in Kempton.

One family in particular, the Lotzkos, who lived on the

main street appeared well-to-do. "When there was plenty of work with good wages and overtime, Lotzko always saved part of his money and is well off now," Mr. Kofaks told me. "Most folks just spend it as they made it and when work got scarce had nothing to show for it."

I became the doctor for the coal-mining families through the efforts of Dr. Milton Gormley, who had an arrangement with the Davis Coal and Coke Company to provide medical attention for the employees, who paid a few dollars out of their wages each month into a fund. This entitled them and the members of their families to medical and surgical treatment.

Obstetrics was not included in the insurance plan. For this I was entitled to charge ten dollars per case. I was also paid five dollars extra for each time I went into the mine to give emergency treatment. My income amounted to about two hundred dollars per month, a little more than at Gallinger. The furnished house in which I lived and my office, drugs and supplies were provided.

The office occupied what would otherwise have been the living room of my dwelling. In it were the usual medicines, antiseptics, dressing materials and surgical instruments for minor surgery. There were a few chairs for patients awaiting their turn or those accompanying them. Except for accidents, office patients were usually seen in the morning.

Most house calls were to a certain few families. A typical way this was done was for a mother to send a little boy to my office with the message, "Mama said to tell you to come up and see the baby; he is sick." The boy would not know the kind of sickness his little brother had. "I don't know, but she said to come right away."

"What is your name and where do you live?"

"Joey Mellani; we live in the top row."

"You can show me where it is. Wait till I get my bag." Off we went up the only real street in town and, after the equivalent of a few blocks, began climbing steps. We passed two rows of houses at different levels, climbed to the third height, and Joey said, "This way."

Neither Mrs. Mellani nor her house was very neat. The breakfast dishes had not been washed and the beds had not been made, although the covers had been thrown over the sheets, which were not completely covered and were rather dingy.

"Come on in," the woman said. "I haven't had time to do anything. The baby kept me awake last night. He's got a bad cold and hasn't been eating right. He has been coughing."

The baby, about sixteen months old, had a nasal discharge and a temperature of 102 degrees. His lungs were clear. After getting what history the mother could give and completing the examination, I advised Mrs. Mellani, gave the baby a dose of medicine and left some for her to give him. I then returned to the office and my temporary home.

Dr. Gormley's home was in Thomas, West Virginia, a larger town with a railroad station, churches, businesses, stores, hotel and a moving-picture theater. His office was over the bank building and when not otherwise used, some of the local citizens enjoyed a card game there.

There were a number of coal mines in the area. The names of some of the other towns were Bayard, Henry, Davis, Albert, Coketon, Benbush, Pierce and Erwin. Several of them were named for the sons of the original owner of the mines, I was told.

Dr. Jason Norton, a contract doctor for one of the mines, brought me out to Kempton from Thomas in his cluttered Dodge, which looked as if it had seen service on unpaved roads. He was well nourished, bluff and apparently wanted to be helpful. He showed me through the house in which I would live and the medical equipment.

"You can look through what is on hand, make a list of whatever else you need, send it to Dr. Gormley and he will see that you get it. Dr. Strauss, who was here before you came, might have let some things get low," he advised me. "If you want to find out about something or need help on a case, you can call me."

Dr. Norton had been engaged in mining practice for many years; it was the only kind he knew and he was compatible with it. "Some of these people will run you ragged if you let them. They think that because the old man gets a dollar or two taken out of his wages every month for the doctor, they own you and will sit on their cans up on the hill and send for you every day. Don't let them get your goat."

In the kitchen he pointed to the blackened ceiling around the stovepipe and said, "That was done by a good German housewife. We have all kinds of people around here. Most of them came from southern Europe, Italy and the Balkans espe-

112

cially to work in the mines. There are lots of Slavs. You will know them. When they have a wedding or a death in the family, they all get together and eat and drink for several days."

The Frontier Nurse, Flora Martindale, stopped to see me one day when making her rounds visiting the sick and injured who were confined to their homes in isolated communities or alone in the mountains. As Kempton was in the area that she covered, I saw her occasionally. She had reason to be proud of her association, which provided nursing service where not otherwise available.

Flora took me in her Ford to see the boat races on the lake one Sunday. She was a graduate nurse, healthy, resourceful, the outdoors type capable of bringing sunshine with her into a cabin where gloom had prevailed. Accustomed to driving long distances on the narrow mountain roads, she amazed me with the ease with which she made the hairpin turns seem like straightaways as we rode through green forests adorned by luxuriant laurel in bloom.

Natural air conditioning made the Alleghenies very pleasant in the summer, but the old-timers kept warning me that it would be different in the winter. "You'll be wading in snow up to your waist and the temperature will be way down below zero part of the time," they would say with a grin as if looking forward to my anticipated discomfort with pleasure.

Once when Flora came by for a chat we were talking about winter in the mountains and I mentioned the little pot-bellied stove that stood in the office. She seemed amused at the prospect of the doctor from the city being all alone in that house trying to keep warm on a wintry night. She laughed and said, "What you need is an armstrong heater." I had not always been a city fellow and, besides, I expected to be in Philadelphia before the snows fell.

When Jason Norton introduced me to Kempton he told me, "The Humphrey family down toward the mine on the left takes boarders sometimes. You could probably get your meals there unless you want to cook and I don't think you do. She's not a bad cook and I think she's clean. It won't be anything fancy but you should have plenty to eat, such as it is. He and the oldest boy work in the mine."

I did as he suggested and found that his description of the family and the food was quite accurate. The home was much like the others but they were a little more ambitious than some.

113

The menfolk worked hard and regularly and Mrs. Humphrey, assisted by the children, was willing to do extra work to improve somewhat their standard of living.

Sometimes before or after a meal, I had a chance to sit on the Humphreys' front porch and talk with one of the family. The lady of the house was the most talkative and would tell me about various Kempton citizens and happenings. She was a large, good-natured woman with plain features and plain clothes that she had washed and ironed.

"Jess Harmon went blackberry picking," Mrs. Humphrey told me. "He was by himself, found a good patch of ripe berries and was picking away when he heard something close, looked up and there was a big bear! He ran nearly all the way home, must have been two miles," she said, laughing heartily.

"Folks here generally seem healthy," I remarked.

"Some of 'em live a long time. Old Mrs. Allen over in the direction of Parsons is 112 years old. She's not very spry anymore but still gets around. I get along very well but am bothered with rheumatism a little sometimes."

From their house I could see the men coming from the mine, dressed in overalls, a head lamp on, covered with coal dust, every man's face black. The Humphrey men went to a wash shed back of the house, took baths and put on clean clothes before coming into the house to eat. They were hungry and the evening meal was ready for them when they came in.

I ate with the family. We did not eat daintily. The food was put on the table in big dishes and we helped ourselves to all we wanted. The meat was fried and the vegetables were boiled or fried. Dessert was usually fruit pie, sometimes pudding or cake, and a few times watermelon. The day's events were usually the conversation subjects. These were local things seen and heard, not something that happened beyond the mountains or what was read or reported on the radio.

"One time a woman got the superintendent to let her see in the mine," Mr. Humphrey said. "Within a week we had three accidents, one of them an explosion. That's the way it always happens if a woman goes in a mine. It's bad luck," he concluded seriously. No one disagreed with him. Mrs. Humphrey, no doubt, was content to stay out of the mine. She had enough to occupy her time above ground, cleaning, cooking, mending and keeping house.

The Kempton mine was a deep one. To get into it we went

down, down, down, by a rather slow work elevator. At the bottom were tunnels running in various directions. In them were small open coal cars on tracks. There was not much space between the cars and the tunnel walls.

Coal was brought up by the elevator hoisted by a cable which passed over a great pulley wheel and to a windlass-like contraption in the hoisting shed. At a certain height above ground the coal car was emptied into the tipple, where the coal was washed, weighed and sorted, then loaded into railroad cars.

Mike Benes dislocated his left shoulder while at work. I examined him and was of the opinion that because of the type of dislocation it would be advisable to reduce it under anesthesia, so I called Dr. Norton and asked him to help me with it. He came and said, "Hello, Mike, so you've done it again. Let me take a look."

Dr. Norton, with a quick maneuver, returned the head of the humerus to its socket. I examined Mike again and found the dislocation reduced and the bones of the shoulder back in normal position. Except for the mention of some soreness, he was uncomplaining.

"That is about the fourth time I've done that for Mike," Jason Norton told me after Mike had gone home to recuperate. "I think that he can dislocate it whenever he wants to, that is, if he wanted to. Maybe he ought to have an operation on it sometime."

Mike did not dislocate his shoulder again while I was at Kempton. Maybe this was reserved for the doctor who replaced me.

A few of the miners seemed prone to have accidents, having one after another. Approximately ten percent of the workers were estimated to have ninety percent of the injuries that occurred while I was there. In my opinion, the reasons why they got hurt varied not only individually but in the same individual from day to day.

One reason that some men received more injuries than others was that their jobs were more hazardous and subjected them to more dangers daily. Another possible cause was that the machinery, the tools or the equipment parts were less efficient and more trouble-prone in some instances than those generally used by most of the men, I theorized when puzzled by why a few men had so many accidents. Lack of concentration on the job could result in an accident.

115

Based on my observations, I believed that some of the factors that contributed to the causes of accidents were impairment of one or more senses such as sight, hearing or touch; lack of intelligence; laziness; carelessness; physical defects; and, one considered important, fatigue. Being tired might not have been due entirely to the work. It might have been accounted for, partially at least, by lack of sleep or proper nourishment, other activities or by a deviation from the normal of which the worker was unaware and which was not detected on examination.

A temporary mental state or aberration could conceivably cause a worker to injure himself, intentionally or unintentionally. Another possibility is self injury as a means of avoiding what the invidual regards as a worse alternative or of obtaining some advantage. Some injuries, of course, are caused by accidents over which the individual has little or no control and resulting from, for examples, carelessness of other workers, explosions or collapse of a tunnel.

Anthracosis, a type of pneumonoconiosis, produced by inhaled coal dust, is a lung condition attended by fibroid induration and pigmentation which may produce symptoms or impair the physical efficiency of a miner, depending upon its duration and extent. As a disease, it is sometimes called "black lung." It was an occupational hazard of Kemptonites.

During the summer there was not much sickness of the kinds common in winter such as influenza, bronchitis and pneumonia. Some days were relatively quiet, so I had some unaccustomed spare time but usually did not leave the office unattended very long. In an emergency the doctor of another mine could have been called. I took the opportunity to read a few books.

A teen-age girl came to the office a few days after my arrival and asked, "Could I keep house for you?" Then she explained, "I worked for Dr. and Mrs. Strauss until you came."

I talked with her a few minutes, then said, "There won't be much housekeeping to do. What little there is, I can take care of, but thanks for asking." She was one of several children in the Stambolov family living across the street not far away. Eventually I became acquainted with most of the townspeople.

A small boy, Jim Nichols, who was very active and inclined to be mischievous, often came to the office and said, "Mama wants some cough syrup." I gave him a small bottle with directions for his mother a few times, but someone told me, "I saw that little Nichols boy stop down the street and drink what you gave him in that bottle."

The next time young Nichols came for cough syrup, I said, "I'll let you have it if you will let me hypnotize you first." He agreed. There was no one else in the office at the time. He was cooperative and appeared to be on the verge of being hypnotized when Dave Moneta came in and broke the spell. The attempt was discontinued. I gave him a little of his favorite liquid anyhow. "That's the quietest I ever saw that boy," Dave said.

"The other day Tony Sabatini and Rizzio called on me to donate to Al Smith's presidential campaign," Dave told me. "They thought that because I'm Italian we must be Catholics but we're not. I came from northern Italy. There were many blond Italians in the mountains where we lived." Like some of the others he liked to talk about the "old country."

The big general store operated by the mining company was the only store in town. It also served as the social and entertainment center where one saw friends and perhaps a stranger or two. In and around it was where much of the action was, outside of the mine. Scrip issued by the company to employees and charged to their wages account was used by many customers to make purchases in the store.

Jake Jenkins was one of the friendliest of the men that I saw frequently in Kempton, at the store or in that vicinity. He did not actually live in town but in a small community at a mine that had closed. Some of the families had moved away but Jake had remained. I understood that he did odd jobs and worked part of the time at another mine, but he was a little vague as to his usual work.

Jake was a tall, lean, big-boned man that some people might refer to as a hillbilly. He was strong but not the silent type. He had a stubble of beard and the unpolished appearance of a man accustomed to roughness yet hospitable in nature. Usually when he saw me he would ask in a jolly way, "How are you, Doc?" Then after a few pleasantries such as, "Are they keeping you busy?" he would say, "I want you to come out to my place some time and have a groundhog dinner with me."

The McCosh family did not live in town, but I had treated some of them and when they had their big family reunion they invited me to have Sunday dinner with them. Tad McCosh came for me. The clan had already gathered. The yard was filled with members of the large family and relatives from miles around, one couple from Beckley.

Long tables placed end to end under the trees were loaded with food, most of it home grown. There were heaps of fried chicken, ham, big bowls of garden vegetables, new potatoes, corn, melons, fruits and several kinds of pies and cake. The chairs were brought out of the house for some of us and boards placed on supports alongside the tables as seats for others.

Men, women and children were seated before quantities of food not often seen, hardly knowing where to start, but soon all were eating in earnest, undisturbed by the banter of their relatives. Eventually we reached our capacities. The women took the dishes and things back into the house, the men talked in groups and the children, now better acquainted with their cousins, began to play, cautioned by parents.

When those living at the greater distances began to leave, Andy McCosh, who with his family was going my way, offered me a ride back to Kempton. The innate kindness, courtesy and thoughtfulness of those whose reunion I shared that day was appreciated and not forgotten.

Thomas, the nearest town by road, was about seven miles away. I got a ride there a few times and went to the movie a time or two, but usually when there were chances to go to other places, I took walks on paths through the bushes in the other direction. It was a treat to see in this way the natural charm of West Virginia. Where unspoiled by man, it still impresses us after traveling extensively on all continents.

At certain places on the ascending paths where the view was unobstructed by trees, I could see the whole town spread out below. If all looked quiet and peaceful I would go further.

A long snake that had been killed lay near the path I took on one walk. When I returned, another snake of similar size, shape and coloring lay beside the dead one and did not move as I approached. It must have been a devoted mate as it would not leave the path until a stick threatened it.

One Sunday I walked to the highest observation point in the area, which was about ten miles away, to get the long view about which people talked. When I reached the mountaintop, it was not just the climb that took my breath. As far as I could see, the wooded ridges and valleys extending to the misty horizon created a spectacle magnificent in its vastness and quiet beauty.

The Appalachian Mountains form a divide between the rivers that empty into the Gulf of Mexico and those that flow into

118

the Atlantic Ocean. One day I went to a spring not far away, stepping over the stream flowing from it in walking around the area. I had stepped over the Potomac River, which forms the boundary between Maryland, West Virginia and Virginia and is joined by the Shenandoah River at Harper's Ferry on its way to the Chesapeake Bay. For its last one hundred miles the river is two to seven miles wide.

Jake had told me about where he lived at the abandoned mine. Not having anything to keep me in the office, I decided to walk over there one of those mild, sunny days when the woodsy paths beckoned. I found the little community. Many of the houses appeared to be abandoned and were in need of repairs, their yards filled with weeds. Other houses were apparently occupied but there was no one in sight. It was like being in a ghost town.

After walking along the few grassy streets and looking at the graying dwellings and old mine, the only living things I saw were two or three black-and-brown, long-eared hounds which were noncommittal toward me although they had barked when I first appeared. I had the feeling of being watched and once thought that I got a fleeting glimpse of someone disappearing from a window.

The next time I saw Jake in Kempton he seemed to be amused. "I walked over to your place the other day but didn't see anybody," I said.

"Yeah, I heered about it!" he replied, laughing. "They thought that you was a revenuer and everybody hid out. Anyway they didn't shoot you. Come back when I'm there and we'll have that groundhog dinner."

I hoped that on my walks alone I would not again be mistaken for a government agent or lawman looking for moonshiners.

Loud talk disturbed the quietness of a warm afternoon as I sat by the window reading a book while waiting for the next patient to arrive. In front of the first house on the side street diagonally across Main Street from me, where the Capeks lived, I saw Mrs. Collins. She was shouting to Mrs. Capeks, who was standing in her front door but not saying anything that could be heard.

"My Tommy is as fine a boy as your Carl; you should be proud to have Tommy play with him," said Mrs. Collins in a voice that could be heard a block away. Mrs. Kemensky, on her front porch next door, stopped rocking to look and listen. Don Cori, who happened to be passing by on the other side of the street, kicking a can as he hurried toward his home, forgot the can and slowed his walk to watch.

Mrs. Capeks said something that I could not understand. Mrs. Collins responded by advancing a few steps, raising a strong arm and saying angrily, "You come out here in the street and I'll show you who is the best lady!"

The challenge was not accepted. Mrs. Capeks disappeared into her house. Mrs. Collins soon withdrew and quiet reigned once more but not for long.

Joe Macek rushed into my office panting from running and said excitedly, "Mr. Brozovic is having a spell. He's hurting and looks real bad," he said.

Mr. Brozovic, the town cobbler, lived not far from the office on the next level above, but his shoe repair shop was on a higher level and toward the mine. "Where is he?" I asked Joe, reaching for my bag.

"At the shop; I'll go back with you," he said.

We quickly climbed the steps to the top row of buildings, turned right and soon were in the shop. Brozovic was lying on a crude bench, with pieces of leather, tools and shoes in disorder around him. His knees were drawn up over his abdomen. He was pale, wet with sweat and making low moaning sounds.

"Where do you hurt, Mr. Brozovic?" I asked.

"It's my stomach—been giving me trouble for a long time. I've been going to Johns Hopkins for examinations and treatment."

The news of Mr. Brozovic's "spell" spread rapidly and in a short time a large proportion of the population was crowding around the little shop. After a preliminary examination, I asked some of the men if they would help me get him home in bed. About eight of them volunteered. We located a bed, lifted the patient gently onto it and prepared to carry him downhill to his home.

"They're goin' to tote him back to his house," someone quietly announced to the crowd outside. "Get back and give 'em room."

Those not needed to carry Mr. Brozovic on the bed followed behind. Nearly everyone else in town, it seemed, was watching as the slow procession carefully made its way down to Mr. Brozovic's home. His neighbors were sympathetic and asked if they could do anything for him. I told them that he would need a way to get to the hospital in Baltimore.

The crowd dwindled to a few friends, whom I asked to wait outside his bedroom while I examined him under circumstances more favorable than in the shop. Now he was calmer and more relaxed so that I could get a better medical history and an account of that day's events and the episode that had caused the excitement. Too, I could palpate his abdomen satisfactorily and determine his general condition.

I assured myself and then him that it was advisable for him to return to the hospital where his records, including X-rays and laboratory reports, were and where he was known. He was given medicine that was indicated and when asked how he felt, he said, "I feel tolerably well now." So did I.

When a sick person lived in a village where there was no doctor and where there was no other means of transportation, it was necessary for me to ride a local train of a few cars that threaded its way through the rugged country. Seen at a distance, moving in a curve on the side of a mountain, it looked like a miniature or toy train. I had to signal to the engineer and wave the train down to get on and then tell the conductor where I wanted to get off. The trainmen were very accommodating, which was fortunate for me and the sick.

People generally were obliging. Like me, many of them did not have automobiles in those days. The ones who did were helpful in case of genuine need. Being without a car at that time did not seem to be such a handicap as it would be considered now. Walking was not regarded as a great hardship.

"Mrs. Watkins is ready to have her baby and wants you to come as soon as you can," Al Oglesby informed me.

I had never seen her, but that was not surprising as many women in rural areas did not expect to see the doctor until time for delivery. "Where does she live?" I asked.

"It's quite a ways beyond me. They live on the other side of the creek. I can take you as far as the road goes. You'll have to walk the rest of the way. If you're ready we can start now. I've got my car."

There was not much obstetrical material except what was usually required. There were no forceps. I left word as to where I was going and why. There were not many well-kept secrets in Kempton, anyhow.

Soon we were on a dirt road through cutover timberland

which was covered with the second growth consisting of bushes and small trees. We passed the Oglesbys' small farm, saw a cow and calf in the pasture, a vegetable garden, two children and a dog in the yard and some chickens, and then the road wound its way into the forest. Apparently it had been used as a logging road and for the use of the few little farms along the way. It gradually became less distinct and disappeared at the creek.

"You'll have to walk the rest of the way," Al said. "Just follow the path, cross over the creek and you'll see the house from there."

I took my bag and followed the path through the woods to the place where it crossed the creek. To get to the other side, I walked across on the trunk of a tree which served as a bridge. A few limbs of the tree had been left. It was no great challenge to one who could walk railroad rails without falling off, but perhaps it insured that only sober people reached the Watkins' home.

After crossing over the rushing mountain stream, the path led to a clearing in the woods which I could now see a little further up the creek. Near the center of the clearing was the dwelling, an old log cabin, with spaces between logs covered by boards. To it, additions had been made in past years. Around it were some apple trees, patches of corn, and vegetable gardens with potatoes, beans, tomatoes, pepper, onions and other plants. Back of it was the barn and behind it an enclosure for livestock. A mule and a milk cow could be seen.

Chickens were clucking and scratching in the yard, a hound lay on the porch and a cat was near the door. I did not see anyone but noticed that smoke was rising from a chimney. Mr. Watkins came to the door and I introduced myself.

"Come in. I'm glad you got here. She seems to be having a right hard time. She's right in there. This is her ma, Mrs. Moseby, who is staying with us." He went to the wood pile to get some more wood for the kitchen stove on which a pot boiled.

The pains were coming at irregular intervals. They were not of constant duration or intensity. My examination indicated that a long wait would be necessary. As Mrs. Watkins needed to be attended and repeated trips to see her being impractical, I remained there that night. Labor would be difficult, it appeared.

The crowing of roosters finally announced the gray dawn after a long night during which no appreciable progress had been made. The arduous hours had tired the suffering woman, who was uncomplaining but whose tortured body could not continue the struggle much longer with prospects of favorable results. It was evident that instrumental delivery would be advantageous.

Dr. Gormley was known to this family, as he was to most of those in the area because of his many years of practice there. Too, he had the equipment needed for abnormal deliveries. I suggested that he be called, under the circumstances. He brought not only the necessary instruments but considerable experience. I regretted not being able to complete what had been undertaken, but seeing the patient get the best treatment available more than compensated for my disappointment in this case.

In one of the obstetrical cases that I had in Kempton, the woman in the last months of pregnancy was found to have tuberculosis. She was given the advantages possible, although the situation was not what one would have planned, and she had a natural delivery of a baby boy who appeared normal. This, however, did not end the problem of the family and the new Kempton resident, a baby with a tubercular mother. Fortunately such problems have become less common.

The sad ending of one pregnancy resulted from the umbilical cord being knotted, in an unusual occurrence. The circulation in the cord had been stopped before birth and the baby was born dead. This was the first time that I had seen this complication in obstetrics.

The superintendent of the mine, J. W. Williamson, was a mining engineer, a quiet man who usually seemed absorbed in facts and production figures. He had his own problems in connection with the mine and dealt with them without outward signs of emotion.

The dinner that I had with Mr. and Mrs. Williamson one Sunday gave me a chance to see mining from a different angle, to get more of a bird's eye view of it. It was an enjoyable meal in a pleasant home that could have been in Charleston or some other city from all appearances. Seeing Kempton when we came out of the house seemed momentarily surprising.

We took a ride in their Pontiac that afternoon, under blue skies and over winding roads to several towns, including Oakland, Maryland, where church conferences were held during the summer. The Williamsons pointed out places of interest we passed.

"Josh, in which one of these houses did Mr. Rockefeller stay when he was here?" Mrs. Williamson asked as we were passing the rows of uniform houses for the miners.

"It was this one here on the end," he said. "He was here inspecting mining property in which he had investments. He came to the mine and talked with some of the men there.

"The miners get paid according to the number of tons they get out. Shale is not wanted and the company pays nothing for it, but it gets in the way anyhow. You see big piles of it around the mines.

"Rockefeller asked one of the miners how much money he got for digging a ton of coal and the man told him. 'And what do you get for this?'

"'We get hell for digging that,' the miner said. The foremen try to avoid mining shale, but it is often found with the bituminous or soft coal that is mined here. West Virginia has some of the biggest soft coal beds in the country, along with Pennsylvania.

"In some strata the coal can be brought out in big lumps with almost no waste. A tunnel follows a vein and may extend for over a mile before it plays out or is exhausted. Some of the coal is so difficult to get that it does not pay to mine it. When one tunnel gives out, we start another and have to be careful that they do not cave in."

"I wish Josh would not work so hard," Mrs. Williamson said. "I'm afraid he will get an ulcer or have a heart attack or something. Sometimes he stays up half the night figuring, then gets up early to see about the machinery, timbers for the tunnels, all kinds of things, and listen to complaints. It's enough to run him crazy at times. I wish that he would take it easier."

"You're exaggerating a little, Doris, I think. It's not quite that bad. Anyway, it's better than digging in the mine," her husband answered.

"I don't know; you're down there part of the time, too," she replied.

The ride had been educational as well as enjoyable. It gave me an inkling of the complexities of coal mining, involving geology, engineering, economics, sociology and health, and a little better understanding of the way of life in a large and important section of our country.

A circuit rider preached in the schoolhouse at intervals of a few weeks as scheduled. At one service, the biblical character, Ham, was a sermon subject. The preacher was an ardent speaker and his voice must have carried well beyond the building walls to assure the congregation of his earnestness.

The annual Sunday School picnic to which I was invited was held in a low meadow several miles from town in a grove of sugar maple trees, an ideal place on a warm, sunny day in July. It was a pretty green spot, covered with grass and surrounded by shady woods.

A dirt road led to the picnic grounds, where there were tables for the food brought by the families in big baskets. There was no parking lot so drivers parked their cars where they wished which, for most of them, was not far from the tables. I had not seen so many Kempton cars before.

The food was spread on the tables and some of the crowd were beginning to eat when the rain started. In a short time it was obvious that the picnic could not be continued. People were hastily putting the meats, bread, salads, beans, fruit, sweets and drinks back into the baskets. The rain was soon coming down so fast that the maples did not give much protection.

Men, women and children scrambled to their cars trying not to be soaked. The meadow was now drenched and wheels sank into the soft mud so that many could not leave until long after the rain stopped, when others could pull them out of the mire. Luckily the car in which I had come had been left near the road and did not become mired, so my return to the office was not delayed.

So many people were still at the picnic ground that there was less activity in town than usual and it seemed relatively quiet. Carl Capeks had skinned his knee when he fell while running. I washed his knee, applied an antiseptic, while he grimaced, and a dressing.

My practice was essentially that of a general practitioner with more injuries to treat than the usual family doctor because of accidents in the mine. As there was no other physician in town and no hospital or specialists in the area, the complaints and conditions with which I had to deal were of great variety, including dental. I was expected to stop the pain of an aching tooth and extract it if necessary.

A midwife was available to assist women in childbirth, I heard, and I asked Mrs. Humphrey if she knew her. "That

125

would be old Mrs. Ashley," she said. "She lives over in that direction," pointing toward Erwin. "They tell me that she has helped a good many women hereabouts, usually when they couldn't get hold of a doctor, and some believe that what she thinks is the dictum."

I specialized in the skin and its contents, including bones, joints, muscles and all organs of the body. Scabies, a parasitic skin disease, is attended by severe itching, especially at night. Untreated cases showed little tendency to spontaneous cure and the condition was often called "seven-year itch." It could be cured rather quickly, however. All skin diseases were not so responsive to treatment. I was reminded of a facetious saying of interns, "Dermatology is a good specialty because the patients never die and never get well."

Miners often got dirt or other material in their eyes, which caused acute pain. Usually these foreign bodies could be removed from the eye without much difficulty but few treatment measures were more appreciated.

The weeks passed and the long summer was almost over. Mothers were getting their children ready for school. The company store was busier than usual. There was already a touch of fall in the mountain air. I had notified Dr. Gormley that I would soon be leaving to enter graduate school in Philadelphia. When I thought of leaving, it was with mixed emotions, including sadness.

Realization of the trust the people among whom I lived placed in me and the friendship that they gave one who had come to them as a stranger a few months before contributed to the gratification and warmth I felt that sunny early fall afternoon when my pleasant reminiscences were interrupted by a shadow which suddenly appeared in my office door.

"Leo Pasic got hurt in the mine! They want you to come down to see him," Emil Stursa informed me. His eyes large and white, in a face dark with coal dust, and his deep breathing emphasized the urgency of his mission.

I quickly got my emergency bag and hurried with Emil to the mine, where the big elevator was waiting to carry me down. At the bottom of the shaft I was directed to the entrance of one of the several tunnels from the large underground chamber, where a number of coal cars stood on the tracks.

"A loaded car ran over Leo's foot," one of the miners standing near him—the foreman, I believe—said.

126

Mr. Pasic was lying quietly, although he was hurting and doubtless vaguely aware of the extent of the tragedy that had struck him. Now he appeared shocked. The pain and anguish would be felt more severely with increase in sensation in his foot and realization of what the accident meant to his future. The nature and extent of his injury had to be determined.

The boot on the injured right foot showed scarcely any damage. He was placed in as comfortable a position as possible on a stretcher and the boot removed. The foot was deformed and was crushed where the car wheels had run over the instep or arched part of the foot in front of the ankle joint. All the metatarsal bones appeared to be broken, as was the skin over them.

"Is it bad, Doc?" Mr. Pasic asked me.

"Some of the small bones in your foot may be broken. You will need to go to the hospital for some X-rays and treatment. How does it feel?"

"It was sort of numb at first but is beginning to hurt more."

"I'll give you something to help you, put a dressing on it and go with you to the hospital. How did it happen?"

"I was by the track when the cars moved out. As I stepped back, my foot slipped on some loose gravel and onto the track under the wheel. Am I going to the hospital tonight?"

"Yes, if you feel like it and we can find a way. I'll check when we get up to my office."

His general condition was satisfactory and the distal part of the foot, that part beyond the injury, seemed to be viable. There was no excessive bleeding. I learned that treatment was available in the hospital in Cumberland, Maryland, and arranged to have him admitted there. Mrs. Pasic was advised and she approved of the arrangements. "Do you think Leo will be all right?" she asked. She was assured to the extent that assurance could be given but was not led to believe that he would soon be well.

Draza Ruzicka, Ivan Mihajlovic, Joe Masaryk and several other miners were helpful in moving Leo by stretcher, getting a car and driver and improvising so that the injured man could recline on the way to the hospital. Stef Mestrovic offered to take him and me in his Plymouth for the night ride to Cumberland. It was near dawn when we reached there.

After Pasic was admitted to the hospital, I waited until the doctor appeared before leaving. Stef went out to get a cup of coffee and doughnuts while I talked with the doctor, a mature man who was experienced in the treatment of serious injuries, especially those resulting from railroad accidents. The maintenance shops of the Baltimore and Ohio Railroad were in Cumberland.

That afternoon, back in Kempton, I went to the Humphreys' house a little early and sat on their front porch while waiting for dinner. The whistle for the end of work for the day crew sounded and I watched the miners, blackened as usual with coal dust, stream away from the mine shaft. Humphrey senior and junior went to the wash house in the back. As the men walked up the street, one or two stopped at each house. At a distance they all appeared alike, but some of them I recognized as they passed.

Sabatini and Collins came by together; then there were Stambolov, Cori, Nichols, Kofaks, Rizzio, Benes, Hotsko, Capeks, Macek, Masaryk, Mihajlovic, Ruzicka, Metrovic, Mellani. Next I saw Moneta and Stursa followed by many others, tired but walking briskly toward their homes to get out of their grimy work clothes and eat a big meal. The kitchen odors were strong now.

Several girls on one of the front porches could be heard talking and laughing. Occasionally one or two of them would look toward the street scene. Soon young Ed Perkins, his clothes already changed, was seen driving slowly up and down the street in his Chevrolet, casting glances from side to side. The young man with him was likely a visitor and it was also likely that two young ladies would be riding with them the next time by, as on other occasions.

Many other things I might have seen here in Kempton before the shades of night fell, but as I watched, for the last time, the sun sink behind these mountains, Mrs. Humphrey, with the supper that she had prepared now on the table, said, "Come and get it!"

The anticipated long, quiet summer in a setting of great natural beauty, adorned with bits of coal dust, had been so enlivened by unexpected events, so enriched by human interest, pathos and humor, that the time had passed all too quickly. A new chapter in my life would start tomorrow.

Graduate Schools
Of Medicine

Dr. John B. Deaver, the senior surgeon of Lankenau Hospital in Philadelphia when I was a graduate medical student at the University of Pennsylvania, in a typical teaching clinic would have a schedule of operations that would have exhausted most men, even those forty years younger than he was.

I liked to sit on the front row as near as possible in order to see as much of the operations as could be seen from the tiers of seats around one side of the operating room. It was necessary to be there early to get a favorite position to watch and listen to the noted surgeon.

This particular afternoon he had done a nephrectomy, removing a kidney so diseased as to be only a menace; had removed through the bladder an enlarged prostate that interfered with the flow of urine; and had performed a cholecystectomy, the removal of an inflamed, painful gall bladder that had become detrimental to health. He made frequent comments regarding the cases and procedures used and on a variety of subjects, including boxers and boxing, a sport which interested him.

A perforated gastric ulcer patient was wheeled into the operating room, lifted from the stretcher, and placed on the table. The woman anesthetist was placing the apparatus in position and making adjustments to continue the anesthetic which had been started in the preparation room. The surgical resident was giving a history of the case.

Dr. Deaver stressed the finding of board-like stiffness of the abdominal muscles after a perforation. "When you palpate the abdomen with a history of an acute, severe abdominal pain and it feels like a board, you can be reasonably sure that there has been a perforation," he said. To emphasize the point, he prodded me in the abdomen and the lesson was not forgotten.

The next case was one of intestinal obstruction. The part causing the obstruction was removed. Reasons were given why a temporary external fistula was generally made for evacuation of the bowel before making an anastomosis later to restore intestinal continuity. This operation was followed by a rectal case, the removal of a cancer.

Being a busy general surgeon, Dr. Deaver performed numerous operations on most parts of the body, but more in the abdominal and genitourinary areas. Commonly seen in his afternoon clinics were those classed as major operations, generally a half dozen or more at one session, such as a hysterectomy or removal of a kidney stone. In addition, the repair of a hernia, an appendectomy and various other operations might be observed here. Clean, uninfected cases were done first and the so-called dirty cases later.

Students from several medical schools came to this clinic. These included some young ladies from the Woman's Medical College, who generally sat in the rear of the amphitheater. Occasionally there would be a mild commotion among them as one or two of them fainted.

Fainting has not been found to be a characteristic of the types of persons regarded as gentle, meek and mild any more than of those who appear to be rough, bold and aggressive. In a line of men waiting for injections, the big, muscular one talking loudly and joking as if to imply that he is not afraid is the one that is especially watched when his turn for the needle comes, in order to catch him so that he will not be injured if he becomes pale and falls in a faint.

"Do you know of any surgeons who do any more operations than I?" the surgeon asked the resident assisting him, in a voice that all in the amphitheater could hear.

"Yes, sir, the Mayos," was the answer.

"Why is it that they do more?"

"There are two of them," the resident replied, just as was expected of him.

To be sure that a gauze sponge would not be left unseen in the incision, Dr. Deaver followed a ritual that was something like the following.

"How many sponges did you start with?" the surgical

nurse was asked before the incision was closed at the end of an operation.

"One hundred," she might say, for example.

"How many do you have left?"

"Twenty-five, unused, on the tray."

"How many in the used sponge count?"

"Seventy-five," would have to be her answer, or a further search would be made until all were accounted for before he would close the incision.

He gave careful attention to the details of each technique used and stressed the importance of germs in the causation of disease. Cultures were taken at each operation and biopsies were routine on all tissues removed.

His statistics were unusually favorable when successes and failures were compared. The mortality rate was very low in consideration of the extent and severity of many of the pathological processes presented. In some instances surgery was the treatment of last resort and in some cases the operation was to correct a previous procedure "that was done elsewhere," to do or undo what had been neglected or done inadequately or inadvertently before.

Surgical success was not always possible and he accepted responsibility for the results of his surgery. He insisted on preoperative preparation for the eventualities that might be anticipated and on anesthesia of sufficient depth to permit necessary exploration and to perform the procedures required. "Handle the tissues tenderly, lovingly," he would say during an operation.

Dr. Deaver, who was an eminent surgeon, is an example of those who were associated with graduate schools who "by precept, lecture and every other mode of instruction" imparted a knowledge of their art to those who had a chance to learn from them.

Seeing abnormalities which can be removed or corrected is heartening. In a few cases the disease or pathology is so far advanced or extensive that excision or corrective measures are impossible and to attempt it wholly impractical.

A rare exploratory incision, after all diagnostic procedures have resulted in uncertainty, might reveal a malignancy so widespread as to dictate that the incision be closed immediately without subjecting the patient to further surgery and that other treatment measures be employed.

The finding of an inoperable condition may represent a failure of the profession but its greatest importance is to the one who has the condition. What it means to the individual, whether or not recognized by him, is realized by the surgeon and stirs his emotions, but he cannot afford to dwell on it.

Feeling the accumulations of the miseries of all his patients would be more than could be borne by one doctor and his usefulness would be destroyed. He can sympathize with these unfortunate ones and hope that each, with the help possible, will be able to bear his or her burden.

Many surgeons or their loved ones have undergone major surgery. This helps them to more fully understand its importance to the ones operated upon and the sensations felt by them and their families.

I found that each hospital utilized for the teaching of graduates, in common with other hospitals, had its variations of the methods used to apply the generally accepted principles of treatment for various conditions, such as gastric ulcer, goiter, hemorrhoids, bed sores, burns or whatever abnormalities the patients might have. As hospitals consist of buildings, resources, equipment, personnel, doctors, nurses, technicians and those other employees usually present in great numbers, they vary in the details of treatment as these essential elements vary.

The Graduate School of Medicine of the University of Pennsylvania used a number of hospitals in Philadelphia for the instruction of medical graduates. While in my second year of training after receiving my M.D. degree, I had decided to specialize in general surgery and had chosen Pennsylvania for further study because of its facilities and the comprehensive course it offered.

Many who wished to specialize preferred to obtain their training in one institution, progressing from one stage to another on the same service. I wished to get experience in a variety of hospitals in different localities and to get the viewpoints of those practicing in various places.

The University of Pennsylvania, an Ivy League school which was founded by Benjamin Franklin, has the oldest medical school in the United States. Its museum has an outstanding collection of archaeology and the history of man. It provided one of the many cultural advantages in the city, established by William Penn and rich in history, with its many institutions of higher learning including four other medical schools, Temple,

Hahnemann, Jefferson and the Woman's Medical College of Pennsylvania.

I chose general surgery as a specialty because it was not restricted to one particular part of the body as many others were. One surgeon I knew, for example, specialized in surgery of the hand. Not only was he limited as to the body area in which he operated but the geographical areas in which he could practice successfully were also limited.

After investigating the facilities for room and board available in convenient locations, I got a room at the Y.M.C.A. in the center of the city. It had a cafeteria, gymnasium and certain advantages which included nearness to transportation and many places of interest. My room was small but clean and contained the essentials. A classmate from upstate New York also roomed at the "Y" until his wife and baby arrived, after which he rented an apartment.

A few Hahnemann Medical College students roomed on my floor. Their institution was located on North Broad Street and I had heard that it was "homeopathic."

"What is the difference in your school and the regular kind like mine that some call allopathic?" I asked them.

"I'll try to explain it to you," Al Bradley began. "The founder of our school believed that disease is cured by remedies which produce in a healthy person effects similar to the symptoms of the complaints of the patient.

"The system of medicine that the school was supposed to teach, according to the founder's bequest, was called homeopathy and according to it drugs were given in minute doses."

In contrast to the neighborliness of Albertville, Alabama, I lived for a school year in the Philadelphia "Y" without meeting the roomer on either side of my room. Occasionally there were social affairs at the Y.W.C.A. several blocks away to which we were invited.

The "Y" was on Arch Street near the intersection of Broad and Market streets, the city's chief thoroughfares, across the square from City Hall with its statue of William Penn. The statue is about 548 feet from the ground on its tower in the center of the city. People who had seen the statue many times, when asked in which hand Penn held his Quaker hat, would usually guess right or left without realizing that it was on his head.

The home of Betsy Ross, the seamstress who was said to have made the first official American flag, was on Arch Street

133

not far from where I roomed. Independence Square was within easy walking distance to the east. It brought to mind that Philadelphia was the national capitol from 1790 to 1800.

Independence Hall and the Liberty Bell, which was rung to proclaim liberty after the signing of the Declaration of Independence, are preserved there. When I touched the crack in the bell it made me feel as if I had reached back in time and come in contact with a great moment in history.

On the square I saw Congress Hall, scene of Washington's second inauguration and his farewell address. St. Peter's and Christ churches, with pews of George Washington and Benjamin Franklin, were of historical and architectural interest to us who tried to visualize their association with people and events about which we had read since childhood. One of my first books was of Washington's boyhood.

Fairmount Park was a pleasant place to walk and to see the Free Library, the Academy of Natural Sciences which was established in 1812, the Benjamin Franklin Institute and Museum, the Philadelphia Museum of Art and the aquarium.

Letitia Street House, believed to be Penn's original building, and Mount Pleasant, the home bought by Benedict Arnold for his bride, Peggy Shippen, are in the park. The University of Pennsylvania crew could be seen rowing on the Schuylkill River.

Rittenhouse Square in a wealthy residential area to the west was another place where I liked to walk. On the way to it I would stroll on Chestnut Street past leading shops and on Pine Street, where many doctors had offices.

When walking in the other direction I would sometimes go through Wanamaker's Store and by the big golden eagle on the street floor. To the south in a section that seemed foreign, I went occasionally to enjoy the duck dinner at a moderate price in a Roumanian restaurant. Going more often would have burdened my digestive system.

A seafood dinner at Kelly's, a Chinese or Italian dinner or even a meal in a Linton's gave variety to my fare. At the "Y" I was introduced to substantial German cooking and to squares of tasty scrapple.

Martha Brandt, a student at the Pennsylvania Academy of the Fine Arts nearby, who came to the "Y" cafeteria for lunch, brought her tray to my table one day. Her brother was in the Wharton School of Commerce of the University of Pennsylvania and their father was a New York broker. "Sometimes we have lots of money and sometimes we're broke," she told me. Fortunately she enjoyed walking, too.

There was not much time for recreational pursuits while taking the intensive course in surgery and studying for the examinations of the National Board of Medical Examiners at the same time. Success in the latter would permit me to practice in most of the states.

The days were filled with hospital rounds, lectures, watching demonstrations and operations and work in the laboratory. Nights were usually devoted to study during the weekdays. Fortunately for this purpose, the city was rather quiet and sedate.

Movies and a few dance halls offered Saturday night diversion. Blue laws closed all places of amusement on Sunday. If one wanted to be amused, Camden, New Jersey, was just across the Delaware River or there might be an invitation to a friend's home. The Arch Street Methodist Church was close to the "Y."

Someone's description of Philadelphia as a cemetery with lights was not intended to be factual, but the city did not claim to be a fun city either. It was still known as the City of Brotherly Love, as in colonial days.

Governor Alfred E. Smith of New York was running for the presidency that year, appealing to the people to "look at the record." He appeared in a parade on North Broad Street with his derby hat and cigar. His good-humored smile was most impressive as the motorcade passed slowly through the throngs of people exhibiting more curiosity than excitement. Franklin D. Roosevelt called him "The Happy Warrior."

"Who are you voting for?" one man was heard to ask another.

"I'm voting for Al Schmidt; how about you?"

"I'll vote for Al Schmidt, too."

The spirit of Philadephia appears rather conservative to visitors from more exuberant cities and not characterized by quick changes, even though the central part of the city has been rebuilt. This spirit or attitude is recognized by its citizens.

Many years after leaving Philadelphia, I telephoned an eminent medical authority there concerning a problem of mutual interest and suggested a conference with him. "I could come to your office," I offered. "Could we discuss it by phone?" he asked me and then commented, "I can't imagine anyone coming to Philadelphia who did not have to."

Nevertheless this old city has much charm and many

unique attractions, in addition to being one of the great medical centers of the country.

Many conventions were held in the huge convention hall near the university west of the river and there were the Quakers' football games in the big Franklin Field Stadium with Brown, Cornell, Columbia, Harvard, Yale, Princeton and others.

On a chilly New Year's Day, among thousands of other spectators with stamping feet and steamy breaths, I watched and listened to the long procession of colorful string bands in the Mummer's Parade. At least each year in Philadelphia begins with much unusual music and a bit of excitement.

The Graduate Hospital was the principal one used for our instruction of a formal nature. Some of the others were the Pennsylvania, founded by Benjamin Franklin; the University; Episcopal; Lankenau; and the Philadelphia General Hospital, sometimes called "Blockley" in those days. We also visited Temple University, Jefferson Hospital and others.

"This patient was admitted last night for a stab wound of the chest over his heart. We found that the knife had entered the heart and that blood was escaping from it. At operation we had the problem of suturing the opening with the beating heart a moving target. Placing the sutures had to be synchronized with the heartbeats," Dr. Jones, the surgeon conducting us through the Pennsylvania Hospital wards, told us. He then continued by describing the technique successfully used to repair the heart wound.

This was long before open heart surgery became common. The man was resting comfortably in satisfactory condition from an otherwise fatal injury, not to mention what it did for the one who stabbed him. He was in an area reserved for clean or uninfected cases.

Lung abscesses, peritonitis, fecal fistulas and various other kinds of infected cases, common then, were seen on appropriate wards. They required frequent attention to drainage tubes and changing the voluminous gauze dressings worn by many.

"This baby was left in front of the hospital in a basket last night," we were told by the doctor on the pediatrics ward. "We have no idea who left her but will take care of her until she is adopted or placed in a foster home or other institution.

"The baby here is one of many that are unwanted and left with us without permission, generally at night. They are usually not in need of treatment except for malnutrition, perhaps.

There are slum areas and many poor people near us. Maybe some think that they cannot afford to keep a baby.

"The situation is not satisfactory but so far we have found no acceptable way to solve the problem. Mothers of illegitimate babies seem to be confident that we will care for them and relieve them of all responsibility."

"Does a mother ever come to the hospital and claim a baby that she has left here?" someone asked him.

"I have not known of this, but several times I have noticed young women walking by the hospital looking anxiously toward this section. Each time I see one she goes slower when there is the chance of a baby being seen. You can imagine how they feel."

This is recalled when there are discussions in which the only reaction to acknowledgment of having illegitimate children is praise for "honesty" and when the virtues of free love, freedom from family ties and state care of children are extolled.

"You have to pay in some way for what you get," someone said thoughtfully.

Mental anguish, as well as the suffering due to abnormalities, disease or injuries, is often witnessed by the doctor even though the sufferer may wear a facade to conceal it.

Each hospital has its individual characteristics. The resources, the grounds, the building and equipment or combinations of these may be the most prominent visual feature that gives one an impression. But the personnel is the essential ingredient which determines its character.

The reputation of a hospital in many instances results from having a famous doctor on its staff. The reputation, in so far as most patients in it are concerned, may or may not be deserved. Often a hospital, especially if it is a small one, is dominated to a large extent by a man or woman who is not necessarily its administrative head or chief of the professional staff but in effect runs it.

The Pennsylvania Hospital, when I was there, seemed benign, calm, relatively peaceful and elderly, but not retired. In keeping with its age, many came there seeking relief from such infirmities as rheumatism and related ailments. Benjamin Franklin would, no doubt, express his pleasure in seeing the contribution to "life, liberty and the pursuit of happiness" that the institution he fostered has provided through the years to the people of his adopted city.

Age of an institution is not a proper criterion for judging its spirit, vitality, capacity to serve, the ability of its staff or the modernity of the methods used to fulfill its purpose. Again, how it functions depends largely upon the qualities of those who work in it and how conscientious they are in doing their jobs. So it is with the efficiency of a hospital and its effectiveness in making people healthier and happier. Individuals and committees consider many factors to determine the acceptability of a hospital for the services it offers.

The Philadelphia General Hospital, one of the nation's great hospitals and complex as well as large, also seemed mature and offered to share its learning with those who came to broaden their knowledge. As at a four-ring circus, there are limitations to what an enthusiastic watcher can see.

In the genitourinary and venereal disease wards were numerous chronic as well as acute infectious cases. Among them were many cases under prolonged treatment that could have been cured in short order with drugs that only became available more than a decade later.

Examples of gonorrhea, syphilis and other so-called social or venereal diseases resulting from sexual experiences, often promiscuous, were there in great numbers and in various stages. A session of viewing these should have been sufficient to curb one's appetite.

The instructor reminded us that such infections were no respecter of personages and illustrated this with incidents. "The only time I ever charged a preacher for treatment was when one lied to me about how he got gonorrhea," he said.

Dr. DaCosta's Surgical Clinic at Jefferson Hospital was a favorite with students in the medical schools of the city. They were held in a large amphitheater before audiences that were even more attentive than they generally were at performances by the noted.

Many of the students gathered there had studied his widely used textbook on surgery and awaited his entrance with an air of expectancy doubtless akin to that felt by aspiring young actors in other theaters waiting for the star to appear. Too, some of the patients to be seen would have unusual, perhaps rare, conditions.

Dr. John Chalmers DaCosta, stricken with disabling arthritis, came into the arena in a wheelchair. No longer able to operate on patients, he could still give them and his students the benefits of his brilliant mind, accumulated knowledge and experience. By his example, he was able to inspire them to persist when faced by adversity.

Patients shown in the clinic, one at a time, were usually representative of problems encountered in medicine, particularly surgery. Often there was a question of diagnosis.

A layman might be surprised to know how often a precise diagnosis is missed, even in an excellent institution. The possibility of obtaining accurate diagnoses has increased with the new aids and improved techniques introduced from time to time.

Lionel Barrymore in the television series "Young Dr. Kildare" played the role of an older doctor confined to a wheelchair but guiding the young one, played by Lew Ayers and later by Richard Chamberlain. He was reminiscent of Dr. DaCosta, from whom I had been privileged to learn early in my career in surgery.

What was learned in courses taken after graduation from medical school was not limited to that resulting from the teaching of those charged with that responsibility. Useful knowledge could be obtained from many sources, not necessarily doctors or educators. One of the sources was classmates, all of whom were graduates with varied backgrounds and experiences.

One of the graduate students told us of an operating-room incident involving a noted surgeon. "During an operation he was impatient with his assistant if forceps or retractors were not held properly or if he did not move his hands out of the way quickly enough."

"Working with him must not have been easy," one of us thought out loud.

"That's right. He had a habit of hitting the resident who assisted him on the knuckles with an instrument when he did not like the position or movement of his hands."

"Didn't the assistant complain?" we asked. "That could hurt."

"One day after getting an unusually hard rap on the knuckles near the end of a trying operation, the assistant walked around the table and gave the surgeon a swift kick in the seat of his white pants."

A frequent subject of conversation in a group of doctors is what one of them refers to as "an interesting case I saw." It might or might not be of particular interest to the others but was out of the ordinary in the experience of the narrator, who often was the hero of the story. Most doctors, when with a group of others in their profession, tend to talk shop wherever they are. Once when there was a chance for relaxation, we were talking about autopsies, recalling odd findings.

"There was a weird one in Bellville," Dr. Woods began, getting our attention. "It was a case of sudden death of a man under circumstances which made the police suspect that he had been killed, but they could find no wound or other evidence of it on the body.

"At autopsy it was discovered that he had been shot in the rectum, a perfect bull's eye, and the bullet had ranged up through the abdomen without leaving an outside trace that could be seen."

"Did they find out how it happened and who did it?" we asked, thinking of possibilities.

"Yes. A neighbor of this man had come home, found him in bed with his wife and shot him while in the position he was in at the time found."

At the end of the school year there were tests to determine whether a certificate for successful completion of the course would be awarded and also if a candidate could continue in the graduate program working toward a degree. The main hurdle was a comprehensive oral examination given individually.

When my turn came to face the examiners, I entered the room to find Dr. John B. Carnett with about six other surgeons, heads of their staffs and members of the graduate faculty, seated around a long table. Each of these authorities was free to ask me any question that he considered as pertaining to surgery in general.

The questions are not recalled but my answers must have been satisfactory as the certificate was received and I was permitted to continue in the graduate program under the direction of a proctor acceptable to the rest of the faculty.

My proctor was to be a distinguished surgeon, a Fellow of the American College of Surgeons, whose hospital was located in Vicksburg, Mississippi. Some incidents of my year in that city will be related later.

Before leaving the graduate study theme, references will be made to a few short formal courses that I took or that took me, depending upon the viewpoint. They gave me an opportunity to observe aspects of surgical practice in various parts of the country.

The Harvard course was taught mainly by Elliott C. Cutler and Robert Zollinger. Dr. Cutler was the professor of surgery and surgeon-in-chief of the Peter Bent Brigham Hospital, where most of the instruction was given.

Traditions and the character of the venerable institutions of Boston inspired respect and confidence. While the practice of surgery appeared dignified and proper, it did not seem essentially different in principle from that which I had seen before coming to Boston.

One nicety in dressing surgical incisions to which our attention was directed was the application of a strip of sterile tinfoil to the wound to exclude possible infection. Operative procedures were performed meticulously.

While in Boston I took advantage of spare time to see the places of which I had heard, especially those of historical interest such as Beacon Hill, Bunker Hill, Faneuil Hall, Old North Church, Old South Meeting House, Paul Revere's House, the State House, Boston Common, which is said to be the oldest public park in the United States, and Old Granary Burying Ground, where I saw the resting places of Revolutionary patriots.

I enjoyed a visit to the Museum of Fine Arts, an evening of music by Boston's famous orchestra and a Sunday afternoon's walk in the Arnold Arboretum, as well as a Harvard-Yale football game where the Harvard accent was the most amusing.

At the Massachusetts General Hospital, the statue honoring William J. Morton, the dentist who in 1846 first proved publicly that ether was a valuable anesthetic, of course did not mention that Dr. Crawford W. Long of Georgia had used it in operations as early as 1842. Giving the credit to Morton is an illustration of the fact that it pays to advertise.

Seeing Plymouth Rock where the Pilgrims had landed, the Minuteman statue at Lexington commemorating "the shot heard 'round the world," the "rude bridge that arched the flood" marking the spot where another battle of the Revolution was fought, Longfellow's home in Cambridge and other memorable spots in the Bay State made the history of this part of the country come alive for me.

Whatever else may attract attention in a particular area, the natives are always of interest, especially if one of them is a cheerful Irish girl, representative of an important segment of Boston's population, who is proud of her city and enjoys acquainting an outlander with its charms. Thank you, Shirley O'Halloran.

The ancestors of those who populated the state after the Civil War, I learned, came from various countries, many of them from Southern and Eastern Europe. The Yankees, who were descendants of the early settlers of English stock, were found to be remarkably similar to the people I had lived among in the South, most of whom had common ancestry with these Yankees, although for several generations far apart from them geographically in the New World.

The New York Post-Graduate Medical School—Columbia University course in orthopedic surgery taught the latest techniques in the diagnosis and treatment of deformities, fractures and dislocations, including open and closed reductions. Taking the course afforded me an opportunity to visit the Presbyterian Hospital and other hospitals in the city.

Equipment for traction and splinting of broken bones, as well as operations for fixing the fragments in normal or functional position, were demonstrated. The care of the patients and their injuries, both before and after surgery, was observed.

Orthopedics had been considered as my choice of the surgical specialties but I decided not to limit myself to bones and joints. For one thing, bones heal slowly and joint conditions are often chronic. A general surgeon, however, frequently is called upon to treat injuries to the skeletal system, particularly in the absence of a specialist in this field.

Fractures, or broken bones, were generally immobilized or held in position by plaster of Paris which was applied while wet and became hard as it dried. This was accomplished, in a general way, by putting rolls of a thin fabric holding the plaster powder into water and, when thoroughly wet, rolling it around the part to be splinted until thick enough to be sufficiently strong.

This was shaped, as it dried, to fit the part being immobilized to make the cast. Before application, the skin was protected by powder and stockinet and then care was taken to make the cast close enough to be effective but not tight enough to interfere with circulation. Skill and experience contributed to the construction of a proper cast, strong enough but not too heavy, that would serve its purpose while the break healed.

Body casts which included the extremity involved, an arm or leg, were frequently employed. This meant encasing the body in the heavy, rigid covering to hold a large portion of the body of the patient, together with his broken part, in corrected alignment, in a particular position for several weeks, sometimes with the legs spread apart if the hip had been broken.

Open reduction and fixation with a metal part did much toward diminishing the need for massive casts. This permitted more freedom of movement for the patient and reduced the chances for complications, such as bed sores and pneumonia.

Another method for getting broken bones into proper position and holding them was by traction obtained through the use of weights attached to a rope which went through a system of pulleys, on a frame over the bed, and was tied to broad strips of adhesive plaster applied to the patient's injured extremity.

The means employed depended upon the location and type of fracture, whether it involved the skin or other soft parts such as tendons, nerves and blood vessels, and taking into account the patient's general condition. Much more was involved than simple carpentry or construction.

Although one learns largely by doing, pitfalls may be lessened by taking advantage of the teachings of those with more experience in a particular area of endeavor. Sometimes we absorb more from exposure to learning than is realized at the time.

Columbia's postgraduate course allowed little time for anything else. My explorations were mostly confined to midtown rather than to the lower east side of the city as before.

The Mayo Clinic in Rochester, Minnesota, offered a course in military medicine which appealed to me as an officer in the Army Medical Reserve Corps. There were a number of other inducements, including the opportunity to see this famous clinic, located in a city which it made unusual, and to profitably use part of a vacation without pay that a government hospital gave some of its staff because of a temporary lack of funds during the worst part of the Depression.

The Mayo brothers, Drs. Charles H. and William J., gave lectures to our group and we watched operations done by the younger Charles W. Mayo and other surgeons such as Waltman Walters. We saw Alfred W. Adson in neurological surgery. Louis A. Buie performed operations in proctology.

Dr. Donald C. Balfour was one of the noted surgeons we had the pleasure of seeing at work. His signature as president of the American College of Surgeons is on my Certificate of Fellowship in that organization. The other officials who signed it were Dr. George Crile of the Cleveland Clinic and Dr. Frederic A. Besley, professor of surgery at Northwestern.

The younger of the two brothers, Dr. Charles Mayo had talked to our class at Tulane years before when on a visit to New Orleans. His talk dealt with the subject of preparing patients for operations, particularly those considered poor risk cases. With proper preparation and timing, the risk could be minimized.

The next occasion I saw Dr. Charles H. Mayo was when he visited in Vicksburg, Mississippi, the year I was resident in surgery there. He came in his yacht, *The North Star*. Many doctors of the city attended the reception given for him in the home of Dr. Maritain, my University of Pennsylvania proctor.

In Rochester, he told our group about the founding of the clinic by his father, William Worrall Mayo, a pioneer in Minnesota when the Indians there were still dangerous. "Our home place," he said, "was surrounded by a high fence or wall. Whenever my father had to be away, the women of the family would attach shiny knives on the ends of sticks and march around the inside of the enclosure with the knives showing over the wall to simulate soldiers' bayonets.

"When my father first came here he was the only doctor in the area. For an emergency he would have me stand on something so that I was high enough to give the anesthetic by drops so that he could do the operation."

Then I knew that my father was not the first doctor who had asked a young son to help in this way.

St. Mary's Hospital in Rochester started with thirteen patients and a staff of three, William W. Mayo and his two sons. These three surgeons founded the world-famous Mayo Clinic a few years later in 1889. Thus began this great medical center.

I read the newspaper account of an interview with Dr. Charles H. Mayo. According to it, the reporter asked him, "Dr. Mayo, you have looked inside a great many people and have examined all parts of the body. Have you ever seen a person's soul?"

The reporter then wrote, "He looked at me with steady, clear eyes and said, 'No, I have not seen it but I know it is there.'"

In the hospital where we watched the various surgical procedures, there were a number of operating rooms in a row, each with an observation gallery which could be entered from the hallway. Generally several operations were in progress at the same time.

Once while we were watching an operation, the condition of a patient in the next connecting room apparently became so critical that the operating personnel became alarmed, giving us an opportunity to see the surgeons, nurses and attendants in action during a crisis, an exhibition of Mayo teamwork.

Those in the operating suite who could let go of what they were doing rushed to aid the surgeon and assistants who were primarily concerned with the patient's life, which hung in the balance. Resuscitative equipment was brought into play and soon the emergency situation was over and the operations continued. The drama of real life-and-death scenes such as we had witnessed exceeds that in the world of make-believe on the theater stage and in moving pictures.

The episode affected all of us doctors in the gallery, but not as acutely as when we had been the active participants as surgeons shouldering responsibility in other operating rooms. One was heard to remark, "I'm glad that it is my turn to watch someone else sweat."

The Mayos, in addition to other skills, had been adept in attracting men of outstanding ability and organizing them into an effective clinic at a time when individual practice was the rule. As its fame spread, many young men were drawn to it for training and some remained with expansion of the clinic.

One of these, Bob Jackson, whose family I knew in Vicksburg, showed me the places of interest in and around Rochester. He pointed out the fine, old homes where the two brothers lived and the smaller, more modern home of "Chuck" Mayo which was further out.

Bob was enthusiastic, talked of the hospitals, the clinic, its influence on the city, and told me about the hotels, in one of which I had a room while taking the course. It was a modest room, of moderate price rented by the week, the meals simple but adequate.

"I had been here only a few days," he recalled, "when Dr. Mayo invited me to his home for dinner. It was all very nice and the organ which he enjoys with dinner was played while we ate."

Our instructors described the procedures used at this great clinic to direct each of the thousands of patients from all over this country and from foreign countries to the proper doctor.

Generally one of the Mayos would not be seen, but at that time if a patient especially wanted to see one of them it could be arranged. The international reputation of the clinic also brought many foreign doctors to visit it.

Patients did not always find what they expected there, especially if they had not seen any large medical institution before. A friend in Hattiesburg, a town many hundreds of miles from Rochester, mentioned such an incident.

"Mrs. Dreyfus had a skin condition on her body that hadn't cleared up under the treatment of the specialist in dermatology here so she decided to go to the clinic and see an expert.

"When she got there, after her history was taken and other preliminaries, she was ushered to an examining room, asked to undress as necessary for the examination, to get ready and wait for the doctor who would be in presently. Who should walk in to examine her but young Dr. Vogel, who was born and raised right here in Hattiesburg, the son of one of her best friends! You know the saying, 'A prophet is not without honor save in his own country.'"

By going away to a large, well-known clinic, one may obtain the advantages of an aggregation of competent specialists and equipment not available where the patient lives. It does not necessarily mean that the doctor who treats this individual has more competence or experience than the home-town doctor.

Some doctors who go into a hospital for training get "The White Coat Habit" and remain there for their careers. Many of these become teachers, especially if the institution is affiliated with a medical school. Generally this provides a feeling of more security than striking out alone and often more prestige eventually as a professor and contributor to the literature.

Taking special courses can be enjoyable as well as a way to acquire more knowledge in a subject that interests the graduate. Making a living, however, becomes a matter of practical concern as well. I considered broadening of the horizon by the contacts made in them one of the fringe benefits of these courses.

"Do you see the fellow sitting near the end of the third row?" a classmate whispered to me before a lecture started, looking at one of the physicians in our class, who was seated in front of us.

"Yes, that's where he usually sits; what about him?" I asked.

"He is Al Capone's doctor," he confided to me. "His body-guard always waits for him just outside the door and if you look you'll see him."

The man was described and, sure enough, whenever we went out, there he stood, ready to leave with the doctor when he appeared, looking at everyone in their vicinity with dark, darting eyes.

Classmates in postgraduate courses represent, as a rule, more diversified backgrounds, years of experience, and wider geographical areas than undergraduates. For example, a doctor from Alaska described for us what his practice in that great territory to the north was like. Another, of Spanish descent, talked of his home and life on a big plantation in Cuba and invited us to visit him. One of German ancestry told us about the nature of his practice in Lima, Peru, and the people and conditions in that mountainous land south of the equator. Another doctor in my class mentioned his kinship with Greek royalty and, by way of contrast, related his experience with a different kind of dynasty in a different world, the Chicago gangsters.

Hospital training and my practice before and after the postgraduate work included serving in a state hospital, municipal hospital, jail, a coal-mine practice, infirmary, private hospital, and as a ship's surgeon; then I served in government civilian and military hospitals, a forest camp, the army overseas in war time, and in private practice.

As a medical corps officer I served in an infantry division, a named general hospital, a station hospital, a dispensary, numbered general hospitals and in special assignments. Before this, however, I was an intern and then a resident.

Surgical Residencies

Dr. Francis Maritain, the University of Pennsylvania Graduate School of Medicine proctor for my second year of training in surgery, was the chief surgeon and chief of staff of the Warren General Hospital in Vicksburg, Mississippi. I was the surgical resident there. It was a private hospital standing nobly in the residential area of this city on the Mississippi River about halfway between Memphis and New Orleans.

The surroundings, as seen from the window of my new temporary home, were quite different from those in the northern city I had just left and I was anxious to see more. Dr. Maritain, I soon learned, was of French ancestry, in which he took pride. He was a gentleman, however, whose position in the class that some people in the Old South regarded as the aristocracy was based more on intellect, wealth and value to the community than on who his ancestors were.

Mr. Bertrand Maritain, brother of the surgeon, was the hospital's business manager. In addition, he managed the approximately eight-thousand-acre family plantation in Warren County. A bachelor, he lived across the street from the hospital.

Dr. Herman A. Fisher, an old classmate of mine at Tulane, was medical officer for the hospital. As he planned to make Vicksburg his home, he was developing a practice by treating patients outside the hospital as a general practitioner and was making satisfactory progress in becoming accepted. When he heard of plans to bring new industry to the city, he said, "I think Vicksburg is big enough as it is."

Herman's favorite sports were fishing and eating. His figure showed that he enjoyed good food, especially that produced locally. Too, he enjoyed conversation, the talking more than the listening, and working with him was agreeable. He did not treat the surgical cases but often helped with the anesthesia for operations.

The hospital staff was composed of physicians practicing in the city. As a rule the operations were performed by Dr. Maritain, usually assisted by me and occasionally by Dr. Politian, who was the chief surgeon as well as superintendent of the State Charity Hospital in Vicksburg. He also had a private practice.

Alan Walton was in charge of the clinical laboratory. He had previously been with the State Laboratory in Jackson. Like many others in that part of the country, he was a fishing enthusiast. Now and then when there was leisure time, I took a walk with him and Lance, his big German shepherd dog that he had taught to heel.

Spanish moss was draped over the limbs of spreading oaks standing before old mansions. Azalea, poinsettia, oleander, wisteria, camellia and honeysuckle bloomed in gardens filled with color and fragrance. Enormous sweet-scented, creamy white blossoms were scattered among the large, glossy green leaves of magnificent magnolia trees that were seen in yards of modest as well as grand homes.

Reverend Mark S. Wright, minister of the First Baptist Church, soon invited me to go fishing with him. We went in a small batteau propelled by oars on a lake not far from town. I did not bring him exceptional luck but it was pleasantly restful. Dr. Fisher attended his church and was paying attention to his daughter Martha, a comely, cheerful girl of marriageable age.

The Lake Country Club had a golf course, tennis courts and other attractions but the activity that drew the largest attendance was the monthly dance. These events afforded an opportunity for me to meet many of the social set and for some of them to imbibe from private stocks kept in their lockers during the time of prohibition.

The girl with whom I had a dance at one of the club affairs was from a prominent family and looked the part. She was resplendent in a becoming evening dress, with jewelry appropriate for the occasion. The orchestra music started. This was our dance. The melody and rhythm could not have been better.

We walked onto the ballroom floor, around which many of the people stood talking, listening and watching the dancers. I quickly discovered that my pretty partner had imbibed too freely. She could hardly stand, much less dance, and did not look as pretty. It was an unusual club happening.

I was wondering what to do—if it would be better to pretend that we were dancing or assist her off the floor or what—while trying to be inconspicuous and not embarrass her. Her brother, seeing the predicament, came over as if to "cut in," an accepted custom, but instead of continuing the dance, the three of us quietly left the floor.

A college for girls which was regarded as "a finishing school" had several parties during the year to which I was invited. The enrollment was not large and the students were no doubt carefully selected. They were fresh, genteel and, at least in the beginning, were considered to be unsophisticated young ladies. I was a bit over age to be included but went along at the urging of a young businessman, whose father was a trustee of the school. I perhaps became almost sophisticated enough to catch up with these girls, if a man ever does. Most of us agree that the female of the species develops faster than the male, socially anyhow.

Dr. Maritain seemed to take a fatherly interest in whatever seriously interested me and, often as not, his tutorial advice was concerned with subjects other than surgery. Once while we were scrubbing for an operation he said, in speaking of associations and friendships among people, "I think that one should associate with those who are his kind of people; many troubles are caused when a person goes out of his class."

He was not specific. Maybe it was a suggestion that I should select my friends from among those that the old families there thought of as blue-blooded, although I never heard such words used. He mentioned no one with whom I had been friendly if he knew of such.

Another day during our conversation of nonmedical matters, Dr. Maritain spoke of a girl that he apparently thought would be suitable for an aspiring young man. "Adele Winthrop seems to be a nice young lady, looks well and is always pleasant. John Wharton is her uncle. He is president of the bank where we have our account." I did see Adele a few times, found her to be as he had said and enjoyed her company, but we did not envision our futures as the would-be matchmaker probably had.

Reverend Wright's maneuver one Sunday reminded me of Dr. Maritain. After the church service he told me that he and Mrs. Wright were taking a young lady of the choir, Matilda

150

Walker, to her home and that I could ride with them if I wished. The four of us went there; then the Wrights, instead of taking me by the hospital on their way home as expected, left me at Matilda's. Their intentions were good, no doubt, and they were appreciated, but Matilda and I were amused by the ruse.

I decided that having a car of my own would be advantageous. Bryan Wayne had the Chrysler-DeSoto agency and suggested that he could give me a bargain. Bryan had married a wealthy girl who had made it possible for him to build a new garage and acquire the agency, but sales had lagged and he was anxious to dispose of an excess of cars on hand.

The Wayne company was struggling to become established and Bryan said that it would be helpful if I took a car. He offered to sell me a two-door DeSoto and deduct the amount of his commission. "Nearly all the parts are interchangeable with the Chrysler," he told me. As a result of his salesmanship I became owner of my first automobile.

Alan Walton saw in this an opportunity to go fishing. One thing I soon discovered in driving was that there were some steep inclines on streets leading to the river but that Mississippi mud could be worse.

There was a series of lakes not far from Vicksburg that were the results of river overflows, I was informed, which had left them well stocked with fish. Some of these, like Reelfoot Lake in Tennessee, had attracted sportsmen from many states.

"When in Rome do as the Romans do," I had heard. Well, I was in Vicksburg. So Alan and I set about making preparations for a fishing trip and at the first chance headed for the lake. I drove north for a while, then we turned left onto an unimproved road. This led us through the woods toward the place where the catfish, black bass, speckled trout and bream were waiting impatiently for us.

Pines, oaks, hickory, gum and other trees shaded the meandering road damp from recent rains which had freshened the forest green. The purring sounds of the motor in my new, shiny car were making pretty music and then it happened—the wheels sank into the mud. We were stuck. Efforts made to go backward or forward only splattered mud over the car and got the wheels in deeper.

We put sticks and tree branches in the ruts under the wheels and finally extricated the car, which no longer looked so new. Back on firmer ground, we reached the small, rustic hotel at the lake, where there were several other fishermen, and got beds for the night. Up at break of day, we had breakfast and, with fishing tackle and lunch bag, set forth across the lake in a small boat supplied with paddles but towed by Sam Watts with his motorboat.

Sam lived at the lake. "I'll take you to where the fish have been bitin' lately. You can give it a try and if you don't have any luck you might paddle over there where the stumps are," he said, pointing. "I'll come back for you this evening when you're ready." He left us. It was a long lake.

We tried for two or three hours in the area to which he had taken us without much success, although we were encouraged by many nibbles and a few little fish less than pan size. "Why don't we try another spot?" I suggested. Two men in another boat about two hundred yards away seemed to be doing better. We paddled over toward the cypress trees and the many tree stumps, some of which we found to be submerged. Care was taken to avoid being stranded on top of a stump or having one tear a hole in the bottom of our boat.

Hungry now, we ate our lunch, then returned to active fishing. Occasionally we saw a fish jump out of the water and frequently a big gar would make the water splash near us. They seemed to be over four feet long and must have weighed as much as fifty pounds.

"We won't have any luck with them around," Alan said gloomily. "They will scare off the fish that we are after. Garfish belong to the pike family. They eat smaller fish and get awfully big here, especially where there are lots of stumps in the water." It was hot in the sunshine. The gars were greedy.

"How much longer do you want to stay?" I asked. He seemed relieved that I mentioned it.

"Let's try one more place. After that I'll be ready to call it a day." We did and concluded that it was time to signal Sam. On the way back I let my lure and hook trail behind the boat. About half way to shore the strike came! I pulled in a big bass. For me the fishing trip had been a success. The DeSoto and I had been initiated into the fraternity of creators of fish stories.

The appearance of the DeSoto when I returned to town did not make it a very good advertisement for the Wayne company. There was another agency in the state that was well established and had a big volume of business. "They got their start with money made in selling bootleg whisky on an island in the

Mississippi River between the two states where neither claimed jurisdiction," my barber in the Vicksburg Hotel confided in my ear.

Alan Walton bought a used car that had served so many years that it probably should have been retired. The first night he parked it on the street. The next morning a policeman came to the hospital and asked if anyone knew anything about the wreck at the bottom of the hill. The brake on Alan's car had not held. It had apparently rolled rapidly down the steep hill and crashed into a telephone pole.

Dr. Politian asked me to be a member of the visiting staff of Vicksburg Charity Hospital and invited me to attend staff meetings which were held at night. On one occasion he did an appendectomy before the staff and requested us to note the time required for it. He finished the operation in approximately seven minutes.

In another operation there, a big ball of hair or bezoar was removed from a patient's stomach. This individual was accustomed to swallowing hair, which had accumulated over a period of time to form a hard mass about the size of a baseball.

I had known Dr. Willis Wentworth, the surgical resident at the Charity Hospital, in college. An unusual case he showed me was a woman with ainhum, a disease which is also called dactylolysis spontanea and is seen chiefly in African countries. Constrictions appeared in some of her toes without known cause. The course of the disease is slow and sometimes one or more toes drop off.

The writing of a paper on a subject pertaining to surgery was one of the University of Pennsylvania Graduate School of Medicine requirements for a Master's degree. In the Charity Hospital was a five-year-old black boy, Walter Adkins, who had an operation for cholelithiasis or gallstones. The literature indicated that this condition is more common in females than males and in whites than in black people and is very unusual in children. I reported this case and used the subject, "Cholelithiasis in Childhood," for my paper, which was approved by Dr. Maritain and the faculty.

George Harris, another little black boy, had swallowed lye in his home. The scarring resulting from this had caused an obstruction of the esophagus, the tube to the stomach, which prevented him from swallowing food. An operation provided a gastric fistula, an opening in the stomach through which he could be fed, and the narrowing in the esophagus was being dilated gradually so that eventually he could eat normally.

This youngster had been in the hospital so long that he felt at home there and enjoyed privileges not ordinarily accorded the patients. He was not confined to the ward and was allowed to visit a little general store nearby. He felt well and his general condition was good. Sometimes he would ask one of the doctors or nurses for money, buy a Coca-Cola at the store and pour it into his stomach through the opening.

Dr. Wentworth was showing me the new babies born in the hospital and stopped in front of one of them to tell me its story. "The mother of this baby was a problem case with poor prognosis. We treated her on the obstetrical ward but she died when she was taken to the delivery room. There was an emergency case being admitted at the time. It was a busy day.

"I left the delivery room and was on my way downstairs. The nurse said, 'Do you think there is a chance that the baby might be alive?' I went back, applied forceps, delivered the baby, got its respirations started and there it is."

During the Civil War the Confederate force at Vicksburg surrendered to Union troops led by General Ulysses S. Grant on July 4, 1863, after a siege of forty-seven days. A National Military Park adjoins the city on two sides and covers over fifteen hundred acres. It contains the remains of forts, many old cannons and hundreds of monuments, memorials and tablets marking positions of the armies. With my DeSoto I was able to explore the park and visit other places of interest in the city and state.

Natchez to the south, founded in 1716 by the French governor of Louisiana and the oldest city on the Mississippi River, contains many antebellum homes, some of them magnificent, built during its golden era of prosperity. Still further to the south, in Louisiana, I visited Dr. Cecil C. Blakeney, a former classmate, practicing in St. Francisville and with him saw several of the outstanding old mansions with their heirlooms, gardens and statuary. I also met the people who lived in them.

The plantation owner living in one of the most impressive of these mansions built during the first part of the last century gave me a bucketful of blackstrap molasses that was made on the place. "It's good for your health; has a large iron content," he said. He spoke of the grayish green Spanish moss hanging in large, loose strands on the ancient oaks and how it grows natu-

rally, nurtured by the air without the need for fertilizer or cultivation. It was gathered for commercial purposes such as use in
upholstery and packing, but the demand for it had decreased
with the manufacture of more of the synthetic materials.

Many of the old plantation homes had been built to face
the river rather than a road, as transportation was largely by
boat during the period they represent. The steamboat would
stop at intervals to bring goods and supplies and to take away
what had been produced for marketing, which then was mostly
cotton. The coming of a riverboat was a time for excitement on
the big plantations.

A banquet at our hospital was attended by many of the
local doctors and some from other towns such as Greenville,
which was north of us. Some of the nurses assisted with serving
the food. One of them spilled a large glass of iced tea on me. I
was not sure if it was an accident or intentional.

The hospital had a training school for nurses. I taught the
class in anatomy. Some of them appeared to have their thoughts
on other subjects during lectures, but all of them passed the
state board examinations so they must have learned something
anyhow, maybe at other times.

Dr. Charles Mayo came to Vicksburg in his yacht, the
North Star. Most of the doctors in the city, it seemed, came to
the stag party that Dr. Maritain gave for him in his home. It was
a decorous but stimulating occasion for us.

Dr. Politian asked me to go with him to a family reunion
dinner in the Amati home one Sunday. The dining room was
unusually large for a private residence and everyone sat at one
long table. After the spaghetti course I felt as if I had eaten sufficiently because it was a large serving covered with a rich, aro-
matic sauce. But I found that this was only the beginning of the
dinner.

Our hosts plied us with quantities of a variety of meats and
vegetables, always urging us to take more, apparently disappointed when we did not take second helpings. The food was
excellent and bountiful. My appetite had been excellent, too,
but my stomach could not hold all that the Amatis seemed to
think it should. Dr. Politian felt of my abdomen and said, "You
have a tumor there." It was a delicious meal with a merry family, but after it was over I felt that I would not be able to eat
again for a week.

"Would you like to go to the plantation with us? Margery

Verne is coming along," Bertrand Maritain asked me one day.

"Yes, I would be glad to see it."

Where I was reared we had farms and farmers, but here there were plantations and planters. Some of the plantations contained several thousand acres. A number of families would live on one of these large holdings.

We rode several miles from town into the country, then turned off the main road onto one leading into the plantation, where it became a private dirt road. "Sometimes we come out here for a day and get one of the women to cook a chicken for us," Bertrand said. He got out of the car and opened a gate; then he drove inside and closed it. This procedure was repeated at different places in the large land area that we toured. On the way we stopped at several homes.

This plantation, instead of being a continuous piece of ground cultivated as one tract, was divided into many tracts of varying acreage. On each was a small dwelling and associated structures for the black family living and working there. The homes were generally of the kind sometimes described as cabins but not in a degrading sense. In general, those living in them appeared to be as happy as those living in mansions I had visited.

Bertrand knew these people, showed personal interest in them and discussed matters of mutual concern. They and Bertrand talked together in a friendly way as people who have known each other for a long time. They depended upon each other.

The plantation, to me, seemed to be a series of adjoining farms with a tenant family on each. The boundaries between them appeared to be somewhat informal and less clearly delineated than when each has a different owner. The farms were defined by a pasture fence, a curving ditch, hedge or other mark. The main products grown were cotton and corn, but there were also many kinds of vegetables. The soil was evidently fertile, judging by the appearance of it and the plants. That Mississippi, among the states, was said to be listed at the top in wealth per capita before the Civil War was understandable.

Patients in the hospital where I was the resident were, as a rule, people who paid for what they got, including medical service. "The kind of people who pay their bills are the most appreciative of what you do for them," Dr. Maritain said. Most of the people treated there were well-to-do. Generally they were less demanding and said "thank you" more often than the charity patients that I had been treating before.

One of the most worrisome patients that we had while I was there was a wealthy planter, reputed to be of a "good family," who lived quietly far out in the country but on rare occasions went on a spree. When he did, he was difficult to manage; he became noisy, unruly, unclean, and did not obey orders, even resenting them. We breathed a sigh of relief whenever he became quiet and orderly. Then he was contrite and again acted the part of a gentleman.

Dr. Politian, a large, jovial man of tremendous energy, participated in many activities, including that of representing the Italian government as consul. His gift to the priest at Christmas was a silver cocktail shaker. Whenever he wanted to get away for a day or two, he drove in his Cadillac to Pass Christian on the Gulf of Mexico.

Most of the people in the city ordinarily appeared more relaxed than those in larger cities in some other parts of the country. Dr. Politian and Dr. Maritain frequently joked with each other. During an operation Dr. Maritain said, "Politian, it would look neater if you mopped the blood more often and cut all the ties even."

"Spoken like a true Frenchman," said Politian.

"Where does that word 'dago' come from?"

"Oh, it comes from 'Diego,' which was the name of an island, I think."

Gus Bridgway, a slender young man whom I treated in the hospital and later at home, was a hijacker who was shot in the abdomen with buckshot by some bootleggers whose whisky he was attempting to acquire in the practice of his profession.

"They thought that they had killed me. It was on the river bank. I fell by the boat and pretended to be dead, didn't move until they got out of sight, then managed to get to the road and somebody brought me here," he told me frankly after we had become better acquainted.

The house in which Gus lived, in common with most homes in Vicksburg and other cities, was not a mansion. It was not in the best part of town either but the attractive Mrs. Amy Bridgway was attentive and devoted to him. "Will my man ever get well?" she wanted to know. He had six or more openings in the abdomen, which drained for several weeks and required many dressings, but he eventually recovered.

Another patient, on the other side of the law, was not so fortunate. One night when I came from my room into the hospital lobby, a policeman in uniform, Officer Westenburg, who had just entered, was holding onto a post and swaying unsteadily, his face white and blood on his uniform. "I've been shot," he said.

We prepared him for surgery at once. It was apparent that he was bleeding internally from abdominal wounds and although an emergency operation was done, he did not survive. The wounds were so extensive and severe that this outcome seemed to be inevitable. Officer Westenburg was one of the very few patients who died in the hospital.

Barney Riley had his left arm pulled off when it was caught in machinery. The injury was mutilating but not fatal. Reparative surgery resulted in healing and his general condition was excellent after recovery, even though he had lost his arm.

While in Vicksburg, I applied for and was granted a license to practice medicine and surgery in Mississippi. I also joined the local medical society and attended its meetings. Each member of the society was expected to appear on at least one program during the year. The subject I chose for one of the scientific meetings, "Intercostal Neuralgia," was one that had come to my attention because of Dr. Carnett's interest in it. This nerve disorder sometimes simulates a surgical condition.

Dr. Claud M. Dawson, an elderly Vicksburg physician and member of the society, congratulated me on my paper and after becoming acquainted in this way we often talked together. He told me of some of the early experiences in his practice.

"When I was a young doctor malaria was very common in this state and its cause not generally known," he recalled. "Most people thought that the disease was caused by miasma or swamp air.

"A court case involving malaria, or chills and fever as many called it, attracted much attention and I was asked to testify as an expert witness. I testified that malaria is caused by a mosquito. The judge and everyone in the courthouse laughed uproariously as if I had told the best joke that they had ever heard. It was hard to convince them that I was serious."

Dr. Dawson wanted me to stay in Vicksburg after finishing my residency in surgery and offered me a partnership with him. I wished to get more surgical training elsewhere before deciding where to practice and declined his flattering offer, although it was appreciated and I had enjoyed the city and its people's hospitality.

I had made regular reports of my work to the Graduate School of Medicine and submitted the paper required for a degree. Dr. Maritain had sent his endorsement of me and I awaited the decision of the faculty as the year drew to an end. At long last, notice of my acceptability was received and I was advised to be present for graduation. For this, I returned to Philadelphia and at the University of Pennsylvania commencement was awarded the degree of Master of Medical Science for Graduate Work in Surgery.

My second year as surgical resident was served in the Matson Hospital in the largest city in the nation, a contrast to where I had spent the previous year. The hospital was located east of Central Park in the upper part of midtown Manhattan. Whenever I wanted a change of scenery from city streets, the pond, lake, green grass and trees of the park were nearby.

Mrs. Cornelia Struther was superintendent of the hospital, and Dr. Arnold Rodwurm, chief of staff. She superintended with the masculine traits that she had nurtured to the extent that not much of her feminine nature remained. The hospital rooms and services were expensive.

Dr. Rodwurm was a born New Yorker. His instincts were influenced by the subconscious need to defend himself and he reacted according to the theory that the best defense is a strong offense. Consequently he was often offensive. Some of the staff members were natives of the city and others came from various places, including Europe.

Dr. Mantegna said that he came from England and indicated that he practiced in London before coming to New York. Included among his patients were many prominent in society and in the field of entertainment. He had a contract to treat the employees of a broadcasting company. His girl friend was the leading lady of one of the most popular plays on Broadway at that time. It was his custom to kiss his women patients when he visited them.

The description that these women would give of Mantegna was that he was "tall, dark and handsome." This view of him must have been affected largely by his affability and the fact that his bedside manner was as much natural as developed. His technique must have been acceptable as he had a large practice.

"Thank you, Dr. Mantegna, for all you did," Mrs. Armentrout said when on morning rounds he had told her that she would be discharged that day.

"All I did was kiss you," he said.

Dr. Sabatini had patients of varied backgrounds. Some of them were sports figures. Apparently he was available to Madison Square Garden. Also among those he admitted were individuals reputed to be gangsters. Nurses told me that they gave them substantial gifts and sometimes I noticed signs of affluence, such as baskets of enormous grapes and other hothouse fruit, in their rooms.

The room of a patient who had many friends or was a public figure might have so many flowers in it that it gave the appearance of a florist's shop. In one I noticed a beautiful bouquet from President Herbert Hoover. At times a patient's room would not hold all the flowers received.

Dr. Aufricht was a plastic surgeon and a skilled one. Many of his patients were Jewish girls who had requested nose surgery. The operation which he did inside the nose altered its shape so that it appeared shorter and straighter afterward. He usually operated unassisted except for the surgical nurse. The moment when a girl took a mirror to see the results was one of excitement and emotion. Generally they appeared to be relieved and pleased.

A famous orthopedic surgeon from Vienna, Austria, had achieved a reputation for correcting clubbed feet of children by a bloodless method. Actually he did make small incisions, only large enough to admit a scalpel blade to cut restricting tissues. The foot structures were then forcibly manipulated into approximately normal position and a plaster of Paris cast applied. The results were favorable in most cases.

The procedures employed by this doctor were carried out under general anesthesia, which was not usually very deep because the patient did not have to be anesthetized very long and relaxation to the extent required for abdominal operations was not necessary.

A child died while the doctor was manipulating the bones and other structures in its foot, which was deformed at birth, in his attempt to bring the parts into normal position. Informing people of a death is an unpleasant, sorrowful duty for a doctor, especially when parents must be told that their child has just died. In this case it was worse because unexpected, occurring during a corrective procedure regarded as having slight risk.

It was my dreaded lot to make known to the mother of this child the outcome of what had been done in an effort to straighten the child's foot. She was waiting hopefully outside the operating room to hear the results. The expressions of her anguish were unrestrained. How all of this affected me was unimportant perhaps, but seeing and hearing this grief-stricken mother added to the misery I already felt.

Sudden death in a hospital is a dramatic and distressing event, but it occurs in only a very small percentage of cases. Some of the possible causes are unusual reaction to a drug or anesthetic, sudden massive hemorrhage, shock, embolism, or an acute cardiac condition such as coronary thrombosis. A few times I have seen a postoperative patient, whose incision has healed and who is ready for discharge, getting dressed to return home, surrounded by his happy family who have come for him, die suddenly as the result of an embolus. The possibility of this rare happening has been reduced by early ambulation and other measures after certain operations.

An attractive couple I met in the hospital and came to know as Phil and Ethel were there for the delivery of their first baby. She was at term and appeared to be in good health, expecting a normal, healthy baby. Instead she gave birth to a dead, macerated fetus with findings typical of syphilis. It was a sad occasion for all, especially at their departure.

The DeSoto that I had bought in Vicksburg could not be used very satisfactorily while living in midtown Manhattan. Driving in heavy traffic was slow and did not afford much pleasure. There was no place for me to park at the hospital. Garage parking in the area was expensive, so I decided to sell my car.

During the Depression, money for buying cars was scarce. Wishing to learn what could be expected for mine, I went to a Chrysler-DeSoto agency on automobile row over on the west side of this city of nearly eight million people. The building was a large one with many new cars on exhibit. There were a number of salesmen. The one who came forward was Phil. I had bidden him good-by only a few days before, never expecting to see him again. It made New York seem small-town.

Sharing a small apartment of two bedrooms and sitting room with me in the Matson Hospital was Dr. Alvin S. Haynes from Syracuse, New York. Several of his friends were in show business or were would-be professional entertainers. One of them wrote lyrics for songs but was having difficulty in getting them published. Some of them sounded rather silly but so do many until, with the music added, they become popular. He said, "I could get them published if I let them go under the name of a writer with a big reputation."

This was during prohibition. It was legal for doctors to prescribe whisky for people they were treating. Alvin learned that a druggist would buy a specified number of prescriptions per month and use them to enable certain customers to get the "medicinal whisky" he dispensed or otherwise dispose of them. Each month Alvin would write a batch of these and, for patients' names and addresses, use some picked at random from the Brooklyn telephone directory. In this way he supplemented his modest salary and was able to gratify his desire to see all the Broadway shows.

New York provided much inexpensive or free entertainment. The best in vaudeville could be seen in the Palace at a price much less than the cost of a ticket for just a movie in later years. In many of the moving-picture theaters, such as the Paramount, stage shows could be enjoyed after the movie. I saw top performers whose names became household words and heard many of the great bands of that era.

At the Ziegfeld Follies I listened to Will Rogers make comments on what he had read in the papers and watched as he circled his lasso over the entire cast assembled on the stage for the last act. From a top balcony of the old Metropolitan Opera House on Seventh Avenue it was a pleasure to see the opera-goers as well as the grand presentations on the stage and hear the wonderful music. The Hippodrome also provided entertainment that was not expensive.

I got to see a few New York Yankee baseball games. Babe Ruth and Lou Gehrig each knocked forty-six home runs that year, but Philadelphia won the American League pennant.

At First Army Headquarters, Governors Island, I saw a polo game consisting of eight chukkers of 7½ minutes each. The players were skilled in swinging their mallets while dashing up and down the 300-yard-long field, but the ability of the trained polo ponies to start, stop and turn quickly in pursuit of the ball was amazing.

The sidewalks of New York, east side, west side, and all around the town, offered a variety of amusements and I gazed upon them from the Battery to the Bronx. These included Greenwich Village; Union Square, where soap-box orators spoke on all kinds of subjects; Times Square with news bulletins in electric lights going around the building and the bright colors of animated signs; the theater district; the German section to the north of the hospital; and Harlem, where I was wont to wander in times of relaxation.

On Easter Sunday I mingled with the throngs of people on Fifth Avenue dressed in their new finery, many of the men wearing high hats. It was still cool and those in summer clothes were shivering, but nearly everyone was wearing a smile. The largest crowds were at St. Patrick's Cathedral, where scores of cameras were clicking.

St. Patrick's Day was another joyful time in New York City. Most of those at the big parade wore something green, whether or not they were Irish. There were dozens of brass bands and representatives of a great many organizations, but one of the most impressive elements of the parade was the rows and rows of "New York's Finest" marching proudly up the avenue in their blue uniforms.

A ride on the Staten Island ferry gave a good view of the harbor, Statue of Liberty and the lower end of Manhattan Island and skyline. In the New York Stock Exchange on Wall Street I witnessed the trading and price changes on the big board and felt the excitement of activity in the financial center of the country. At Trinity Church, Broadway at Wall Street, I visited the little cemetery where Alexander Hamilton and Robert Fulton are buried.

A few of the other churches visited were John Street Methodist Church; "Little Church Around The Corner"; St. Mark's In-the-Bowery Church; St. Paul's Chapel, the oldest church standing in Manhattan, where George Washington and Governor George Clinton had pews; and "The Church of All Nations." In Riverside Church I climbed to the bell tower, saw the seventy-four-bell carillon and had a fine view of Upper Manhattan. From the church I walked to Grant's Tomb on the high bank of the Hudson River.

One Sunday I rode in the subway to Battery Park, began walking up Broadway and continued on it to Van Courtland Park at 242nd Street. On the way I passed City Hall, Union, Madison and Lincoln Squares, Columbus Circle, Columbia University and Columbia Presbyterian Medical Center and much more. There were so many things of interest to keep my attention that it did not seem too far. I came back on the elevated train. When visiting Brooklyn and Coney Island I went by subway. I could walk anywhere in the cities then without feeling uneasy.

Christmas time in the city was a special period in the year when the better dispositions of people became visible. In the big stores on Fifth Avenue and in shops large and small everywhere, adorned in the season's colors, glowed countless luminous bulbs shedding soft lights on the displays.

Most shoppers hurrying along the busy streets in snow-flecked coats and carrying bright, gift-wrapped packages radiated happiness, although some appeared to be concerned. The more biting the cold, the warmer they looked. Seeing groups of people having fun together at such a time, I missed my family and old friends. When later I told a new friend, who knew only New York, that one could be more lonesome in a big city than anywhere else, she did not understand.

The Fourth of July was quiet in the city. Many took advantage of the holiday to go to the Catskills or to a beach. Coney Island was teeming with vacationers who barely had room to walk on the sand without stepping on someone. Walking by a group of firemen sitting in front of a firehouse on an almost deserted street in Manhattan, I heard one of them say, "This is the time I like New York best, when everybody leaves town."

While at Matson Hospital I received a letter from the War Department stating that there were openings for doctors in the Army Medical Reserve Corps and offering me a commission in the corps as a first lieutenant if physically fit. I applied, was given an examination and was soon commissioned. After that I attended weekly meetings at night in the army building on Whitehall Street at the lower end of Manhattan near City Hall. There was no pay for attendance, but we were advised that because of our training we would be advanced a grade over that which we held at the time if ordered to active duty in the event of a future war.

We were expected to go to a summer camp for two weeks of training after a year in the reserves. I did not want a career in the regular army but did wish to be prepared for duty in case of a national emergency. To remain in good standing in the corps, it was necessary to take correspondence courses taught by the army. This was time consuming and exacting. There was no remuneration for this, but promotion to a higher rank in case of war was expected to compensate us, and patriotism to motivate us.

The hospital sometimes received emergency calls from people in the vicinity or from the broadcasting company. When a call from the company came I would put an overcoat over my white uniform and go downtown to the broadcasting building by taxicab. Once it was to see a man who had fainted. On another trip I treated a hand injured by a machine used to simulate the sound of a locomotive. One time it was a man who had been cut when he fell on a glass door.

Dr. Mantegna phoned me one night and asked, "Will you go over to Park Avenue and see a girl for me?" I was agreeable but then he said that she had been bitten by a dog and made suggestions as to treatment. He paid me for making calls at night when it was inconvenient for him to go.

In the large apartment at the smart address he had given me, I found a party in progress and no one feeling pain. A girl, however, showed some lacerations on her face where a poodle that she had held had bitten her. After treating her wounds in a room away from the crowd, I was invited to join the party but had to return to the hospital. Although the party was missed, the gratuity was generous.

Another night Dr. Mantegna asked me to go over to Central Park West to see Kathleen Riley, a servant girl, whose employer had called. A few couples were playing cards in the sumptuous apartment when I arrived. The game continued quietly while I was directed to the rear of the apartment proper to the servants' quarters, where there was a row of small bedrooms. Kathleen, a maid who appeared to be about twenty years old, was in bed in one of these rooms. She was distressed. Her complaint was vaginal bleeding.

I questioned Kathleen regarding her menses. She said, "My menstruations have been fairly regular every month at near the same time. They may vary a few days but I've never had any trouble before." Asked if she had skipped any month prior to the present flow, she answered, "No."

The amount of discharge, though not alarming, was excessive and if it continued would jeopardize her. For adequate treatment she needed to be hospitalized and her general condition would permit her to be moved. I phoned Dr. Mantegna and advised him of the situation. He told me to get her to the hospital by ambulance and that he would see her there. Her employer was informed and he was very cooperative.

On examination of the patient, Dr. Mantegna found that she had had an incomplete abortion. He took the necessary steps at once and she responded to the treatment favorably. The next morning when I went to see Kathleen she was greatly improved, not only physically but in her attitude as well.

"I want to apologize for not telling you the truth last night," she said. "You knew that those were lies all the time. I was trying to keep my condition secret because of wanting to go back to my home in Ireland on a visit soon." Fortunately her indiscretions had not made it impossible for her to see the auld sod of the Emerald Isle again.

I returned home once during the year, going by steamship to Savannah, Georgia, and from there by train. An unexpected passenger on the ship was a nineteen-year-old girl with a cast on one foot and leg, a patient of Dr. Lorenz who had just been discharged from our hospital and was accompanied by her sister.

In Savannah, the first settlement in Georgia and one of the chief southern ports on the Atlantic Ocean, were many old homes of the previous century. Juliette Low's brownstone home, birthplace of the Girl Scout movement, was where the first meeting of the Girl Guides was held. The city is the chief naval-stores center in the United States and the train from there ran through pine forests, where I saw pails attached below V-shaped cuts in trees to catch the oleoresin, or turpentine.

At home I found Mama and Papa well and still active but on a reduced scale. Mama was bothered with rheumatism from time to time in varying degrees. "You're a doctor. What's good for it?" she said to me. I was sorry that there was nothing new to offer. She did not complain much.

Papa still practiced medicine, mostly by prescribing for people who came to him, as he did not make house calls much any more. He managed his affairs mainly from his room at home, where hired men and others came to see him. During the day he was talking with one or more people most of the time.

"Come in; sit down and talk to me," Papa would say to me. He was not overly interested in New Orleans, Washington, Philadelphia or New York but wanted to know about me and what I had been doing. He might ask me how the farm crops looked along the way from where I had come.

Doctors should not get sick, according to the way some

people think. Mrs. Struther, the hospital superintendent, was one of those. I was ill once with a severe cold and was not fit to be with patients even if I had felt able. However, she tried to induce me, not very subtly, to perform as usual. Such tactics did not endear her to the hospital personnel.

A hospital resident is supposedly carefully selected and is respected. Ordinarily a doctor in this position is immune to any possible machinations of the visiting staff versus the administrative individuals. Once, however, Dr. Sabatini got me into a squeeze between him and the chief of staff. He asked me to assist him with an autopsy on one of his patients who had died in the hospital, leading me to believe that he was following the approved hospital routine in the matter. I helped him. Later, Dr. Rodwurm, who had not been consulted regarding his approval for the autopsy, and apparently offended by his authority not being respected, complained to me instead of to Dr. Sabatini, saying, "I can't do anything to him." No doubt he had problems as chief of which I was not aware but his lack of tact caused me to foresee the future more clearly and predict that he could not do anything to me much longer.

When I first came to Matson Hospital I talked with Dr. Rodwurm regarding my opportunities for doing operations in connection with my other duties. He had said, "The amount of surgery you do depends on you." I found that nearly all of it was done by the surgeons in private practice who sent their patients to the hospital, so my participation was mostly in the role of assistant. I did, however, get to assist some of New York's outstanding surgeons, which perhaps was of more value to me at that stage than being the operator.

Alvin, my associate, was amiable enough and kept me informed concerning his friends in the theater world. He mentioned one from upstate New York who wrote a play, got it produced on Broadway and invited his parents down for the opening. The parents were shocked by its daring and embarrassed that their own son had written it.

New Yorkers, I discovered, were not only the native kind but came from all parts of the country as well as other countries. A large proportion of them had immigrated from Europe or their parents had. Many of the others had come there from the New England states, the South or Midwest. Some of these would return to the places from whence they came. I met a few from Alabama.

Alabamians were even found on Wall Street. Edgar Harrison from Cullman, Alabama, invited me to have lunch with him in the Executive's Dining Room of his bank on the street. The quietness and dignity of the room contrasted with the bustle of the neighboring streets swarming with people at noon. Wyatt Patton from Huntsville was in the Sullivan and Cromwell law firm. He described his work with this large firm of many members. What I was doing at the hospital seemed more exciting to me.

Another young man from back home holding a minor position in a big bank invited me to his apartment on Fifth Avenue, where he lived with two other young men who had similar positions. The apartment was unusually large and had the appearance of being very expensive, not the kind that I had expected one who was only a beginner in banking and finance to rent.

"How can you afford it?" I asked my friend rudely. "Not that it is any of my business."

"Well, it's like this," he said. "The apartment belongs to a rich lady who does not like to live alone and wanted to help us."

Back at the hospital, Alvin, who had grown weary of the everyday drudgery associated with his duties and wishing a change with more independence and money, told me that he was leaving. In order to have a steady income until he could become established in private practice, he had arranged to be the doctor for a taxicab company and would give the drivers their physical examinations.

Dr. Antonio Hertilinni, a graduate of the University of Naples, took Alvin's place. He showed me his artistic diploma granted by King Victor Emmanuel and enlightened me on many aspects of life in Italy in which appreciation of history, art, music, well-seasoned food and wine played a large part. He was ordinarily warm natured like his native Napoli and as volatile as Vesuvius, but at times he could be as depressed as Pompeii covered with ashes.

Tony was one of those people who could not be ignored when present. He was not present much, however, when off duty as he soon found a girl over in Jersey, a kindred soul, to whom he became attached. He showed me the ring that he bought for her, a heavy one embellished with red and green stones. To me it appeared gaudy, but everyone to his own taste.

"In Italy it pays to be a fascist," Tony said in his Neapolitan accent, smiling and gesticulating. "You get the best of everything, even discounts at the whore houses. Mussolini has done much for Italy."

The clientele of Matson Hospital was unusual. Here celebrities could enjoy privacy not possible in certain other institutions. "Guess who came in tonight?" the nurse on admissions might ask when I returned from a show. The name of the new patient would be one that was familiar to people all over the country. Famous individuals in need of care that we could give, and certain ones who visited them, added to the interest of a day's work.

The rich and celebrated may often get more attention than those not wealthy or well known, but this does not necessarily mean that they have better medical treatment. Operations for them are performed in the usual way. A society surgeon in some instances may have less skill or knowledge than the average surgeon not known to the fashionable set.

In Matson Hospital I was able to learn how a titled nobleman, the so-called beautiful people, or a noted novelist, athlete, humorist, singer or comedian looked and acted when sick. Usually they behaved admirably but, understandably, one who is humorous professionally may be glum when ill. I had learned much more while gaining experience in surgery, but felt that it would be preferable to extend my field of operations, and the sea enticed me.

Brenda Bartlett, secretary to the dean of the Graduate School of Medicine, University of Pennsylvania, while I was a student there, had moved to New York and was secretary to the dean of the Columbia University Medical School. She advised me of a possibility for surgical research there and suggested that I investigate if interested. I discussed it with the dean but nothing materialized from this. Full-time research did not particularly appeal to me.

New York City, being a center of world shipping and passenger traffic, had many steamship line offices, which made it advantageous for me to apply for a position as ship's surgeon. The office of the chief medical officer of the American Export Lines, a company to which I had applied, asked me to come over to New Jersey for an interview. An appointment was made for a certain hour. Getting across the Hudson River by ferry took more time than anticipated and it seemed certain that I would be late for the appointment until I remembered that New

York was on daylight saving time and New Jersey was not. As it was, there was a short wait.

"You helped me do the cholecystectomy Tuesday," the chief medical officer said when I was ushered into his office. It was Dr. Barcroft, an excellent surgeon who operated at Matson, but I had not recognized him in a business suit instead of operating-room garb. He had on his desk a thick stack of applications for the opening, but I received an offer of employment as ship's surgeon on the steamship *Excalibur* cruising the Mediterranean and, after a brief consideration, accepted.

While preparing for my new position, I gave advance notice of my departure from Matson Hospital to Dr. Rodwurm and Mrs. Struther. I obtained a New York state license to practice medicine and surgery, had ship officer's uniforms made by a tailor on Fulton Street, and secured a Seamans Protective Certificate from the Bureau of Navigation showing proof of citizenship. I bought a large steamer trunk for my clothes and other belongings.

As the time approached for leaving the hospital, I anticipated with pleasure my first trip abroad while recalling events and associations of the past eleven months. Fifth, Madison, Park and Lexington avenues had become as familiar to me as Baltimore Avenue and Main Street in Albertville.

I could associate such names as Gould, Vanderbilt, Sinclair Lewis, Ring Lardner, Bobby Jones, Rudy Vallee, George M. and Georgette Cohan with real flesh-and-blood persons just as I did Baker, Brooks and Brown back home. I remembered how Freeman Gosden and Charles Correll appeared and sounded when not playing radio characters in "Amos and Andy," one of the most popular shows of that period.

There was so much to remember but so much more lay ahead.

Ship's Surgeon

The *Excalibur* of the American Export Lines was docked in Hoboken, New Jersey, and being prepared for its next Mediterranean cruise when I reported as ship's surgeon nearly two weeks before the date for sailing. This gave me time to become acquainted with the ship, officers, members of the crew, medical facilities, equipment, and supplies.

Alfred Erickson, the steward assigned to the hospital, was very helpful in assisting me with my preparations for the voyage. He was a veteran of the sea and also experienced in his paramedical duties. The ship's nurse was Natalie Lindsay. She, too, had crossed the ocean many times.

The surgery was equipped with large steam sterilizers, an operating table, surgical instruments, suture and dressing materials, anesthetics and other items needed for operations. I found that metals tarnished easily on the sea and required more attention to keep them brightly polished. There was paraphernalia and solutions for embalming.

On deck was a box-like structure, the size of a small room, for fumigating. It was not used but I was told that it was required by some country that we would visit. The lifeboats and apparatus for launching them were in position, as were the fire extinguishers.

The ship had a trim, attractive and eminently seaworthy appearance. Like others of the line, its name began with "Ex" and the capital letter "E," the line's insignia, was painted on the smokestack. The *Excalibur* carried a cargo of manufactured goods, such as automobiles, as well as passengers. All staterooms were first class. Mine was in the hospital section.

171

Roy N. Turner, the ship's officer second in command to the captain, did much to advise me concerning the functioning of the ship and its crew and the rules. He introduced me to the customs official that I would have to pass often while we were in port. "I'd like for you to meet Dr. Hall, our ship's surgeon. He will have to pass through here often, going back and forth to the ship. This is Mr. Downey."

Mr. Turner made my transition to shipboard life easier than it would have been otherwise. To him a ship was home. Above average height and without any excess weight, he was quiet, efficient, confident, firm, and respected by the crew. His wife was a Frenchwoman. If she took a voyage, it was on a ship other than his. He was fluent in French as well as English and had a speaking knowledge of a few other languages, including Arabic.

Jules Villon, the purser in charge of the office for accounts, finances, tickets and such, was from New Orleans, considered me as an old friend and liked to talk of experiences in the city where his family had lived for many generations. "We always spoke French at home," he said.

Mark Marino was the radio operator charged with maintaining communications with shore and other ships. He was a tall, black-haired young man, interested in electronics and dedicated to the proposition that a sailor should have a girl in every port, the main one at his home base. "My special girl is in Camden," he confided. "I usually buy her something on a trip. We might get married when I settle down.

"One night I went to see a girl who had a regular boyfriend—a great big fellow, a mean, jealous guy. He knocked on the door while I was there. She was scared to death and I didn't feel exactly at ease. At first I thought of being a tough, merchant seaman and bluff him as I had done before, but decided I was due back at the ship at once, grabbed my clothes and went out the back window."

The chief engineer was Eric Grieg, a broad, muscular man who talked mostly about cycles, revolutions per minute, gauges, velocities, temperatures, the situation at two bells, speed in knots, and things like that. I did not see him much except at another table in the dining room.

Four large tables in the dining room were for the captain, first officer, chief engineer and surgeon and certain passengers assigned to each of them. The rest of the passengers ate at the

172

smaller tables. The four officers acted as hosts at meals and other times when not otherwise engaged. We were not expected to show favoritism or romantic involvement.

Captain Jonas Sampson was a heavy, grizzled man with ruddy complexion who often reminisced over happenings of his lifetime on the shipping lanes of the world. "Once you get salt water in your blood, you're never satisfied on land," he said. When with him one thought of the expression: "He talks softly but carries a big stick."

One of my duties was to keep a log in which I recorded events of the day, routine and unusual occurrences, and conditions of the sea and on-board ship. I also had to keep medical records of the crew and passengers. For my ship-related duties I was paid a salary. It was permissible to charge passengers for medical attention that they requested personally, such as continuation of treatment started before coming on board or for individual complaints.

Clyde Wilbur and Evan Griffith were two of the junior officers that I met in port and would see frequently. One of Clyde's duties was to oversee the lowering of the gangplank after the ship and those on board had been cleared for landing at a foreign port.

At last the date for departure arrived. The cargo had been loaded in the hold, fuel and food taken on and everything was shipshape. The passengers had come on board, their luggage had been placed in their staterooms, the parties were over and all visitors had left the ship after the warning of "All ashore that are going ashore!" It was night. The ship's deep-throated whistle sounded.

The gangplanks were removed, the hawsers released and with the ship no longer moored or tied to land, I felt it gently vibrate as if coming to life, and new sounds were faintly heard. Then the ship began to slowly move and the distance to the dock increased. Our voyage had begun.

We passed other ocean liners at their lower Manhattan docks along the Hudson River, the Statue of Liberty, entered the Lower Bay, hesitated at Sandy Hook, where the pilot's boat left us, and then we were moving faster. The skyline of the city and its myriads of lights, making luminous the sky above, had faded and the Atlantic was before us.

New York seems more impressive on arrival and departure than when staying there. The grand view is more inspiring than the sensations felt when you are one of the millions in the city's noisy canyons. The ocean seems different, too, when there is no land in sight. I observed that the further the ship was from shore, the smaller it became.

"I just got a radio request from the *Nantucket* for you," Mark Marino informed me, handing me a typed message which stated: "Seaman Tarbell has pain right side low and hurts when touched. Nauseous. Please advise."

"What kind of vessel is the *Nantucket* and why did they radio you?" I asked.

"It's a freighter and has no doctor. We often get messages that way."

I advised for Tarbell rest in bed, liquids only, a towel-covered icecap to the lower right abdomen, medicine for pain if necessary and suggested hospitalization as soon as possible. Mark said that they would have first-aid material and ordinary drugs, including some kind of pain pills. He would let me know if he got any more radiograms.

Mark talked a while, as he liked to do, after the *Nantucket* request had been satisfied. We had gone into rough water and the ship had begun to roll from side to side a little. This was becoming worse. "The first month on the ship I was seasick every day and kept a bucket by me all the time," he said, looking out at the waves.

I noticed that Mark's face had lost color and that he was becoming paler as the ship rolled more, taking on a sort of greenish tint. "Well, I'd better get back to work," he said. Before long I learned how he felt. At first I had an uncertain feeling of dizziness as the ship rose and fell and there were sounds of the fall of objects that were unsecured. Then came the nausea.

Chairs in the dining room were held in place by chains underneath them. The sides of the tables were equipped with walls a few inches high that could be positioned to prevent dishes sliding off. Beds had side boards to keep one from falling out. I repaired to mine. It was a bit embarrassing to have the only doctor on board sick, but that was not my main concern at the time. At first I was afraid the ship would sink, then was afraid that it would not.

Alfred Erickson, my loyal helper, seemed to be immune to mal de mer but was sympathetic. He brought a tumbler of cognac to me and said, "This will make you feel better; it helps."

At the moment I would have tried almost anything, so I drank it. It did not end the seasickness but after that I did not mind it so much. Luckily we were soon out of the rough seas and those indisposed were happy again.

Back in my blue uniform and on deck breathing the fresh, sea air, my mood had changed and I could contribute to the morale of the passengers. The uniform was like that of the other officers, the stripes on the sleeve designating the duties and rank of the wearer. On mine were three parallel gold stripes with a red stripe above and below the middle gold one.

Medical duties of a routine nature were usually taken care of in the morning when I held sick call and wrote records and the reports required by regulations. I gave particular attention to the reporting of accidents as the details might have a bearing on legal as well as medical matters. For example, should a seaman be rendered unconscious by a blow on the head with a monkey wrench, various officials could become concerned.

Certain personnel, including the doctor, were permitted on the passenger decks. We were expected to see to the comfort and well-being of our guests on the cruise. Deck stewards provided games, reclining chairs and refreshments for them.

In the evening there was entertainment which was often provided by the passengers themselves, each one adding his or her talents. One of the volunteer entertainers, Belle Willis, was a young lady from New York who was very companionable. We enjoyed looking at the moonlight on the waves together until it was called to my attention that I was supposed to stay with the program.

Matt Hamilton, son of the chairman of the board of a large shipping line, was a junior engineer on the *Excalibur*. This industrious young man was learning ships from the water up and got as greasy as anyone in the engine room deep in the bowels of the ship. He was preparing for examinations required of the engineers in testing their qualifications for promotion. One of the subjects was first aid and he asked me to help him with his studies. I was pleased to do this.

Wilma Vandergrift, one of the most comely of the passengers, was also one of the most reserved except when Matt was with her. He asked the captain for and was given permission to see her on the top deck at appropriate times when not on duty. "We are learning French together," he informed me. This study was appropriate as French is said to be the language of romance as well as of diplomacy.

The time we spent with the passengers was intended to make the trip more enjoyable for them. It probably benefitted us more. Each had personal stories of the past and forecasts of the future to be elicited. Some had traveled much; others were feeling the excitement of crossing the ocean for the first time.

Paul Vonyer was a world traveler and a mining engineer by profession. As the representative of a great oil company seeking new fields, he had worked in many out-of-the-way places. Now he was going to Baghdad and from there would make trips of exploration. The Middle East would become one of the main sources of petroleum.

The passing of a ship was an event when none had been seen for several days and land was still out of sight far beyond the horizon. Porpoises often kept us company, leaping, diving, and performing as if putting on a show for us. We watched the flying fish at play and were amazed to see water birds far from shore. The phosphorescence in the water when seen for the first time at night was strange and reminded me of "swamp fire" seen long ago.

We reached the Strait of Gibraltar after cruising for ten days. The sight of land again after seeing only water for so long was wonderful. To our right was Tangiers, Morocco, on the north coast of Africa and closer on the left was the Rock of Gibraltar. I found that this tall, rocky promontory looked like the pictures of it only when viewed from a certain angle, but seeing it in this way thrilled everyone.

Marseille on the southern coast of France was our first stop. Before docking, we stopped in the harbor to be cleared by the French officials. A rope ladder was dropped over the side of the *Excalibur* to a small motorboat below. Mr. Turner informed me that I was to accompany him to the harbor master's office to vouch for the health of the passengers and crew. This was a safeguard to prevent bringing in contagious diseases. He descended the ladder first and beckoned to me. I had never been on such a ladder before but had used the one to our barn loft many times so followed him. Although the ladder hung loose, perpendicular to the water on which the little boat below was bobbing, I made the transfer and we proceeded to the office where clearance was granted.

The *Excalibur* was at the docking place when I returned to it, walking along the wharf. The passengers were lined up along the rails and members of the crew, with the deck officer Clyde Wilbur, were ready to place the gangplank to let the passengers off but apparently were waiting for something—what, I did not know. Clyde seemed to be signaling in my direction.

I had set foot on foreign soil for the first time and now watched the passengers disembark after a short delay. Clyde met me. "Why didn't you give me the high sign?" he asked impatiently.

"What do you mean?" I inquired.

"When you find out we are cleared, you are supposed to signal me so that I can lower the flag to show that we are not quarantined and let the people off. You can make a sign like this."

He reached above his head, made a grasping motion and pulled his fist down as if pulling on a rope. We had no further difficulties, and, anyway, Belle Willis thought that I had performed my duties well. "I was proud when I saw your uniform among all those Frenchmen on the wharf," she said.

Captain Jonas Sampson was not so happy. He had problems and sent word that he would like to see me in his cabin. "Do you have any Eno's salts?" he asked me. It was a vegetable laxative. The only kind in the ship's pharmacy was Epsom's. I think that the main thing he wanted was someone to tell his troubles to.

"When we came into the harbor to dock, the ship struck the piling and the hull was damaged. It does not seem to be serious but we don't know yet and it will delay our departure.

"We had a French pilot guiding us in but that makes no difference. It's my responsibility; I'm responsible for everything that happens to the ship even if it's not my fault. I'll catch hell when we get back to New York," he said downheartedly. It was evident that he wanted to talk and I was a good listener.

"I've been making this cruise around the Mediterranean from the start," the captain said. "We had a tough time at first. Some of these petty officials are hard to deal with. Some of them expect to get some graft.

"An official came on board at one port and pretended that we had not complied with all their regulations and said that they could not give us the papers we needed. I knew he had the documents; I saw them in his inside coat pocket but he would not turn them over to me. Finally I threw him down on the deck and took them away from him."

177

The captain described other incidents in his career on the seas. "One time a man died and we had to have the burial at sea at night. The departed was prepared and weights were attached at the ankles to keep the remains submerged. We had the prescribed ceremony, I read the ritual, and the body slid off the plank into the water in the usual way. The sea happened to be very rough that night and the next big wave washed the body back onto the deck.

"The wet corpse, with eyes wide open, lay there as if staring at us in the pale moonlight. The weights had become detached. We had to fasten others more securely and consign the body to the deep a second time."

Marseille, the main seaport, second largest and possibly the oldest city of France, was alluring. Jules Villon asked me if I would like to go sightseeing. Thinking that his fluency in French would be advantageous, I went with him. Walking along the waterfront of the old port, we saw a boat almost ready to leave for Chateau d'If on a nearby island featured in Alexander Dumas' novel, *The Count of Monte Cristo*. So no sooner than we were off the *Excalibur*, we were on another vessel.

That night Villon and I were walking on a busy street a few blocks from the waterfront and were mistaken for naval officers. A French colonial soldier unexpectedly gave a military salute that to us seemed exaggerated. Stopping at a news stand, Jules talked with the vendor and assured himself that he could converse satisfactorily in the language as spoken in France.

Panders or pimps would come to us, fall in step, and show their licenses or permits to act as go-betweens. From what they said, we understood that the government licensed them to solicit customers for houses of prostitution and that the houses were also licensed and regulated, the prostitutes being given medical examinations regularly.

These bold ones were persistent in the presentations of their sales pitch, which was about the only thing that could be said in their favor.

Before our arrival at Marseille, prophylactic medication to prevent venereal disease had been issued to the seamen. The purpose of it became apparent soon after we arrived. Because of this and other reasons perhaps, venereal disease was not often seen.

"You see the one in the red dress over by the rail?" Mark asked me one day and continued, "She wanted to come to my cabin. I don't know exactly what it is about the sea and ships that makes women that way, but they want to get with a man when they are on board."

"Maybe they are looking for husbands," I suggested. "Or perhaps what they have read about adventures at sea, pirates and all that, makes them feel stimulated that way."

"I think it's the salt air and the kind of life we lead. If I have a date with her it will be to meet on shore, not on the ship."

The longer I served as ship's surgeon the more important and extensive my duties seemed to me. Sanitation, hygiene, preventive medicine and attention to the physical and mental health of all on board were areas in which I could be of service.

In Marseille I went with one of the passengers to a hospital in the city for some diagnostic studies including chest X-rays. I was pleased that the taxicab driver could understand my French, that the cab fares were lower than in New York, and that the patient had nothing abnormal that was serious.

The water in the Mediterranean was calmer than in the Atlantic and in the Strait of Gilbraltar and the weather had become warmer. We changed to our white uniforms and by then I was more familiar with nautical terms such as starboard, meaning the side of the vessel on the right when facing the bow, opposed to port or larboard, and knew that the stern was the rear end.

I had seen some unusual things. For instance, several of the stevedores on the wharf wore red sashes with their work clothes. These were commonly worn by men from a certain part of France, I was informed.

The old harbor, rectangular in shape, was used mainly by the smaller vessels such as ferries, excursion and fishing boats and other small craft. Large ocean-going ships were anchored farther out. On three sides of the harbor were streets lined with business houses, shops, hotels and many restaurants specializing in seafood, including that delectable dish, bouillabaisse, that the French season so well as to make the mouth water by just thinking of it.

We left Marseille with a tinge of regret, but there were other harbors, cities and people to see. Jules Villon, with a number of the passengers, was standing with me at the rail watching as our ship moved away from the port past many other ships and out to sea again. Our destination was Genoa, Italy.

179

"Did you get any souvenirs?" he asked.

"No, maybe I will when we come back."

"I got some cards," he said, reaching into his pocket. Some of them were the kinds of pictures not often seen in the United States at that time. "A character sold these to me on the street. He offered to take me to a place where movies like these are shown."

It was a bright, sunny day. I had not noticed before how blue was the Mediterranean. The ship's prow was slicing through the water and the waves it made were spreading out on each side. Looking back toward the harbor, the only building that could be distinguished was a cathedral high on a hill.

Genoa, or Genova, one of Italy's largest cities and foremost port, is in the center of the Italian Riviera. It is strung out along a narrow coastal plain and in width spreads out only about a mile, this east of the old port. It is hilly, so steps and funiculars often replace streets, and tunnels carry some streets under hills.

I went to see the sights of Genoa with some of the passengers, bought a Borsalino hat at a fraction of the New York price, and had a tasty dish of spaghetti in a little restaurant. We hired a driver and horse-drawn cab. This was not the fastest way to see the city but allowed us to sightsee unhurried.

The Ducal Palace, over seven centuries old; banks; business establishments; the Academy of Fine Arts; and the Teatro Carlo Felice stand on the Piazza de Ferrari in the center of town. Not far from it is the Cathedral, which was begun in 1100, with its black-and-white striped facade and representing Gothic, Romanesque and Renaissance styles.

Palaces di San Giorgio, Pagano Doria, Palazzo Reale and others are near the port. Many old churches and monuments were seen, but the house that interested me most was the one where Christopher Columbus was said to have been born. Seeing this spot stirred memories of the stories I had read of the explorations of the remarkable man credited with discovering America.

Leghorn (Livorno), one of Italy's chief ports, was our next stop. The city, ten miles south of the mouth of the Arno River and the city of Pisa, is an industrial center known for the manufacture of Leghorn straw hats. It is an important railway and highway center, several canals run through it and there are beach resorts nearby.

The Leaning Tower of Pisa in the Piazza des Duomo or Cathedral Square had a familiar appearance as if I had seen it many times before. Built of white marble as the bell tower or campanile of the marble cathedral nearby, it is an eight-story structure, fifty-two feet in diameter. I learned that work on the tower began in 1174 and that it was designed in the decorative style known as Romanesque.

I climbed the inner stairway of 296 steps to the observation platform near the top and recalled the story long believed that Galileo dropped weights from here in his studies of the effects of gravity on the acceleration of falling objects. The tower tilted about seventeen feet, or more than five degrees, from the perpendicular and it was said that the tilt which began while it was being built continues to increase each year. As I looked down at the ground, the possibility of it falling occurred to me.

Naples or Napoli, our next port, spread out fanwise above one of the most beautiful bays in the world, its white buildings gleaming in the sun. The third largest city in Italy, it forms a crescent around the Bay of Naples. Beyond to the east could be seen menacing Mt. Vesuvius, the only active volcano on the European mainland, rising from the shores of the bay to a height of almost four thousand feet.

Evan Griffith saw me looking at Vesuvius and said, "I was here on a ship in 1929 when the volcano erupted. It was throwing out so much smoke and stuff that we were afraid the ship would be hit by rocks so we moved out of the harbor. You never know when there will be another eruption. It was about five hundred feet higher than it is now, before the one in 1906."

Several passengers and I engaged a guide with a car to take us on a tour of the city and on an excursion to other points of interest including Sorrento, Pompeii and Amalfi, to which we ascended over winding, narrow, mountain roads. We had to have much faith in our ebullient, hornblowing driver. The marvelous scenery took most of our attention, however.

At the base of Mt. Vesuvius we saw what remains of the ancient city of Pompeii, which was there for seven centuries before Christ and was buried under about twenty feet of pumice stone and ash when Vesuvius erupted in 79 A.D. We could see parts of the forum, temples, administrative and business buildings, theaters, sport structures, public bathing establishments and private homes, enough to make me want to return and explore more.

We wondered what the fate of the towns still fringing the base of the mountain might be. We saw gardens and orchards flourishing in the remarkably fertile soil. Above these, on mountainside terraces, were small vineyards laden with purple grapes. The barren and lava-covered upper slopes of Vesuvius reminded you of the threat of tremendous force inside which is capable of hurling fire and brimstone at any time.

Our climbing road, steep and twisting, ended at a small restaurant perched on a high point where, with the food served in the clean, open air, we could enjoy the scenic beauty of the rugged green terrain over which we had come, the clear sky above and the blue Mediterranean far below us.

We were not alone in this picturesque spot, however. Those at the table next to us were German tourists and there were people of various nationalities at other tables to be seen and heard. After feasting on the food and scenery we almost forgot about going back to the ship until our driver suggested, "We'd better get started back as soon as you're ready."

The descent to the bay was faster than the climb. There were some narrow misses when we passed donkeys, goats and other cars but we returned unscathed from our unforgettable excursion.

Jules Villon and I, together with a few passengers, took a walk on one of the principal streets of Naples at night. We heard the sounds of music with the characteristic rhythm and melody inherent in these people, natural in this setting. Soon a brass band swung into view marching down the street. "They are the Fascisti," a proud Italian informed us. I thought of Hertillini back at Matson Hospital and of the values that he revered.

After returning to the ship I talked with Mark Marino. "Conditions in Italy are much better under Mussolini than they were before," he said. "He has done a great many things to improve the country. For one thing the waterfront area has been cleaned up. This part of Italy is poor but the people are working now."

Eric Grieg, one of the *Excalibur* officers, checked people coming on board to see that unauthorized persons did not have free access to the ship or that objectionable things were not brought on. He also noted those going ashore.

"Used to, when we docked here there were beggars all over the place," he told me. "You couldn't go on shore without them crowding around you. Since Mussolini came into power, you don't see them any more. It's not the kind of government we like but it seems to work for them."

The American flag and other representations of our country, such as a ship from the United States or the sign of a U.S. firm, gave one a depth of feeling not experienced when the same objects were seen back home. I had observed some Americans abroad, however, who, by their appearance and behavior, indicated that if they realized they were representatives of the United States in foreign countries, they did not care what kind of impression they left with the foreigners who had the misfortune to come in contact with them.

From Naples we went south, around the toe of the Italian boot past Sicily and many small islands that I had not seen on a map. Then we turned southeast toward Alexandria, the chief seaport and second largest city of Egypt, founded by Alexander the Great. A British officer, an Egyptian official in the motorboat with him, met us when the *Excalibur* came to rest in the main harbor and there the landing formalities were executed. At that time Egypt was a protectorate of the British Empire which covered so much of the earth.

In Alexandria I felt as if we had landed in another world. From the ship I saw that it was a great city. In view were an ancient fort, warehouses, modern shipping facilities, custom offices and large buildings. I think that the main difference in this city and others seen before was in the appearance of the people and the way they were dressed. Here the East and West met. On the wharves I saw people wearing loose-fitting robes and women with their faces covered except for their dark eyes. Some of the men wore fezzes, red felt caps with a tassel dangling over the side.

Alexandria, seen on the Nile delta as the gateway to Egypt, revived the stories of its past when it was the center of Greek learning and civilization, the place where Euclid lived, the city celebrated for its great library, its School of Medicine and the famous lighthouse known as the Pharos of Alexandria, one of the seven wonders of the ancient world and nearly one-third as high as the Empire State Building in New York City.

Gaius Julius Caesar, while visiting Alexandria, restored Cleopatra to her throne. Their romances and the association of medical history with them were recalled. It has been asserted that Julius Caesar was brought into the world by removal from

183

the uterus through an incision in the abdominal and uterine walls, hence the name "Caesarian section." I was reminded of his death on the Ides of March when he received more than twenty wounds from the daggers of Brutus, Cassius and other "friends." I was also reminded of Antony, who was led to suicide by Cleopatra, and of her suicide by the bite of an asp. There was not much time for reverie, however, because an Egyptian was approaching me.

Mohammed Asan, a dragoman, or interpreter, who had come on board to organize a trip to Cairo, presented me with his business card. He asked me to go with him and a group of passengers by train to the capital of Egypt, the largest city in Africa. He would make the arrangements and be our guide.

The railroad station activities seemed confusing to us. Vendors were selling hard-boiled eggs in the shell which, to me, seemed appropriate. There was much rushing, noise and loud talk in the excitement of boarding the train. It was the occasion for arguments between Asan and others—why, we could not understand—but eventually we were seated in what we presumed to be our proper seats. Then the train moved out to start the 130-mile trip to the southeast.

We went through a rich agricultural region where primitive methods were still employed. Buffaloes or oxen were being used for hauling, to pull plows and draw water for irrigation. For the latter, the animal walked in a circle while hitched to a contraption which raised the water. I saw women carrying large jars of water balanced on their heads with excellent posture and carriage. In the fields were workers, including boys and girls, in large numbers, usually in line, side by side. They were followed by an overseer who carried a long rod. Camels and donkeys were seen on the farms and roads, many heavily loaded.

In Cairo, Asan called our attention to Shepheard's Hotel but checked us in at a smaller one, then took us on a tour. He told us that over ninety percent of the people were Moslems and that Arabic is the national launguage. However, we saw representatives of many countries and races and found that many, especially those with wares to sell, could understand English.

In a shop specializing in small luxury items, the proprietor asked us to sit on ottomans or stuffed footstools, clapped his hands, and a servant brought strong, black coffee in small cups. Into some of these he put a bit of powder that he smilingly said was an aphrodisiac before showing the articles he offered to sell.

"Do you feel anything?" one tourist asked another after sipping the coffee.

"No. Do you?" he answered laughing.

We were not very good customers although someone bought a bottle of expensive perfume. Maybe that individual did have a feeling.

While showing us the sights Asan spoke of the history and customs of the country. "I am permitted to have four wives if I can afford them," he said. "If I want to divorce one of them I tell her so three times and that does it."

"What would it cost to get a date with a girl tonight?" one of the men asked him.

"One would charge me fifty cents, you fifteen dollars," he said.

He pointed to a place on the bank of the Nile and said, "That is where Pharaoh's daughter found Moses in the little bulrushes boat."

We saw reminders of a civilization going back more than six thousand years. Looking at the magnificent collection of Egyptian antiquities in the museum, including those taken from the tomb of Tutankhamen, I thought of "Sheik," my old classmate at Tulane on whose land an important tomb was discovered.

Cairo, about the same latitude as New Orleans, was warm and sunny but, with the Sahara Desert not far away, was not humid. In this city of contrasts we visited the modern European part and the old native quarters with twisted, narrow streets, and bazaars with tiny shops and mingled scents. We gazed at the king's palace, the Citadel, and many beautiful examples of Arabian architecture. Numerous towers, called minarets, ornament the mosques, Islamic places of worship.

The Pyramids of Giza and the Sphinx were the most impressive of all the sights. About five miles from Cairo, the three gigantic stone pyramids tower above the Nile Valley at the edge of the desert. They are said to have been built between 2720 and 2560 B.C. as tombs for the pharaohs. The Sphinx is said to have been built before then. The Cheops or Khufu Pyramid, the largest of the three, over four hundred and fifty feet above ground and as tall as a forty-story skyscraper, covers more than thirteen acres. Its base is large enough to cover more than eight football fields. Like many other visitors have done, I rode around it on a protesting, jolting camel.

A little boy sold to me a small scarab, an Egyptian symbol in the form of a beetle carved from stone, as well as a tiny statuette in the shape of a figure of Ramses, or so he said. He claimed that he found them among relics of ancient times.

The Great Sphinx standing near the Great Pyramid, about sixty-six feet tall and two hundred and forty feet long, appeared to be staring, the face badly scarred and part of the nose missing. "Napoleon's soldiers damaged it," our guide said. The base of the sphinx was partially covered by sand, which streams of chanting workmen with baskets were removing from between its paws and legs. The head and body were carved from solid rock. One of the most famous monuments of the world, it has seen conquerors come and go for almost five thousand years.

Many more pyramids could be seen by looking up the Nile Valley towards Memphis to the south. This seemed a little strange, as pictures of the area usually showed only three. It whetted my appetite to see more of Egypt and the continent of Africa, but this would have to be postponed. Our ship was waiting at Alexandria.

Jaffa (Joppa) on the seacoast and Haifa on the slopes of Mt. Carmel and the bayshore in what was then Palestine were our next ports. The country was ruled by the British government under a League of Nations mandate. The Union Jack in harbors and Tommies on shore reminded us that "Britannia rules the waves."

Palestine, the Holy Land of the Bible, of historical interest for over five thousand years and sacred to three great religions, Judaism, Christianity and Islam, deserved much more time than our cruise allowed. We were at the door of Jerusalem, Bethlehem, Jericho, Nazareth and many other places of which we had heard all our lives, but they would have to wait for another visit.

Tyre and Sidon were passed on our way to Beyrouth (Beirut), the cosmopolitan capital and chief seaport of Lebanon, which was then under French rule. Like in many cities of the Middle East, part of the people wore the loose clothing characteristic of the East and others were dressed as Europeans. About half of the population of Lebanon is Christian, it was said.

At the ports where facilities permitted, there was an exchange of cargo. This was generally done while the passengers were sightseeing. Nearly all that we ate and drank on the cruise

186

was from the supplies taken on board in the United States. Before starting the return trip, the ship was refueled through hoses into the tank below.

Eric Grieg was on deck during the refueling. "On one ship we were taking on fuel oil and I was in charge of the hose," he told me. "At the same time they were having a big dance on the deck with all the passengers there dressed in their best party clothes. The hose was under pressure, got loose, and covered everybody and the deck with oil. I didn't wait to get fired, so just left."

One day we were anchored offshore and some of the crew took advantage of the opportunity to go swimming, diving from various points and heights and defying any sharks that might have been lurking below. It was a bright day, a fun time for swimmers and onlookers. The one diving from the highest place on the ship was Matt Hamilton. I imagine that his friend Wilma was the most ardent spectator.

Mr. Turner, perhaps wondering if I planned a career on the sea, spoke of the way it had affected him. "Once the sea gets a hold on you, you never feel content on land anymore," he said. "A few years ago I decided to quit and get a job that would let me stay with my family. After a short time I couldn't stand it anymore and came back. There's something about it that you miss when away, the challenge maybe."

Before leaving New York I had had a letter from Dr. Lemmon with whom I had interned at Gallinger Municipal Hospital. After leaving Washington he had obtained a position with the Veteran's Administration as a medical officer in a hospital. He wrote that there were openings for surgeons in veteran's hospitals and in view of the Depression, he thought it would be well for me to apply. "Doctors in private practice are having it tough now and the V.A. offers good opportunities. I like what I am doing," he said.

I filled out the Civil Service forms at the time, applying for a position as a surgeon, but had heard nothing from the application before leaving Matson Hospital. My experiences as a ship's surgeon were interesting and stimulating, but I felt that a greater volume of surgery was desirable for continued development, although I was progressing in my acquisition of sea legs and nautical lore.

At a Middle Eastern port we had taken on board the body of an Egyptian diplomat who had died at a remote place and had been brought across a desert by the men who were accompanying the body to Alexandria. These somber men were tired and haggard. The one in charge had slept little for several nights. They were swarthy, their turbans and flowing robes dusty, eyes reddened. Now resting, they sat on the deck floor, legs crossed, and smoking their hookahs, which are pipes with long stems so arranged that the smoke was cooled by passing through water.

As the *Excalibur* neared the Alexandria wharf we saw a large crowd gathered there. Fezzes were so numerous as to remind one of a Shriners' convention. Then we could see a delegation of men apart from the others and two lines of soldiers forming a passageway from the wharf to a waiting special train. The reception was in honor of the personage who had died while representing Egypt in another country and whose remains our ship bore.

A few solemn officials came on board and were met by Mr. Turner. At first, I thought that this was an expected formality but the earnest discussion which followed, while the expectant crowd and soldiers at attention waited, indicated that something out of the ordinary was taking place.

The officials demanded that the casket be opened so that they could see the body before it was moved onto the wharf. Their wishes were complied with, which caused a short delay. After a brief ceremony on shore, the coffin was carried between the two lines of soldiers and placed on the train to be taken to Cairo.

"Why were they so anxious to view the corpse; what was it all about?" I asked Mr. Turner later.

"One time we brought a body here under similar circumstances. It, too, had been brought across the desert and we picked up the casket at the seaport. The Egyptians opened it, however, when not expected to and found no cadaver inside. It was filled with contraband drugs, narcotics, and hashish. Somewhere on the way to the coast a switch had been made. Today they wanted to be sure. This one attracted more attention because of being a high government official and received with military honors."

At Alexandria I had a cablegram from the Veterans Administration offering me a position as surgeon in the Veterans Hospital of Memphis, Tennessee. I accepted and notified the American Export Line's officials so that my replacement could be secured before the *Excalibur* returned.

On the trip back we had some new passengers. Among them were Osa and Martin Johnson, the motion-picture explorers and writers, who were returning from Africa with several gorillas and other animals. Reclining in a deck chair, listening to the telling of their adventures while gliding over a gentle sea, was a pleasant way to spend an evening.

The Johnsons were married when he was lecturing about the voyage he had made to the South Seas with Jack London on the *Snark*. The stories of the Johnsons' travels to the South Seas, the Hebrides, Borneo and Africa were told in Osa's books, *I Married Adventure* and *Bride in the Solomons*.

"Richard E. Byrd was a classmate of mine at the Naval Academy," one of the passengers said. "Instead of regular naval service he has been exploring and has flown over both the North and South poles," he mentioned. I seemed to detect a note of envy. Byrd was then preparing for a second expedition to Antarctica.

"What was your last assignment?" he was asked.

"I was Naval Attache at our Embassy in Athens," and so the conversation went.

The animals were entertaining during the day when I could find the time to watch them, especially the gorillas. A big male would loudly beat his chest as if to show how great he was. A mother and a baby were most amusing in their human-like behavior. I even saw her spank the little one on the bottom when it apparently misbehaved. Mrs. Johnson sometimes carried a young gorilla in her arms on her walks around the deck. I provided medicine for the animals a few times but Martin administered it.

The tour had been enlightening for me in areas beyond my professional duties. I had been able to get a peek at old-world countries and what remained of important ancient civilizations. Mediterranean cities, their white buildings with red-tiled roofs basking in sunshine just beyond the blue water, exhibited only beauty when viewed from afar. When seen at close range they revealed areas of squalor, poverty and soiling of picturesque scenes.

On certain narrow streets one needed to be aware of the possibility of being smeared by garbage thrown from a window above. We found that plumbing facilities and sanitation were often below the standards to which we had become accustomed. These defects did not lessen our interest in this part of the world or our resolve to return, learn more and sample it more fully. Little did I guess that a great war would bring me back here.

The *Excalibur* stopped at Gibraltar for a woman passenger. Mr. Turner and I landed there, going in by motorboat, then rode through the narrow streets of the town of approximately twenty thousand people, mostly of Spanish and Italian descent, to the British government office. The officer in charge, dignified, cool and proper, asked us to sit while he examined the woman's papers and offered us a drink. All seemed to be in order and he gave his stamp of approval.

Our stop here enabled me to get a better look at the rocky peninsula at the southern tip of Spain which has been occupied as a British colony and fortress since 1713. "The Rock" is a limestone promontory which covers an area of about two square miles and rises approximately fourteen hundred feet above the water. It is connected with the Spanish mainland by a low isthmus a mile and a half long and less than a mile wide.

Martin Johnson went for his camera when we reached Gibraltar and took a picture at a point from which it had the familiar appearance. "I don't know why I'm doing this," he remarked. "I've done it a dozen times." Certain scenes are very compelling.

Back in the Atlantic again and with no land to be in sight for a few days, the passengers were doing whatever was appealing on shipboard. Some played shuffleboard; others liked bridge, reading books, talking or sleeping. Most enjoyed the meals of delicious and abundant food in great variety, as well as the tea times on deck. However varied the activities of the days were, dinner was a time of conviviality when all got together in a festive atmosphere with the captain as host.

One morning at six bells (eleven o'clock) I noticed that the ship was beginning to roll a little. Looking out a porthole at the choppy water, I could see the side-to-side motion of the ship. The waves had become larger and there were more whitecaps (wave crests breaking into white foam) than usual.

When sick call was over at seven bells I went outside the hospital section, looked around forward and aft and saw that the seamen were battening down the hatches. All movable objects on the decks had been removed or secured. A man from the galley, only his head showing above the stairwell, was scanning the horizon apprehensively. Stormy weather complicated kitchen work.

Mark Marino appeared to be concerned when I reached the communication area. "We got word that we are going into a storm. Looks like we've reached it." Waves were then slapping against the ship's hull and throwing spray onto the decks now deserted except for the few who had duties there. These held onto the rail or other objects whenever it was necessary to move. I returned to my quarters and talked with Erickson. All portholes had been closed and everything was in place. Although near eight bells or noon, it seemed almost dark on the ocean and sheets of water were blown by the wind.

"I don't think that it will last long," Erickson said calmly. "We should get through it soon." Listening to his quiet, optimistic forecasts was so reassuring that I was barely conscious of the fore-and-aft rocking motion or pitching of the ship, even without cognac.

"I've been through a lot of these," he continued. "They're usually not so bad this time of year. I won't be doing this much longer. I'm retiring in a year or so to live on my little farm in New Hampshire."

I had difficulty in picturing Steward Alfred Erickson on a New England farm after associating him with life on the briny deep. What Roy Turner, another old salt, had told me about the time he left the sea came to mind. Alfred was right in his prediction concerning the storm. Before the dinner chimes were heard the rain had ended and shafts of sunlight shone through slits in the silver-lined clouds. When time for sleep came, the good ship rocked gently.

We had smooth sailing to New York. My practice as ship's surgeon on the return trip was similar to what it was like over a month before en route to the Mediterranean but was followed with more familiarity and, I trust, greater proficiency. An exceptional case was a man with elevated temperature who complained of being restless, constipated and weak. He had a coated tongue, a slight cough, joint pains and other symptoms which, together with his history, led to a diagnosis of Mediterranean or Malta fever. Other names for the disease are brucellosis, undulant fever and goat fever. He made excellent progress in recovery.

I recovered from the seasickness, a miserable state, but felt that I had contracted a chronic condition called wanderlust and could become a peripatetic physician. The cruise had been enjoyable, exciting at times and, moreover, I was being paid for my participation in it. But the Statue of Liberty was a thrilling sight.

After my duties as ship's surgeon were completed, I served as a general surgeon in several Veterans Hospitals, the first one being in Memphis, Tennessee, which will be included in a later chapter. I was doing well in the Memphis facility for the treatment of our war veterans when a number of the doctors, including me, were given extended vacations without pay because of reduced appropriations at the height of the Depression.

I went to Cuba and Central America on a banana boat during my enforced vacation from the hospital. It was a freighter which would bring back many thousands of green bananas in its refrigerated hold but which had accommodations for about thirty passengers.

Before leaving on this voyage, I asked officials of the shipping line if they would employ me as the ship's doctor for the trip but was informed that there was not a sufficient number of passengers to justify this. Members of the crew, however, had heard that I was a doctor and brought their medical complaints to me. Refusing to give them advice would have been difficult and fortunately their ailments were not too troublesome for me.

The ship, American owned, had been built in Scotland. The captain was an Englishman and many nationalities and colors were represented in the crew, most of whom were from countries to the south. The flag flown was that of a Central American country.

"It is registered in another country," the mate, Lloyd Glendower, who came from Wales, explained to me, "because the requirements of the U.S. regulations would keep the company from making any money. They specify so many cubic feet of space for each seaman and have so many unnecessary rules that it works better to have the registration in a country that is not so strict."

We sailed from New Orleans in pleasant weather. Our first stop was Havana, the largest city in the West Indies, where we passed the fortress Morro Castle, a landmark of Spanish colonial days, on entering the large, beautiful harbor. In the dock area were many people, some youngsters, who were trying to extract money from the ship's passengers in various ways, offering goods, lottery tickets and services.

192

Carmel Sharett, a girl from Chicago, showed mild interest in the strings of beads that a hawker carried strung on his arm. "Would you like some nice beads? They don't cost much," he said to her.

"How much?" Carmel asked, a little more interested.

"Only four dollars for a string," he said and she started to walk away, saying, "Too much." He followed, still talking and gesturing.

Later Carmel was seen with several strands of the beads. "I bought three," she said, "all for three dollars and think that he would have come down more." Apparently she was pleased with her souvenirs.

Our guide, Juan, spoke English almost as well as Spanish and explained, "I worked in Miami a while." In a tour of the city and countryside, he showed the old part of Havana with its wall dating from the early 1600's, buildings of the colonial period, the governor's palace, Columbus Cathedral and a Dominican convent about four hundred years old.

In the modern part we saw the wide Alameda de Paula, a popular promenade lined with palm trees extending along the bay shore and the pretty boulevard Paseo de Marti, or the Prado, leading to Colon Park. Juan pointed out several mansions that were owned by wealthy Americans.

The capitol building, although smaller, was strikingly similar to the capitol in Washington, D.C., an example of the close relationship and friendship between the United States and Cuba, the neighbor that we had helped gain independence from Spain. It was in Havana harbor that the U.S. battleship *Maine* was blown up, an event which was one of the causes of the Spanish-American War.

Riding out into the lush, green countryside brightened by fragrant blooms, we visited a sugar cane plantation where the large stalks, thick in long rows, grew tall in the rich soil of this tropical island known as the sugar bowl of the world. Along the road grew coconut palms and in the fields, bananas, dates, pomegranates, papayas, avocados and mangos.

"The telephone poles are mahogany, this wood is so plentiful here," Juan said.

Whenever we stopped to look at something of interest and walked past a group of Cubans, Juan would greet them cheerfully and after a few pleasantries would say, "O.K." The Cubans would look at us in a friendly way, grin and shout, "O.K!"

Most of them seemed to be of Spanish descent but white and all gradations of coloring were noted in the crowds of people seen and, in public places at least, there were no racial distinctions apparent to us. "There is no color line in Cuba," we were informed, "and persons of mixed blood may call themselves either Negro or white."

Yellow fever, once a serious problem, the cause of which was discovered by the Walter Reed Commission on which the Cuban physician Aristides Agramonte served, was practically stamped out during the American occupation, but there were still malaria and typhoid cases on the island. To a visitor it was evident that crops other than sugar and tobacco and improved sanitation and housing, among other things, would have been useful health measures for the general population.

Returning to the city, we saw mills, factories, a large brewery, and establishments where sugar, molasses, alcohol, rum and other products were made. In one factory we watched the women workers make Havana cigars. The women, perhaps fifty to a room, were seated on stools at long tables on which they rolled tobacco leaves into the shapes of cigars of uniform length and covered them with larger leaves of superior quality. As they worked, a woman seated in a chair on a small, low platform in a corner of the room read to them.

"Each worker pays a few cents to the reader to keep them entertained through the long hours at the workbenches," we were told.

In each room through which we went, the women were rather plainly dressed in dull workclothes except for one or two who were noticeably better dressed and obviously used cosmetics more effectively than their fellow workers. No one explained the conspicuous difference. Possibly these few had additional duties or were forewomen.

When we passed a cemetery some gravediggers had just opened a grave and we were amazed to see them removing the bones from it. Juan stopped and told of a custom strange to us. "The family who rented that plot where a member was buried failed to keep the necessary payments made, so the body is being moved to the burial ground for paupers.

"Here the families rent space instead of buying a lot and they pay so much at regular times. If they do not, the body is removed," he said in a matter-of-fact way and drove on.

At a convent he showed us an opening, nearly a yard wide,

in the brick wall which surrounded the grounds. This gap in the wall was occupied by a platform having sides and partitioned at the center into two parts, which could be rotated. A bell was near it.

"When a mother has a baby that she does not want to keep, she can bring it here in a basket, place it on the receptacle platform, turn it inside the wall, ring the bell and leave it there.

"One of the Catholic sisters will come out and get the baby and they will take care of it until it is adopted or as long as necessary before a place is found. Many babies are left here every month."

One night we went to a club where there was Spanish-type music and dancing and those from the ship sat together. Rum cola was a popular drink with the tourists. A young businessman from Texas became enthusiastic over the charms of Cuban girls. "When I'm ready to get married I'll come to Cuba for a wife," he announced with feeling.

"Yeah, they're usually cute and curvy when young, but you'd better take a look at her mother before you decide," said one of his fellow travelers, who was also observant but more objective or perhaps looking in another direction.

When we sailed out of Havana harbor, away from all the beauty and from the sounds of joyful Cuban music on shore coming to us across the water ever fainter like a siren song luring us back to a tropical paradise, we could not foresee a day when we would not be welcomed. We were looking forward to Panama when the languid, yet sometimes lively, enchanting island of the fandango had faded out of sight.

In Panama we went from Colon on the Caribbean, or Atlantic, side of the isthmus to Balboa on the Pacific side by train. At some points the Panama Canal or "The Big Ditch" as some called it, was in view. Seeing an ocean liner moving through what appeared to be a jungle was a strange sight. Before going to Panama we had thought of the canal as running from east to west but discovered that its direction was more north to south and that the Pacific end was actually about twenty miles east of the Atlantic end.

Panama City, adjoining Balboa and on the borderline of the Canal Zone, is the largest city and capital of the small republic. Near it are the ruins of Old Panama, which was destroyed by the notorious pirate Henry Morgan in 1671. Here were seen what remains of the oldest church in the Americas, built in 1537; the Royal Government houses; jail; slave market and town hall.

A magnificent gold altar which escaped the pirate's fire and was saved from theft by a hastily applied coat of whitewash is in the San Jose Church, to which it was moved from the Convent of San Jose in Old Panama. Along Avenida Central are the rows of balconied shops with merchandise from all over the world.

The Canal Zone, which the United States controls, is ten miles wide, the waterway approximately fifty miles in length. There are locks near each end. We saw ships in the locks being raised and lowered and other ships awaiting their turn to go through. Before the canal was dug, Panama was described as "one of the hottest, wettest and most feverish regions in existence." By the time it was completed, the former pest hole had a better health record than New York City or Washington, D. C.

William Crawford Gorgas had been in charge of the sanitation work and the experience in Cuba led to his victory over yellow fever, malaria and bubonic plague in Panama and made possible the completion of the canal without the terrible loss of life suffered by the French in their unsuccessful attempt to build it. Control of the mosquito carriers of malaria and yellow fevers had been the main problem.

Tropical plants, flowers or fruits in great variety were seen growing luxuriantly wherever we went in a trip through the country. Drainage ditches in certain areas prevented collection of water that might afford breeding places for mosquitoes and on many tree trunks was seen the black oil that had been used to prevent mosquito proliferation.

A great column of army ants on the march was seen near the road at one point. Their movement had the appearance of a long carpet being pulled across the countryside by an unseen force. It was said that "they are blind but fierce fighters afraid of nothing and unless stopped by fire will eat every living thing in their path including poultry, pets, rats, snakes, cockroaches, and even human beings flee from them when they invade a village."

Some children at a roadside stop had some animals that they offered to sell, including monkeys and an iguana, a giant lizard that is sometimes eaten by the natives. At another place Cuna Indians from the San Blas Islands near the coast were selling framed panels of cloth, called molas, in various color designs which represented birds, turtles and other objects that have special significance for them.

The wealth of Central and South America, including gold, silver, pearls and emeralds, brought many adventurers to this narrow isthmus connecting two continents. People from many countries have mingled here. More than half the population are racial mixtures of whites, Indians and Negroes. Many American military people were seen and tourists were numerous, especially in the main shopping streets.

Spanish is the official language, but most of the Panamanians with whom we came in contact also understood English. They did not appear unfriendly to us, but in conversation were quick to remind us that their country is independent. The interdependence of the Panamanians and their nothern renters was recognized.

The man who conducted us on a sightseeing tour had said, "My name is Carlos. The rest of it is so long that you wouldn't remember it. You know we use our mother's family name too."

American tourists often make thoughtless remarks before those in whose country they are visiting, forgetting that people in other countries have pride, too. Travelers learn that food or drink to which they are unaccustomed may "upset the stomach" and that untreated water or food that is either raw or not freshly cooked may cause diarrhea or dysentery because of the type or the amount of contamination.

Located in the Torrid Zone, Panama has a tropical climate but ocean breezes contribute to comfort. We learned that from December to April is the best time of year for a visit as this is the relatively dry season. At a place on our tour where drinking water was available, a woman in our group who was warm and thirsty was heard to remark, "The water must be all right since this is one of our possessions."

"The water is supplied by your army. If it is not pure, you are to blame," Carlos said. "But the United States does not own Panama. You only rent the Canal Zone from us."

At Puerto Cabezas, Nicaragua, a cargo of green bananas was loaded into the hold of our ship. "We have 36,000 bunches," Captain George Wyatt said. He conducted us into the refrigerated hold to show them to us after they were properly placed. "They will be unloaded in New Orleans."

This small Nicaraguan port consisted of a village with a wharf, docking and loading facilities and a large banana plantation, which was run by a Mississippian and guarded against bandits by a small detachment of U.S. Marines commanded by a young lieutenant from Illinois. The lieutenant was sitting on a grassy knoll facing west and was looking toward the horizon as we talked. "Bandit bands were making raids here before we came to protect the people and property nearly two years ago," he said to me. "It seems like a long time. I'll be glad to get back home.

"A mail plane from Managua, the capital, comes once a week. I'm waiting now to see it come in. It's the only contact we have with the outside except for an occasional boat." I did not have the heart to tell him that I had overheard someone say at the company building, "The plane is not coming today."

The dwellings were dull wooden buildings, all made according to the same general plan. Near the harbor was a clubhouse maintained by the banana company for its employees and families. Soft drinks, food and various small items could be obtained there and on a warm Sunday afternoon the place was merry with music and dancing. To us visitors to this Nicaraguan port, the dance was unusual.

Many of the male employees were white and from the states. The native Mosquito Indians were largely integrated with Negroes from the nearby West Indies and a sprinkling of Europeans. All seemed to be enjoying the pleasures available in this relatively restricted area.

The only paved road extended just five miles. Beyond the end of it was the jungle, so most travel was by foot. Docking of the boat meant a period of increased activity and excitement.

Loading was done expeditiously by an experienced crew overseen by a black man. At noon they ate a lunch of rice and beans. Any banana that showed a yellow spot indicative of ripening was pulled from the bunch and tossed onto a large pile of those discarded, so that it would not be conveyed into the ship. The workers took this rejected fruit for their use.

"Only all green bananas are taken; otherwise, some of them would become too ripe before they could be sold," Captain Wyatt told us. "Tarantulas are sometimes seen during the loading, but none were found this time." Much later I saw one of these large, fierce-looking, hairy spiders on the side of a road in Louisiana. The bite of a tarantula is painful and was once thought to cause a peculiar disease called tarantism, which was supposed to make its victims dance until they fell exhausted.

The tarantella dance got its name from this and was said to cure the disease.

Our Caribbean excursion was under blue skies most of the time and the seas were not tempestuous. The days were warm but tempered by soft breezes. Nights on deck were clear and cool, the stars bright with constellations easily recognized and the moon's path on the water shining, that is, until the night we neared the Gulf of Mexico. After dinner the sky darkened, the winds became strong, rain began to fall and large waves now splashed against our ship, sending spray over the decks. With the rolling and pitching of the vessel, we felt giddy. Some of the passengers were nauseated, pale and sweaty, a few hanging over the rail seasick, but most had retired to their cabins.

In my bunk, behind the board on the side which prevented rolling out, I listened to the waves. They made the ship shudder whenever a big one struck solidly broadside. I had the sensation of rising and falling as the ship was raised and lowered by the raging sea, but eventually I slept.

The next morning was sunny and fresh and the sea calmer. The storm was over or we had passed through it and all were smiling again. "When I woke up," ship's officer Holden said, "there were several inches of water in my cabin and some of my things floating around or wet, but we came through it all right."

Reaching the wide mouth of the Mississippi, the sailing up-river was smooth and New Orleans only about a hundred miles away. There I would have a chance to walk again along old streets and pause at familiar names such as Canal, Rampart, Esplanade, Bourbon, Chartres, Conti, Dumaine, Royal and St. Louis before resuming practice on land.

Memories of my early experiences as a seafaring doctor to the Mediterranean and to the tropics would be cherished and the incidents often relived in the years ahead. But these were preliminaries of events to come.

Veterans Hospitals

World War I veterans, as well as some who had served in the Nicaraguan expeditions, on the Mexican border, in the Philippine insurrection, the Spanish-American War, the Chinese Boxer Rebellion, and even several who had fought in the Indian wars or in the Civil War when very young, were treated in the veterans hospitals before I was called to duty in World War II. The first of these hospitals in which I practiced general surgery was in Memphis, Tennessee, where I went directly after my tour as a ship's surgeon.

The Memphis Veterans Hospital was a large general hospital with medical and surgical services, each subdivided into the usual specialties except for obstetrics and gynecology and pediatrics. There was one emergency obstetrical case. A woman happened to be at the hospital at the time of delivery and her baby was born there.

Dr. Best, a young otolaryngologist, introduced himself soon after my arrival and said, "Dr. Briggs is operating now. I'll show you around. You will find veterans hospitals different from the ones you have been in before. Many men that you will examine come here to establish disability claims for compensation or to increase benefits that have already been awarded by the Veterans Administration. So your diagnoses and the degree of abnormality you find will have a bearing on the amount of money the man will get if he is entitled to it by law. He is unlikely to minimize his symptoms or the extent of the disability.

"Some of the veterans are not getting compensation to which they are entitled. We have a service officer here at the

200

hospital to help them with their claims. A rating board determines if a claimant is eligible and what is proper after considering the evidence. You will have all kinds of forms to fill out. I've been here six months and I'm no dummy, but I don't know all the regulations yet."

The visiting otolaryngologist was Dr. Wilkins, who had been graduated from the University of Tennessee Medical School and had stayed in Memphis for his training and to practice. Occasionally we scrubbed for operations at the same time and talked for the ten minutes of this procedure.

"Do you like to go deer hunting?" he asked.

"I've never tried it and probably couldn't pull the trigger if one stopped in front of me."

"Several of us go together. Each one takes a stand in the woods where deer are likely to be and keeps quiet until a buck comes along. Jim Haley went with us one day and after waiting about an hour, got tired and came through the bushes toward me, making noise, of course, that would scare any game away. I pretended to mistake him for a deer, threw up my gun and aimed it at him suddenly. 'Don't shoot!' he yelled, white as a sheet. That cured him of leaving his stand."

Dr. Waggoner, manager of the hospital, had long been an administrator. He had to deal with the Central Office in Washington, city officials, consultants and personnel. Budgetary and most other problems were handled with apparent ease. He was present at the doctors' weekly staff meeting, where difficult and unusual cases were presented. Deaths and autopsy findings and other matters of interest to the staff were discussed at these meetings.

Informal discussions frequently took place in addition to the formal meetings held each week. Dr. Waggoner would talk authoritatively on almost any subject introduced. Once, for example, he described the differences in the dueling methods in France and Italy. On one occasion, to test the efficiency of the Memphis Fire Department, he gave an alarm and then timed the arrival of the fire trucks. He did not do that any more.

Dr. Walters, chief medical officer, gray-haired and near retirement age, was second in administrative command. He was closely associated with the professional staff and although he did not treat patients himself, kept informed concerning them. He often made a point with an anecdote such as, "In court this injured man claimed that since he was hurt, he could not raise his arm higher than his shoulder.

"'How high could you raise it before you were injured?' the man was asked. Without thinking, he raised his arm straight over his head."

One morning when we arrived at the hospital, Dr. Walters' face was not only wreathed in smiles but he was beaming and passing cigars to one and all who would take them. His wife, much younger than he, had presented him with a son. Everyone shared their joy.

The full-time doctors in the hospital were employed under the Civil Service System. None lived at the hospital but one, at least, was there at all times. Night service was by rotation, with the others on call for emergencies. The surgeons, as might be expected, were called much more often than those on the medical service.

Some of the consultants came to the hospital at regular times to examine or treat patients, but a number of them on our list came only when called. One urologist, for example, saw patients regularly, while a general surgeon who was available rarely operated but was occasionally consulted.

Dr. Benjamin Eisenstein, a graduate of New York University, was the full-time urologist. "I've found it most congenial here and am getting very good experience," he told me, but often spoke of New York as if homesick for the big city.

"We lived in Brooklyn. My mother used to go to the fish market and stores with a big basket and get them to give food that she would take to hungry people in our neighborhood. When I was at N.Y.U. I could have a hot dog and orange drink at a Nedick's stand for a few nickels. Ketchup and hot water in the automat made fairly good soup, and coffee with plenty of sugar in it wasn't bad."

Dr. Nolan, a consultant in general surgery in another hospital, figured in a celebrated case that was pronounced as an instance of miraculous cure by certain churchmen, according to news reports. At an operation he opened an abdomen, diagnosed what he saw as inoperable cancer and closed the abdomen. The patient recovered and the event was reported as a miracle, although doctors sometimes see a malignancy heal for reasons not understood.

We who read this, based on the facts stated and our knowledge, suspected that this was a case of mistaken diagnosis, as many unproved diagnoses are incorrect. Perhaps the surgeon had mistaken inflammatory or benign lesions for malignancy. We had seen cases of abdominal tuberculosis that had recovered after an exploratory laparotomy, or opening of the abdomen by a surgical incision, with nothing more being done except for closing the incision.

Dr. Briggs, chief of the Surgical Service, welcomed me to share the burdens, grief and rewards of working with him in behalf of those who had served their country in wars or during national emergencies. He acquainted me with the service and how it functioned, the equipment, assigned personnel and patients. I learned that the operating rooms and wards were well equipped. It was evident that the hospital's resources were greater than those that many other hospitals had available. On a tour of the surgical division, Dr. Briggs spoke of various extraordinary cases we saw. Some wounds or their results dated back to the last war, while others were of recent origin. Many patients had the same kind of abnormalities that are usually seen in general hospitals, such as appendicitis, kidney stones, gastric ulcers, hernias or hemorrhoids.

"This man has an old war injury that keeps giving him trouble from time to time. X-rays show some pieces of metal, probably shrapnel, that we'll remove," Dr. Briggs said of one patient.

"The amputation stump of this man's thigh will have to be reshaped. He is not able to wear his leg like it is," was his comment about another veteran.

One man had a recent bullet wound between and near his eyes. "This is a strange case. He is lucky to be here. The bullet ranged downward and is lodged under the mucosa in the back of his pharynx. We'll take it out shortly," Dr. Briggs said. The man was able to talk.

"How did it happen?" the man was asked.

"I was on the other side of the door and he shot me through the door with his pistol. The wood must have slowed the bullet a little," was his answer. "Guess I just lucked out."

"You can never tell what all a bullet will hit or where it will stop after it strikes the body," Dr. Briggs remarked. His experience with gunshot wounds was considerable.

Dr. Boykin, my counterpart on the medical service, asked me, "Do you have any pull?" We were in a bull session with several others in the Officer of the Day's room. "If you should ever want to use any, you'd better be sure you have enough," he said.

"No," I answered. "I'm just rated as a general surgeon by the Civil Service Commission. Do you belong to the Army Medical Reserve Corps?"

"No, I don't want to get tied up with that," he said. "There are things I'd rather do at night than go to reserve meetings."

I had to go downtown one night each week to attend a class conducted by Major Wolfe of the regular army in a building where the recruiting office was located. The correspondence courses on various military subjects sent from army headquarters were studied on other nights and weekends. While I was in Memphis the adjutant general of the army informed me of my promotion. I was now a captain in the Medical Reserve Corps and assigned to the 94th General Hospital.

The Veterans Hospital area was uptown and surrounded by a high, strong, wire fence. At the gate was a small guardhouse, where patients who were permitted to go outside the enclosure could show their pass. One of the guards, Bryan Holcomb, related a few occurrences that he had seen from his post.

"A few nights ago I watched a patient walk out of the hospital using his crutches. I thought that he would come by here and show a permit slip to go out, but instead he cut across the lawn to the fence, put his crutches on the ground just inside, climbed the fence and took off for town.

"I've noticed that some of the patients walk much better when they think nobody is watching. The ones who are trying to get more compensation, I suppose. They probably deserve it, considering what they went through during the war," Bryan said, then thought of the employees. "It's funny on payday to see some of the men passing their checks through the fence to their wives waiting outside."

Willy Wiler, an elevator operator, was a short, humpbacked black man with large jaw and relatively long arms. He was pleasant, quiet and mild mannered—not suggestive of his previous occupation. We talked a little nearly every day.

"I used to be the 'Wild Man' in a circus," he told me. "I was in a sort of cage, acted wild, jumped up and down and pretended I didn't understand anything. They would tell the crowd that I had been caught in the jungle," he added smiling.

"How was the food and all that?" I asked.

"They said that I ate raw meat and would toss it in to me,

but it was cooked some, just kind of rare. It was not bad."

Mrs. Diggs was in charge of the hospital records and her section was very efficient, which was especially important in a veterans hospital. Her files were kept in order and when a patient returned for more treatment, as frequently happened, his previous clinical records were quickly located.

Dr. Knight, our orthopedic surgeon, had previously been with Dr. Campbell in the Willis C. Campbell Clinic Hospital. There were a great many orthopedic cases among the veterans and he got very good results with them. Some of these were chronic cases, even going back to World War I, but there were many recent fractures also. Knight's favorite recreation was fishing in Reelfoot Lake.

A problem case presented at one weekly staff meeting was brought into the room in a wheelchair. He had been in the hospital several weeks and the cause of his inability to walk had not been discovered, although X-rays and many tests had been made. When not in bed he stayed in his wheelchair and went to various parts of the hospital in it.

The patient was placed on an examination table in the staff room. Dr. Knight suspected that the man's mental state was involved in his disability and that perhaps he was suffering from a condition other than an abnormality of the musculo-skeletal or neurological systems, possibly hysteria. He decided to practice suggestive therapeutics. He felt along the patient's spine which, incidentally, was apparently normal.

"I've found your trouble," he announced. "You have a bone out of place but I can get it back into the proper position; then you can walk again."

He placed his left hand over the vertebra that was supposed to be misplaced and struck it with a sharp blow of his right fist, then palpated again. "That got it back into line and relieved the pressure on your nerve that kept you from walking. Now you can walk!"

The man got off the table, walked out of the room and back to his ward without the wheelchair. It was a dramatic "cure" by suggestion.

Patients with chronic conditions sometimes remained in the hospital for long periods and the staff became accustomed to seeing them. Those with regular jobs or farms that depended upon them were more apt to ask for early discharge. A few who did not accept the treatment offered were asked to sign a form indicating that they left the hospital against medical advice. We had an occupational therapy department where patients could make objects from wood, leather and other materials. Many of the men enjoyed this.

One of my learned and talented patients made for me an unusual paperweight, inside of which was a quotation from Shakespeare in old English: "He jests at scars that never felt a wound." It is on my desk.

When not operating, I was on the surgical wards most of the time changing dressings, doing examinations, listening to complaints, writing orders, trying to reassure those in need of reassurance, and occasionally just enjoying briefly the pleasure of their company. Operations were scheduled for each morning except Sunday and often it was mid-afternoon before we finished. Many emergency operations were done at night.

My patients were of interest for attributes in addition to the abnormalities which brought them to the hospital. Most of them came from Tennessee, Mississippi and Arkansas, but many other states were represented. Among the patients, one of the most melancholy in appearance was a circus clown. He was tall and rather thin. One day he was visited by a "fat lady," the largest I ever saw outside of a sideshow, and he seemed almost overcome by her enthusiastic embrace.

One night a patient with a fracture managed to remove his body and leg cast with a bed crank and pocket knife and left the hospital without waiting for a discharge or signing out against advice. We had all kinds of patients. Most were cooperative, but a few insecure ones liked to exhibit their toughness.

Malingering was a possibility that we had to keep in mind when examinations were being conducted to establish eligibility for hospitalization or certain compensations based on percentage of disability. This was more likely to be in regard to the degree of disability rather than in respect to diagnosis.

A criterion for establishing a diagnosis of active pulmonary tuberculosis, in addition to X-ray evidence, was positive sputa, the repeated finding by the laboratory of tubercle bacilli in the sputum. A small glass dish for collecting specimens would be placed on bedside tables. For a verified specimen, the nurse or laboratorian would have the patient expectorate into a container in their presence. Dr. Boykin said that there had been instances in which a patient who wished to establish a diagnosis of the disease would obtain sputum from a fellow patient with active tuberculosis just before collection time, hold it in his own mouth, and then in the collector's presence expectorate it into the container handed to him.

I occasionally saw patients expectorate dark sputum suggestive of black lung, although such cases were not generally treated on surgical wards. When seen, it reminded me of the West Virginia coal mine where I had practiced.

The nurses were all graduates and generally experienced and efficient, especially those assigned to surgery. Ann Brooks, a very competent, composed and compassionate individual, was in charge of the operating rooms. In my early stages of becoming a veteran surgeon, she did much to assist me. She made certain that everything that might be needed for an operation would be ready, anticipating rather than waiting for the need to arise or to be asked. Her presence was always reassuring.

Morene Collins, the pretty redhead who helped me with the surgical dressings, was very capable but too sympathetic for her own good. She married a disabled man who was bedridden, abusive and drank excessively. When not busy at the hospital she was nursing him at home whenever he was not hospitalized. Perhaps his need of her was what made him appealing.

Ray Seward, white, and Bert Turner, black, were regular operating-suite attendants, both young and quite capable. Ray, the older of the two, usually assisted with the orthopedic cases and was an expert with plaster of Paris.

Bert, a deacon in his church, several times invited me to services when there was special music he thought I would enjoy. He would meet me at the door and show me to a seat down front center. On one occasion the preacher left the pulpit, stood in front of where I sat and said in a strong voice, "If a member of my congregation has a baby with light hair and blue eyes, I know something is wrong!"

The singing was done with more vigor, ardor and movement than that to which I was accustomed. Too, it apparently provided more pleasure for the singers as well as expressing their sentiments. The order of the worship service was similar to what I had seen before, except that the collection was repeated several times, but I felt enriched by having participated.

All was not work in Memphis. Whenever Dr. Rosenkranz took his family for a long ride on a Sunday afternoon, he would ask me to come along. After looking at Main Street, Overton Park and the Pink Palace again, we would cross the Mississippi

River bridge to West Memphis, Arkansas, and beyond, going by several of the great cotton plantations.

Dr. and Mrs. Boykin sometimes asked me to go in their car when they rode out into the country. He was color blind and had to note the position of traffic lights to know when to stop and when to go.

Alma Southey once invited me to go with her to the family country home in Mississippi for a visit and Sunday dinner. Her people were hearty and had prepared for the meal accordingly. The main dish was a big fat possum and there were sweet potatoes, turnip greens and other delectable things in abundance. That night my overwhelmed stomach reminded me that one pays for indiscretions.

Memphis, named after the ancient Egyptian city on the Nile River, lies on high bluffs on the east bank of the Mississippi River, which is one-half mile wide here. The largest city on the river between St. Louis and New Orleans, it offered many diversions.

Hernando De Soto, Spanish explorer, discovered the Mississippi River at this point in 1541. He was followed by French explorers, including Father Jacques Marquette and Louis Joliet. Spanish, French, English, United States and Confederate flags had flown in succession over Memphis. The city experienced a number of severe epidemics of yellow fever in the period from 1855 to 1879 before a modern system of sanitation was installed.

When I went to Memphis it had become one of the world's largest cotton markets, an industrial center, an important inland port and a distributing point with a pleasant residential district and many parks. A remainder of its past was a showboat on which we could see the old dramas, hiss the villain, shout encouragement and advice to the hero and admire the beauty of the virtuous heroine and her courage in adversity.

The Goodwyn Institute provided outstanding speakers. As there was no admission charge, it was necessary to go early in the evening to get a seat. One of those I heard was Richard Halliburton, a Tennessean and author of such works as *The Glorious Adventure, The Flying Carpet, Seven League Boots* and *Royal Road To Romance.* Swimming the Panama Canal was among his exploits. One of the stories he told was of his visit to a headhunter chief who gave him a collection of human heads. On the return trip by a small airplane, in order to maintain altitude, he had to dispose of excess weight and it became necessary to drop the heads overboard one at a time.

Another explorer whom I was privileged to see was William Beebe, the scientist who won fame for his deep-sea explorations, reaching a depth of 3,028 feet, farther below the surface than any man had gone before. His book, *Half Mile Down*, had greatly increased public interest in the strange deep-sea creatures. Other books he wrote include *Jungle Peace, The Arcturus Adventure, Beneath Tropic Seas,* and *Book of Bays*.

Beale Street, immortalized in song and story, was one that I often saw when going downtown. This was where W. C. Handy composed his famous "Memphis Blues" and "St. Louis Blues." It was some years later, however, that I had the opportunity to see him and hear him play.

The Cotton Carnival was an important occasion of the year in Memphis, a time in May for music, dancing, garden tours and other events. Naturally the queen wears cotton dresses.

Bridge games were the usual social affairs for the hospital doctors and their wives. These were played regularly in their homes according to a schedule. I was invited to one of the bridge parties soon after my arrival in the city and accepted, although not an expert. This was my mistake. Certain players took the game very seriously and keenly felt the importance of winning. To me it was a diversion of which I did not feel a particular need, but I was aware of the tenseness of those around me.

One of the younger doctors, wishing to be helpful, made some suggestions concerning particular plays. His wife exploded with "Let him play his own game; he's supposed to know how." By the time the family argument subsided, I had decided that playing bridge was not a form of relaxation for me.

I sometimes walked downtown in the evening, saw a show, came back by the *Memphis Commercial Appeal* plant and got an early-morning paper hot off the press to read before going to sleep, reading Arthur Brisbane's syndicated column first.

My apartment was a few blocks from the hospital and I took my meals at a boarding house nearby. The food was served family style. Those around the large table included a traveling salesman, a newspaperman, an engineer, a secretary and a men's clothing salesman in the largest department store, who let me know when I could get a good bargain in a suit. A few married couples ate there. All had stories to tell, especially the newspaperman, who gave us his version of the news like it was before being edited.

The rotund cook also put the food on the table and contributed to the conviviality with her whimsical witticisms, appreciating the heartiness with which her dishes were received. "You all inhale them biscuits faster'n I can bring 'em in," she would say accusingly. Then she would ask with a big smile, "Are you all ready for the hereafter?" in reference to her generous calorie-laden desserts.

Money for investments was scarce during the great Depression. Mr. Ernst, a stockbroker, frequently came to see if by chance part of my monthly salary might be left and if he could get it in exchange for unlisted stocks that he would describe in glowing terms.

One offering was for shares in a company which owned patents on basic television parts which, according to him, were essential in making sets. The practical application of these patents seemed so remote at the time that I did not invest, but some years later television was a reality. At first, neighbors would gather with one who had this marvel of sights and sounds that brought entertainment into the home.

Mr. Ernst, a polished, polite and persuasive man, induced me to buy stock in an insurance company that had an impressive name but folded before getting off the ground. About all the tangible assets at liquidation was one typewriter.

Another company in which I invested had more liquid assets. It manufactured shoe dye and white polish that was sold in bottles. Mr. Ernst took me to the plant to see it in operation and to meet the employees. "The chemist is a very competent man when he is sober," I was informed. Sales were being made to country stores in the area. Mr. Ernst had told me that the business was expanding.

The next thing I heard about the business was that a merchant had called the plant and excitedly demanded that someone "get out here in a hurry and take these bottles of shoe polish out of my store. They are exploding and throwing white polish all over the place!" No more bottles of the chemist's concoction were sold. The plant recovered its dynamic inventory and quietly closed its doors, lucky that no more damage had been done.

Dr. Walters called me to his office one day. He was not his usual cheerful self. "Dr. Waggoner will talk to you," he said, pointing to the manager's office adjoining his.

"I don't usually explain my actions," he began, holding a telegram in his hand, "but I just got word from the Central Office in Washington that you are one of several doctors that we have to put on involuntary leave without pay for an indefinite time. This is due to lack of funds. We have to let all nonveterans go. I put it off as long as possible. You will be recalled when and if the funds for it become available."

With unexpected free time on my hands, I took a short course at the Mayo Clinic in Rochester, Minnesota, did some traveling and visited with the home folks in Albertville, Alabama, before going on active army duty in the Civilian Conservation Corps program, to which reference will be made later.

Not only was I unemployed when I left Memphis but wherever I went were signs of the Depression. People were out of work and discouraged, with many factories closed, deserted, their furnaces cold and the sky over the smokestacks clear. Many men unable to find jobs in their areas would try other parts of the country and I often saw them in large numbers riding on freight trains.

A haggard man standing with a box of apples on a street corner trying to sell them to passersby was a common sight. In many cities could be seen lines of hungry men waiting to get food at temporary soup kitchens set up by some charitable groups. Those living in rural areas where food was grown were generally more fortunate.

Dr. Showner had a large general practice in a small city in Ohio and wished an associate qualified in surgery. When I was released by the Veterans Administration, he wrote asking me to meet him in Chattanooga to discuss a possible partnership. I met him and his wife at their hotel. His offer was tempting except for one provision.

"Should our partnership be dissolved at some future time, I would want you to go somewhere else to practice. This would be part of our agreement," Dr. Showner said frankly.

The proposition was not agreeable to me for obvious reasons. Therefore, instead of becoming a resident of Ohio, I continued in army service. I was stationed at Ft. McClellan in Anniston, Alabama, until recalled to the Veterans Hospital in Memphis, which happened as soon as its appropriations permitted.

Dr. Briggs, who had remained the months while I was

away, greeted me with, "I'm glad to see you back. It's been tough here and to make it worse, we've had more emergencies than you could shake a stick at."

A cobbler's children go without shoes, it is said. Surgeons often do not undergo surgery for conditions they have that might be corrected by operations. Dr. Briggs, for example, mentioned a surgeon who had an inguinal hernia for which he wore a truss.

We took care of the emergency cases and then began on the backlog of elective surgery that had been postponed from time to time and the ever-present cases with disability claims pending. There were always new ones to take the place of those for which appropriate disposition had been made.

"You never can get completely caught up," Dr. Briggs said. "You might as well expect to see all of a river flow by as to see the last of these cases coming through here."

Practicing surgery in Memphis again could be appreciated more, however, than before I had been away for many months. But my stay would eventually end unexpectedly.

"How would you like a transfer to New York?" Dr. Walters asked me one bright morning. "They have an opening for a surgeon in our Bronx hospital."

"Can you tell me more about it?" I asked.

"It's the largest of our general medical and surgical hospitals after Hines in Chicago. They need a general surgeon and have offered you the position at a higher grade than you have here. It would be a promotion. If you want to accept we will recommend your transfer, although we would like to keep you."

I talked with Dr. Briggs about the offer and he said, "Congratulations, it is a chance to get ahead. I hate to see you go. We'll try to get a replacement for you and keep plugging away." This I appreciated more than if there had been a formal ceremony on leaving. Boykin, Knight, Rosenkranz, Best, Miss Diggs, Ann Brooks and the operating room crew were some of those I told goodbye. A few of them I would see again.

"Put in a good word for me up there. I've asked for a transfer but have not heard anything encouraging. Maybe a recommendation from you would help," Eisenstein suggested, and I promised to do what I could.

The Bronx Veterans Hospital, I found, was similar to the one in Memphis on a larger scale, with the same admission requirements, organization, clinical forms, routine procedures and such. However, there were important differences, especially the location. The main red brick building, not new, sat on one of the highest elevations in New York City overlooking the Hudson River on Kingsbridge Road west of the Grand Concourse.

Poe Cottage, which is near the intersection of these two busy thoroughfares, was occupied by Edgar Allan Poe for the several years just before his death in 1849 and is furnished as it was when the poet lived there. In it he wrote "The Raven," his mournful masterpiece that I had studied in high school, and I looked for the cottage shortly after coming to the Bronx.

"Can you tell me where the Poe Cottage is?" I asked a man whose business, I found later, was only a block or two from it.

"I don't know Mr. Poe," he answered. I soon learned that many people in the area were better acquainted with Europe than with things American.

Mrs. Mellovitz, my landlady in whose home near the hospital I rented a room, had come from Russia with her husband soon after they were married. Before long they had a grocery store in an Italian section in lower Manhattan. In addition to Russian, she could speak Yiddish, Italian and "Bronx."

They had three sons, Aaron, Nathan and Jerry—a lawyer, a buyer for Macy's Department store and a student, respectively—who generally spoke English without unusual accent but had some understanding of the other languages spoken by their parents at times. All attended regularly the nearby synagogue, which I understood was orthodox.

"How about letting me go to the synagogue with you sometime?" I asked her.

"You wouldn't like it," she said. "Gentle people don't go there." She always used the word gentle for gentile.

Every morning for breakfast I had a quart of milk, which I drank in my room. It was delivered by a milkman from his horsedrawn wagon, usually long before dawn. The big gray horse knew the route and would stop in front of each customer's house. I ate lunch in the hospital cafeteria as a rule, except on Sunday. I ate dinner in restaurants, generally in the Kingsbridge area during the week, but often in midtown Manhattan, as when going to a show. Then I had a great variety from which to choose, including those specializing in dishes of other countries such as Japan, China, India, Hungary, France and Mexico.

Mrs. Mellovitz never asked me to eat with them, but sometimes on a cold night she would bring me a big bowl of hot soup filled with vegetables and pieces of beef. This, with a substantial chunk of crusty bread, was sufficient for a meal and still makes my mouth water whenever I think of it.

The Bronx Zoo was said to have the largest collection of animals, birds and reptiles in the Western Hemisphere. Another attraction of the borough, of which I occasionally took advantage, was Yankee Stadium.

More major operations were performed in the Bronx Hospital than in the one from which I had come. It was the Veterans Administration's main tumor center for the eastern part of the United States and we received patients from as far away as St. Louis. Prominent specialists including Ewing and Adair were present at the weekly tumor conferences.

Cases of Buerger's disease (thromboangiitis obliterans), named for a New York physician and believed to be more common among Jews, were numerous. A ward was reserved for the treatment of these and patients suffering from other circulatory impairments of the extremities associated with such conditions as diabetes and arteriosclerosis, or hardening of the arteries.

Smoking, because of its deleterious effects, was prohibited for the patients with disturbances of circulation in the extremities, but some patients persisted in the harmful habit even though it worsened their condition. One of the results frequently seen in these patients was gangrene of the toes. In some instances the disease process had advanced to the point that part of a lower extremity became lifeless and amputation of the leg became necessary. One of my patients who had this operation was a former general. Fortunately his life was saved.

One emergency operation vivid in my memory was that for a perforated gastric ulcer. Large particles of undigested food, expelled from the stomach through the perforation in the stomach, were found free in the abdominal cavity. The patient's brother, a doctor from Lennox Hill Hospital, watched the operation closely, breathing over my shoulder. When it was over he graciously said, "Well done."

The Veterans Hospital in Lyons, New Jersey, treated mental diseases and not much surgery was done there except for minor procedures. Once in a while, however, we were called upon to operate in their surgical unit and were pleased to oblige. We had a few mentally disturbed patients in the Bronx facility as in other large general hospitals.

"A man jumped out of a top floor window last night and

killed himself," I heard some say when I went into the hospital one morning. "It was a heart patient. They said that he got to the window in his wheelchair and went out quickly."

It happened on the medical service and to a patient I had never seen. The dead and dying were ever present, but we never forgot this tragic event.

The Army Reserve unit to which I belonged in New York was the Ninth General Hospital. The meetings were at night and usually held in a building that the army used near the Battery. Two weeks of field training were given each summer.

For one summer period I went to Pine Camp in upstate New York for simulated war maneuvers. An army field hospital was set up and first-aid stations were established after sites had been selected that were appropriate in view of the terrain and an estimate of the situation. Living in a tent in the woods was quite a change from my usual Bronx routine. A minor injury to my eye resulting from the sharp end of a dry weed stem was very painful and I was a patient in the tent hospital overnight. Examination at the end of the encampment showed no impairment of vision.

I had two weeks of army training at Plattsburgh Barracks the following summer. On a Sunday afternoon I heard of an excursion boat to Burlington, Vermont, across Lake Champlain and asked a military policeman for directions to the dock.

"You don't have much time. I'll take you there on my motorcycle," he said and did, as I tried to hold my ballooning coat on. So I got to see a little of the largest city in the Green Mountain state and its university, little dreaming that later Vermont would be my home for a while.

Vilhjalmur Stefansson, the arctic explorer, was one of several stimulating speakers who spoke to the reservists and added variety to our programs. The periods of time that he had lived north of the polar circle added up to seven years, he told us.

"Before going to the far North, I did not think that I could eat fish, but found that this was the principal food of the Eskimos with whom I lived, so I learned to subsist mainly on it," he said. "The fish were caught in the short summer, were left outside and became frozen. At mealtime a woman brought in an armload of them, being careful not to drop and break them.

"When thawed to about the consistency of ice cream, a raw fish was given to each diner. A fish caught early in the summer that had partially putrefied was considered to be a delicacy, in the nature of dessert."

Stefansson did not believe that vegetables were necessary for health. To demonstrate this, as an experiment he once lived on meat alone for months in a New York hospital. He said that Eskimos who ate only native foods, the fish and animals they took, never had any dental decay.

Publications by Stefansson include *My Life with the Eskimo, The Friendly Arctic, The Northward Course of Empire, Hunters of the Great North, The Adventure of Wrangle Island, The Standardization of Error,* and *Unsolved Mysteries of the Arctic.* Hearing this remarkable man talk to us in person as one of our small group, however, made the stories even more enlightening.

I went to the Army Reserve meeting by subway except when able to ride with a reservist living beyond me. Sometimes I rode with a man in the real estate business who lived in Rye, New York. His company often acquired houses that were in need of repairs or improvement and gave employment to many men during the Depression.

One night while we were stopped for traffic a man, apparently able to work, asked the realtor for money and was told, "I'll do better than that; I'll give you a job if you will come to this address." He gave the man his card but never saw him again.

Dr. Eisenstein got his transfer to the Bronx Veterans Hospital. I did not know if my recommendation helped, but he and Mrs. Eisenstein gave me a fine dinner in their apartment soon after they moved from Memphis. A few weeks later I assisted him for the removal of a kidney stone from a patient in the Lyons Veterans Hospital. The insane, subject to the same diseases as the sane, were sometimes more difficult to manage, but in this instance there was no special difficulty. Occasionally a person mentally confused will remove a surgical dressing if not watched closely and possibly contaminate the incision.

One of the requirements for becoming a Fellow of the American College of Surgeons, to which I had applied for fellowship, was to submit acceptable reports on fifty major operations performed. I selected these from among the hundreds that I had done in general surgery in Memphis and during my first service in the Bronx before having the responsibility of brain surgery. The diagnosis and treatment of brain tumors, including the surgical techniques involved, were very demanding. Many of the cases were almost hopeless when we first saw them and the results in cranial surgery were often disappointing, but in certain instances there was dramatic improvement.

Mr. Boland from the Midwest had been gradually losing his vision and was nearly blind because of a growing tumor in the optic area. The tumor was removed in a delicate operation that involved risks, but we were rewarded by being able to contribute to the joyous satisfaction that Mr. Boland experienced on being able to see again and to rejoice with him.

One of the diagnostic procedures used was to X-ray the skull and its contents after gradual replacement of the cerebrospinal fluid with air, about five cubic centimeters at a time, by means of a syringe with needle inserted in the spinal canal. Changes in contour of the brain due to an abnormality such as a tumor would be revealed by the X-rays. These findings would add to the evidence gained by the history, neurological tests and other studies.

Dr. Masson from Memorial Hospital was the visiting surgeon on this service. He was rather young, well trained in the specialty, skilled and meticulous. The precise trim of his mustache and his care in grooming reflected his professional work.

"This brain abscess should be drained now, but I'm not able to operate because of my cold. Will you do it?" Dr. Masson asked me one morning. I had only been first assistant before, but had learned how to make the U-shaped scalp incision, open the skull, control the bleeding and maintain asepsis and other fundamentals. I agreed to do the operation.

"I'll stand by to advise you if necessary, but it will be up to you to do it."

Dr. Bates, the chief medical officer, and Dr. Huntley, chief of the Surgical Service, were also among the spectators. The operation was done in accordance with standard technique and fortunately the patient recovered. Months later, after much more experience, when I was considering leaving the Veterans Hospital, Dr. Masson suggested to me, "If you would like to practice brain surgery in New York, I'll help you get established." Being limited to this specialty did not particularly appeal to me, however. I preferred to be a general surgeon.

Dr. Henry Watson, the full-time doctor in charge of the patients with tumors other than those of the cerebrospinal system or largely involving a nerve, was unusual in that he was not only a competent surgeon but also administered radiation therapy. I was pleased when he asked me, rather than a specialist in plastic surgery, to repair the damage when his face was cut in an accident. Whenever another doctor trusted me in this way it was like a vote of confidence.

Dr. Scannell, anesthesiologist, who often gave the anesthetics for us, had engaged in pursuits quite different earlier in his career. As a researcher in the Rockefeller Foundation program for the investigation of malaria, yellow fever and tropical diseases, he had lived for many years in such out-of-the-way places as the Congo and the Amazon Valley. "There was nothing to spend money for where I was, so my monthly salary was deposited to my account in a New York bank," he said.

Mr. Malloy, the operating room attendant who prepared most of my patients for operation, was generally efficient and thorough in the performance of his duties but he was unusual in one respect. His whole body except for his face and hands was covered with tattoos in a variety of colors but mostly in shades of blue. There were flags, mottoes, snakes, dragons, an eagle, doves and numerous other figures, many of them works of art, worthy of a museum. "They were acquired over a period of years until I ran out of space," he said with pride.

The Bronx Veterans Hospital, in an area of dense population, was a busy one. The work, hour after hour, was strenuous both physically and mentally, but at the end of a day means of relaxation in a variety of ways were available. The theaters, moving-picture houses, opera, concerts, dance halls, sports, Madison Square Garden and the city streets always had new entertainment to offer.

"Would you like to go to the Army-Navy football game in Philadelphia? My brother at West Point sent me two tickets," Laura Warwick asked me one fall day, a week or two before the big event. She was one of the girls whom I had been dating.

"I would be glad to go, but will have to check the O.D. roster to see if I'm on duty that weekend."

"Maybe you could swap with somebody," she said.

I did. It was a cold day in the huge stadium to which we went in a special train. Except for her and the heavy lap robe that she had the foresight to bring, I would have nearly frozen, but it was a great show. The midshipmen and cadets marched in and with them were their mascots, the Navy goat and Army mule.

The President and his party were in the fifty-yard-line box. Many prominent people, government officials, officers of high

218

rank, generals and admirals were among the more than one hundred thousand people there. Music by the bands from the academies and frequent cheers, loud and clear, reverberated in the stadium. On the field the Navy team of blue and gold clashed with the Black Knights of the Army.

We knew that regardless of the records of these two strong teams before this day, they would fight to win the season's big one. The bands' rousing tunes such as "On Brave Old Army Team," "Navy Blue and Gold," and "Anchors Aweigh" made spines tingle. One hardly knew whether shivers were from the cold or excitement and when a touchdown was made Laura said, "That will not hurt his career at all."

On Monday and the days that followed I was engaged in the usual activities which at times seemed like drudgery but were generally interesting with different people with their varieties of problems calling for ordinary but individualized attention or perhaps new solutions. At times the work was stimulating, even exhilarating, and was especially that way when I got the good news. The American College of Surgeons notified me that I had been accepted for fellowship and invited me to be present at their next congress in San Francisco. Leave of absence from the hospital for the occasion was easily obtained and a few extra days gave me a chance to get a glimpse of Los Angeles and the West Coast before the scientific meeting.

I got an inkling of the size of California on learning that the state extends as far south as Tuscaloosa and further north than Plymouth, Massachusetts. On a sight-seeing tour of Los Angeles, including Hollywood and Beverly Hills, I saw the homes of many movie stars and some of the motion-picture studios. We were shown a water tank which was used for making exciting scenes in epics of the sea.

In a section made beautiful with a great variety of trees, green shrubs and flowers, we were told, "All that you see growing here was brought to this area and its growth made possible by irrigation. Southern California has plenty of sunshine, but most of the water is piped in from great distances."

San Francisco was captivating, resting on steep hills at the end of a peninsula with the Pacific Ocean on one side and bay on the other and overlooking one of the largest harbors in the world. One afternoon, going away from the city to a quiet hill, at the summit of which I discovered a spot of surprising beauty, I had the memorable experience of watching the kind of glorious sunset in the harbor entrance which gives it the name of "Golden Gate."

Chinatown, cable cars, the Embarcadero, Telegraph Hill and Coit Memorial Tower, the Presidio, Fisherman's Wharf, Nob Hill and the civic center are a few of the things seen on my first visit to San Francisco that were remembered. The Fairmont and Mark Hopkins were the headquarters hotels for the thousands of surgeons from the United States and Canada attending the congress. Meetings, demonstrations and clinics were held in various hospitals of the city.

The candidates for Fellowship in the American College of Surgeons assembled one morning in the Gold Ballroom of the Fairmont Hotel for the necessary instructions and to sign the Fellowship Roll. That evening our Fellowships were conferred at the convocation in the Civic Opera House. Seated on the stage were local dignitaries, officers of the College and distinguished foreign surgeons who were to be honored.

Each of the young surgeons given recognition appreciated the importance of the occasion. It was the first meeting of a national professional society that most of us there had ever attended. We knew some of the men on stage by reputation or through the study of surgical literature. The president of the College gave the main address.

The ceremony was impressive, conducted with solemn dignity. "Pomp and Circumstance" as played by the orchestra sounded appropriate for the buoyant pride taken in what we had accomplished, but a more lively cadence would have been in keeping with the way we felt that evening. Testimonial that I was qualified in the art and science of surgery had been given by the oldest accrediting body of surgeons in the Americas.

My pledge, as a condition of Fellowship in the College, to live in strict accordance with all its principles and regulations had a sobering effect. Soon I would be back on the wards and in the operating room trying to deal with each patient as I would wish to be dealt with were I in his position.

The Bronx seemed familiar now. Talking with Mrs. Mellovitz on my return she said, "It was not like this when we first came here. Where Webb Avenue is now, used to be a country lane to a farm where there was a fence with a gate."

She lived in a private home, a dwelling built for one family like the other buildings on the block, but nearby were rows of big apartment houses. Back on Kingsbridge Road I was

220

reminded of the crowds of aggressive pedestrians. Some were not averse to pushing me off the sidewalk if I happened to be in the way of progress.

"Sometimes I feel like charging into one of them who does not give me my share of the sidewalk and bumping him aside," I said to Dr. Scannell.

His response gave me food for thought. "If you do, you'll become like that."

At the next staff meeting I made a report on the American College of Surgeons Congress in San Francisco and reviewed a paper that had been given there concerning medical aspects of *Mutiny on the Bounty*. In 1790 nine mutineers from the sailing ship landed on remote, uninhabited Pitcairn Island in the South Pacific with six men and twelve women that they had brought from Tahiti. Survival of the nine men was almost miraculous. A study of their descendants, in which the effects of isolation and intermarriage were considered, was of scientific as well as romantic interest.

"Dr. Kline, the chief of the Surgical Service at Newington Hospital, is leaving and they have no replacement for him yet, so you will be on temporary duty there for two weeks starting tomorrow," Dr. Bates informed me one wintry day. "It is a general hospital near Hartford, Connecticut."

Chief Surgeon

"New-ing-ton! Newington!" the conductor on the night train from New York called out as the train slowed for the stop. There was no railroad station and I was the only passenger getting off. It was dark and I could see no lights. Waiting there with my suitcase, I thought that after the train passed I would see the town on the other side of the tracks. The train passed and I could still see no lights except in a small watchman's structure where a road crossed the tracks about fifty yards from where I stood in the cold wind.

"How can I get to your Veterans Hospital?" I asked the man inside the little shed.

"A bus will be by in about fifteen minutes. I'll flag it down for you." He did this by waving a lantern when the bus approached. It took me to the place where, for a while, I would live, work and gain experience as a hospital's chief surgeon.

The hospital was about one-third the size of the one I had just left but was very active. A room in the building was provided for my use. My bed was the kind used for surgical patients. I was pleased to find it comfortable, although not very wide for practical reasons. Altogether, I have spent considerable time with beds in a great variety of hospitals, fortunately not much as a patient. One crank at the foot could be turned to raise or lower the head of the bed and another could be used to elevate the legs. With a light above my head, it was excellent for reading.

As acting chief of the Surgical Service, I had a chance to see the sort of problems with which a chief must contend, one being related to the personnel on the service. Doctors need experience in performing operations to become proficient surgeons, but the chief is charged by the administration to see that the surgery is proper and that it is correctly done. He also feels his responsibility to the patient.

The medical officer of the hospital, next in authority to the manager, who was also a physician, was Dr. Pafford. He was a native of Georgia who had been with the Veterans Administration for many years. He was helpful in initiating me to my new duties and also had an automobile in which I could sometimes ride. One Sunday we went with Matilda Allbright, who was in charge of the hospital's Social Service, to Andover, Massachusetts, and had dinner with her brother, a member of the Academy faculty.

After the end of two weeks my temporary assignment was twice extended for two more weeks, so that I was in Connecticut for six weeks and had a chance to see more of the state than expected. The Children's Hospital was not far from us. Newington is southwest of and a suburb of Hartford, the state's capital and largest city, which I visited several times. The capitol on a hill with other state buildings, the Travelers Insurance Company Tower and the Equestrian Statue of Lafayette were among the more impressive sights in the city.

The Central Office in Washington, D.C., made the assignments of Veterans Administration doctors, as needed, to the various hospitals over the country. In doing this, consideration might be given to the doctor's wishes.

Several months after my return to the Bronx, we learned that I was slated to be chief of the Surgical Service in a new hospital to be opened shortly in White River Junction, Vermont. The chief medical officer would be Dr. Pafford, my Newington friend. I accepted the position when it was offered.

It was necessary for me to be present a few weeks in advance of the opening date to secure surgical equipment, instruments and supplies and to prepare the operating rooms and wards for the reception of patients and give attention to many administrative details. The main building was not quite completed when I arrived, but the work was progressing on schedule.

Always before when I had reported for work it had been to an equipped, functioning hospital with patients already in it. This time what I saw was a new, vacant structure resting on a hill in a rural setting a few miles from town. Deer from the nearby forests sometimes wandered onto the hospital grounds.

Dr. Pafford and I, together with other early arrivals, set to work to change this empty red brick building into a hospital and to activate it quickly so that disabled veterans in a large area of New England, then without a general medical and surgical hospital for them, would have a place to go for treatment.

Eventually the power plant was functional, the nurses' home was ready for occupancy, the kitchen and dining room were prepared to serve meals, the administrative and record rooms were in order, the laboratory was fully equipped, beds were made on the wards, linens were stacked, record forms and clipboards were in place and medicines in the cabinets and other items were checked.

In the surgery section the sterilizers had been tested and found effective; instruments, dressings, bandages, drapes, gowns, rubber gloves, utensils, powder, solutions and such were sterilized and put in proper places; operating tables, lights, water supply, machines and devices were examined and their efficiency determined, and anesthetics, oxygen, needles, sutures and other materials were checked with Miss Whipple, the nurse in charge. The floors and walls had been carefully cleaned. Everything had a new and sparkling appearance.

"We are ready to operate," Miss Whipple said and I agreed that this appeared to be true. There were always new pieces of equipment that would be desirable, but actual need in the foreseeable future had to be considered. I was guided by my experience in other hospitals in making requisitions, which proved to be a good guide.

Prominent Vermonters and Washington officials came for the hospital opening. The administrator of the Veterans Administration spoke. A large crowd was there and most of those present were shown through the main building. Various pieces of equipment were demonstrated for them and the citizens appeared to be pleased with their new facility. Something new had been added to the Green Mountain State that was blessed with natural beauty.

White River Junction at the confluence of the White River and Connecticut River was also a busy railroad junction with over thirty passenger trains per day at that time. It was also a point for bus connections. Going there by highway from the west, you go through Woodstock, reminiscent of an old painting of a pretty New England village; by the Woodstock Inn; and then past a red-walled covered bridge at Taftsville and over deep Quechee Gorge.

Just across the Connecticut River in New Hampshire was the small town of West Lebanon and beyond it, Hanover, the home of Dartmouth College, to which Miss Mildred Guay and I sometimes walked and then enjoyed dinner in the Hanover Inn. There are many handsome colonial buildings on the campus, the scene of a winter carnival held early in February, for which the students sculpture huge statues of snow.

Ski jumps are near and winter sports are popular. At a meet I discovered that ski jumping and slalom competition, skiing in a race against time on a zigzag downhill course, could be as cold for spectators as that Army-Navy football game had been. A colorful sight on winter afternoons was a throng of rosy-cheeked men, women and children in bright attire skating on a frozen lake.

We often took long walks in the snow through scenery like the wintry pictures on postal cards or that you see in your mind while dreaming of a white Christmas. Here Mother Nature honors the seasons dramatically. She crowds into a short summer the favors that are bestowed with her warmth. Hints of change come early when, in her glory, she flaunts the new flaming reds and yellows with the first touch of frost.

Each wooded hill becomes a bouquet in which the vivid colors of autumn for a while mingle with the evergreens in overwhelming profusion. Then before long the winter wonderland returns, when all is covered by a white blanket until finally the frozen brooks break to flow again and flowers bloom in the brilliant new world of spring.

One pleasant evening Miss Guay and I climbed to a hilltop from which we had a wonderful view of the town, river, roads and homes, all far below. As we rested, talked and looked, twilight veiled the blush of sunset and slowly ascending darkness enveloped us. After a lapse of time in which we seemed above the earth, a glow appeared in the northeastern sky.

"Look!" we said together. Bands of light extended above the glow and beams, which began to shoot upward, kept changing their positions and their brilliance quickly. Shifting sheets of light almost covered the sky. The colors varied, green predominating, usually pale, with flashes in shades of red.

We watched until the streamers of light faded, marvelling at the beautiful aurora borealis display that we had witnessed.

225

Mildred, from Maine, said smugly, "I've seen northern lights before." It was my first time.

"And you've skated on thin ice before, too, but did you ever see a cotton field?"

"Sometimes when we skated on the pond in Sanford too soon I could feel the ice sway under my skates," she said. "At night we would make torches of the long cattails and hold them when we went skimming over the ice. How does cotton look in the field?"

"The leaves of the plant are large and green; the flowers, a creamy yellowish-white at first, turn reddish-purple and fall in a few days, leaving a green boll. There may be as many as a hundred of these on a stalk. They are cone shaped and become about the size of a golf ball. When mature they split open, the cotton inside expands to a white fluff near the size of a tennis ball and the field from a distance would remind you of snow."

Hotel Coolidge, opposite the railroad station on the main business street, was where I roomed and had my meals. Dr. Pafford stayed there, too, and we rode to the hospital together. When he saw the road sign with the words "Hospital" and "Slow" on it, he said, "Our hospital is not so slow." Near the rear entrance was a weather thermometer on the wall.

"Well, what is your guess this morning?" he would ask as we walked toward the building from the parking lot. In the winter our estimates were usually the number of degrees below zero.

"Thirteen below," I might answer. Then he would make his guess.

One cold day I was talking with a truck driver who drove between Burlington and White River. "The temperature got down to forty below last night," he said.

Once when it was thirty degrees below zero I took a walk and areas of skin near my knees where least protected became chapped and almost frostbitten. The cold could be cruel at times.

Mr. Valin was brought to the hospital after his legs had been frozen. While drinking, according to his account, he had gone to sleep in a shed. When he was discovered, both his legs were hopelessly damaged. He was treated and, during the days that would determine at which levels amputations would have to be done, we tried to get him into condition for surgery.

His general condition improved but his legs were discolored below the knees, the feet purple, and some toes came off. Mr. Valin's health had been fairly good but his peripheral circulation had apparently been somewhat impaired even before the freezing. Now he had no feeling in the distal part of his legs and only above the knees was there adequate blood supply for surgery.

"We will have to operate," I advised Mr. Valin. He must have already realized that this was necessary and tried to be philosophical concerning the tragedy that had come into his life, which could now only be saved by drastic measures. The necessity for amputation of his legs was explained to him. He was agreeable.

"Go to it, Doc, whenever you're ready. I'll be glad to get it over with. They're no good to me like they are."

"We'll fit you with ones that you will be able to use when you are healed," I tried to assure him. We prepared him for surgery the next day.

Instead of doing a quick emergency-type, guillotine leg amputation near the line of demarcation between viable and nonviable tissue and waiting until later for a more precise operation to fashion the stump, I amputated above the knee through the upper end of the lower third of each thigh. I had learned that this allowed sufficient length for the prosthesis, an artificial leg, to function well.

I made the anterior flap shorter than the posterior one so the scar would not be on the end of the stump. It was always regrettable when I had to remove a limb, but I made an effort every time to leave the patient with a stump that would be most adaptable for use with a prosthesis. The bone was sawn across at a higher level than the soft parts which were retracted, the bone end being made smooth, and special attention given to the nerves and blood vessels. In this case Mr. Valin got two serviceable stumps and eventually learned to walk very well.

A few veterans with chronic conditions, possibly service connected and treatable, liked to be in White River Junction during the summer but tried to get treatment in a Florida hospital in the winter. This was possible under certain circumstances as in an emergency, for example.

Insignia, found on a patient with a complexion of copper whom I was examining, had not been seen before by me and appeared strange.

"What does it mean?" I asked, indicating the decoration.

227

"That is my Indian sign."

"What is your tribe?"

"I am a Mohican."

"A book I read was called *The Last of the Mohicans.* According to it, they were all killed."

"A few of us were left," he said.

One winter night when I was Officer of the Day and sleeping in the hospital, I was awakened and given an alarming message: "The nurses' home is filled with smoke. It's so thick we can't see where it's coming from."

"Call the fire department while I get dressed," I said, while thinking that where there is smoke there is fire.

The town firemen arrived quickly. They said that the smoke was caused by an overheated transformer, apparently a defective piece of electrical equipment, and there was no disaster. Our hospital manager, Mr. Grof, was aroused, too. The next morning he said that the hospital personnel should have taken care of it. I still think that it is wiser to call for professional or, at least, experienced firemen and to do this quickly, rather than either not at all or too late under such circumstances, especially when the lives of patients may become involved.

There was not a sufficient number of Army Reserve officers in the area to have separate instructional meetings for each branch of the service. Most of the officers in the meetings that I attended were engineers. The instructor tried to be helpful and I also took the correspondence courses that were required, even solving artillery as well as medical problems.

While living in Vermont I tried to learn as much as I could about the state and neighboring New Hampshire. I had heard that these Yankees were rather cold natured and that it was difficult to become acquainted with them. If generally so, there were exceptions; for example, a businessman invited us to his country place for a picnic, where we met other local citizens.

Mr. Heard, the state Y.M.C.A. secretary, and his wife quickly became our good friends whom we saw often. They invited us to the summer camp that he conducted at Lake Ely, a most enjoyable spot near Fairlee.

I came to appreciate the industry and thrift of the people, the democracy of town hall, the unique flavor of real maple syrup, the integrity of fieldstone fences, the character of granite and marble after seeing the quarries, the simplicity of white frame buildings with black trim and a neat village square where stood the modest church with its tall steeple, freshly painted.

After the long winter which kept the earth blanketed with ice and snow, we were more appreciative of the wild flowers covering the meadows, the gurgling sounds of a brook, the aroma of sweet grass, warm sunshine, fresh green leaves, the song of a bird, ducks on the pond and cows once more grazing contentedly on the hillside.

The new Veterans Hospital being built in Montgomery, Alabama, would be opened before long, we heard. It was larger than the one where I was and much nearer home. I asked for a transfer there as Chief of the Surgical Service.

After many New England winters, Dr. Pafford wished to return to the South, where he would be near his son and daughter, who were in Georgia. He, too, applied to the Central Office in Washington for a transfer to Montgomery. We were hopeful that our requests would be approved and were in a celebrating mood. The following Sunday he, Mildred and I climbed Ascutney Mountain.

We had the satisfaction of having seen the Vermont facility, which was not even furnished when we arrived, become an active, successful general hospital, approved for the treatment of medical and surgical cases. Our results had been uniformly good and we felt that the veterans of Vermont and the neighboring states had been well served. Now we anticipated starting another hospital.

Mildred and I did what sightseeing we could whenever the situation permitted me to be away for a few hours. Some of the places we visited in Vermont were Brattleboro on the Connecticut River, a year-round resort surrounded by hills of the Green Mountains; Rutland, the "Marble City"; and Montpelier, the state capital. Those in New Hampshire included the capital, Concord, on the Merrimack River, and Laconia, which borders Lake Winnipesaukee, one of New England's popular vacation spots and headquarters of White Mountain National Forest. While waiting for a decision on my transfer application, we enjoyed the attractions where we were and planned our honeymoon.

A letter from Washington confirming the transfer eventually came to relieve our suspense. The effective date allowed us time for a June wedding and a trip lasting a month before moving to Montgomery. The only cloud in the sky was the war in Europe, which was spreading with Hitler's invasion of Poland in

1939. Dr. Pafford received notice that he would be the Chief Medical Officer in the new hospital. It was reassuring to learn that this officer would be a person I knew.

President Franklin Roosevelt had been in office since March 4, 1933, when the great Depression had frightened the nation. In his inaugural address he had said, "All we have to fear is fear itself." Many new laws had been passed as reform measures and the economic situation was improving. Train travel was relatively inexpensive then and the railway agent had prepared tickets for Mildred and me to Vancouver, B.C., across Canada, and back through the United States.

Our wedding was at noon on a bright Sunday in June. We and our guests ate in the Hanover Inn and then they came to the station to see us off. On the train we were still getting rice out of our clothes.

The first stop was Montreal on the broad Saint Lawrence River, the second largest French-speaking city in the world, a great port and headquarters of the Canadian National and Canadian Pacific railways on which we were traveling.

St. Joseph's Oratory on the slopes of Mount Royal, one of the most celebrated shrines on the continent, was included on our tour of the city. Here we saw a number of praying men and women, some crippled, ascending the many steps leading up the side of the mountain to the large domed building. Inside, on the walls and stacked on the floor, at each side of the altar, were scores of devices, crutches, braces and such that had been left there as tokens of faith by people who had come there to be healed.

In Ottawa, the capital of Canada, we went to see the Parliament Buildings which formed three sides of a quadrangle on the summit of a hill overlooking the river. By now White River Junction seemed far away.

At Port McNicoll we boarded a Great Lakes steamer to cross Georgian Bay, Lake Huron and Lake Superior, going through the locks at Sault Ste. Marie. We returned to train travel at Fort William. In Winnipeg, Manitoba, we did a little shopping in a Hudson's Bay Company store. Our alarm clock sounded two hours before intended in Regina, Saskatchewan, and there was hardly a person in sight when we went outside. We walked through the quiet streets until a restaurant opened.

We went through Moose Jaw and Medicine Hat on the way to Calgary in the Province of Alberta, where the annual Stampede was in progress. As no hotel rooms were available, we stayed in a private home in this city then filled with rodeo cowboys and visitors.

After leaving Calgary we soon entered the Canadian Rockies and saw mountain scenery such as we had never imagined. We arrived at Banff early on a day when the surrounding snow-capped peaks shone brightly in the sunshine. The clear, cool air was invigorating.

This small resort town is in the Banff National Park, which is located along the eastern slope of the Rocky Mountains and extends to the Continental Divide on the west. The ranges and variations of color in endless succession were a revelation.

Little homes with pretty lawns in Banff, forests and wild flowers around the town, and the Bow River were pleasing features. Shops along the main street featured Indian-made goods and curios. We got two Royal Canadian mounted policemen to pose for pictures, one in his service uniform and the other in full dress, as we had most often seen them pictured.

Lake Louise, forty miles west of Banff, was one of the most beautiful spots we saw in the Rockies. A view of the lake with Mount Victoria and glacier towering more than eleven thousand feet above it is unforgettable.

From Lake Louise we went to Jasper National Park by bus over the newly opened Columbia Icefield Highway through the wilderness and past glaciers. We stayed in the small resort town of Jasper inside the largest national park in North America, a region of virgin forests, waterfalls, cascades, lakes in various tints of green and blue, deep canyons and countless majestic peaks.

The Cascade Falls on Mount Wilson and the Athabasca and Sunwapta River falls were outstanding among those we saw on the Banff-Jasper Highway. Mount Athabasca, from its peak to its base, is covered with a tremendous glacier that stems from the Columbia Icefield which covers one hundred and fifty square miles. One of the most interesting of the other glaciers that we saw was the Crowfoot Glacier, which resembled a bird's foot in shape. We had excellent views of many mountains from the highway. Some of the most striking of these were Mt. Kerkeslin, Mt. Fryatt, Mt. Wilcox, Mt. Kitchener and Mt. Edith Cavell, named for the English nurse whose tragic death made her a martyr of World War I.

Some of the animals that we saw on this part of our trip

were coyote, deer, moose, mountain sheep, elk, bears, marmots and Rocky Mountain goats. On a walk through the woods away from Jasper we saw a bear high in a tree and then were surprised by an unusually large one in the bushes. We had heard that the vision of bears is not the best. Maybe this one had a keen sense of smell. We did not tarry when he showed interest in us. I did not hesitate when Mildred said, "We'd better go!"

After Lake Louise, we went to Vancouver, B. C., where we boarded a boat for Seattle, Washington, making a stop at Victoria, B.C. From Seattle we went to Tacoma, Washington, on our way to Mount Rainier National Park. The day was clear and the mountain could be seen for many miles with the July sun shining on its snow.

We visited Portland, Oregon, after Tacoma and then Spokane, where we spent the night before leaving for Livingston, Montana, by way of Boise, Idaho, and Butte, Montana. The next day we followed the Yellowstone River into Gardiner, Montana, where we entered the Yellowstone National Park through the north gate to see the wonders in this, the first of our national parks.

We had lunch in Mammoth Springs Hotel dining room, saw the Hot Springs, Terraces, Museum, a big pile of antlers and other sights on a tour in the afternoon. We stayed in the Old Faithful Inn, an unusual structure of logs and stone with a ninety-two-foot-high lobby in which was a huge clock over an enormous fireplace.

Mildred and I especially enjoyed watching the four-minute displays of the Old Faithful Geyser, which spouted a white cascade of steaming water about one hundred and sixty feet in the air approximately every sixty-six minutes. Some of the other interesting geysers were the Riverside, the Daisy, the Beehive, the Castle, the Grotto, the Giant, the Grand and the Lion.

The hundreds of active geysers in the park make it the greatest geyser region in the world. Some of the most remarkable scenes, we thought, were in the Norris Geyser Basin, one of the six principal basins. The odors from several of these and the hot bubbling pools reminded me of the hydrogen sulphide that had overcome me in the University of Alabama chemistry laboratory.

Forests, natural fountains, sparkling lakes and rivers, deep gorges, high cataracts and animals in great variety and numbers are some of the attractions of this wonderland, which is about two-thirds of the size of Connecticut. The view of Yellowstone Canyon is one of the most beautiful in the park. Under a blue sky we saw, against the surrounding forest green, the splashes of yellow, orange, brown, red and white on the canyon walls. Water of the Lower Falls drops over three hundred feet into a gorge which is more than a thousand feet deep.

Our stay at the Canyon Hotel, at an altitude of about eight thousand feet, was most enjoyable with horseback riding in the morning and dancing in the attractive lounge. I noticed a difference in my respiration on exertion in the rarified atmosphere at that elevation, being accustomed to lower altitudes.

"Do you feel any shortness of breath?" I asked Mildred while we were dancing.

"When we do the fast ones I breathe a little harder, but I've had a good time here."

"Let's come back some time with our children."

We resumed our journey eastward with reluctance but still had much to see on the way. At Mandan, North Dakota, there was a party of Sioux Indians in colorful dress. In Bismarck we walked through business and residential sections and to the skyscraper capitol. We flew to Aberdeen, South Dakota, in stormy weather. It was a bumpy ride but we saw two rainbows on the way.

From Aberdeen, we went by bus to Jamestown, North Dakota, where we boarded the train for Fargo, North Dakota, and St. Paul, Minnesota. On the way to Jamestown we rode through flat country where fields of golden wheat stretched to the horizon and the only trees in sight were a few occasionally seen at a distant, stark farmhouse. The Midwest was suffering a heat wave at the time and we were surprised to be in temperatures of over one hundred degrees that far north.

We spent several days in Chicago exploring sections as varied as Michigan Boulevard and the Stock Yards, shopped a little in big stores such as Marshall Fields and saw a few shows.

In Detroit we went on a sight-seeing trip which included the main points of interest, parks and industrial areas. We visited the Ford Plant, as well as Greenfield Village in Dearborn, where Henry Ford had collected old buildings of historical or other interest and memorabilia such as a grist mill, glass plant, silk mill, tintype studio, Wright cycle shop and the laboratory in which Edison made the first electric light.

Niagara Falls, the goal of many honeymooners before us,

was our last stop. We arrived there at night in time to see the falls illuminated by colored lights. By day we saw the Horseshoe Falls, the Bridal Veil, sat on the rocky projections in the Niagara Rapids and, in the sunshine and mist, held close the happiness of the moment while sharing our dreams of a future together.

Hitler's panzer divisions, fast-moving mechanized forces extending the blitzkrieg, or lightning war, had been successful in France. In North Africa, Field Marshal Rommel, the "Desert Fox," had brought the Africa Korps almost to Cairo. Hopes of Americans to stay out of the war were fading. Organizations and plans were being formed to cope with major medical emergency problems in contemplated disaster areas.

The Montgomery Veterans Hospital, a handsome, four-story brick building, was larger than the one in White River Junction and on spacious grounds northeast of and a few miles from the state capitol. It was almost completed when we arrived. Maxwell Air Force Base is on the opposite side of the city. Another air force base, Gunter, was originally used for training pilots but became a school for aviation medicine.

Carpenters, electricians, plumbers, painters, glaziers and technicians were putting the finishing touches on the main building. Much of the standard equipment had been installed. Yet to be done were removal of the usual debris after construction is completed and the job of cleaning.

My work in getting the Surgical Service ready for patients was almost a repetition of what I had done in Vermont, only on a larger scale. I was pleased to learn that the nurse who would be in charge of the operating suite was Ann Brooks from Memphis. Mrs. Diggs, another old friend from the Memphis Veterans Hospital, was to have the responsibility of the records section. Dr. Pafford, Chief Medical Officer, was already busy with administrative duties. He had quarters in a building on the grounds, as did the manager and his wife, Mr. and Mrs. Shields.

Mildred and I went househunting, aided by a real estate man. We found a furnished two-bedroom, white frame house for rent in a quiet residential neighborhood on North Capitol Street. It had a wide front porch and shade trees, which appealed to us. We also liked the family across the side street who owned the house and quickly made us feel at home.

The first night in our new home I awoke and heard what sounded to me like running water. "Mildred, it sounds like I hear water running," I said to my sleepy one.

"It must be your imagination; go back to sleep," she replied, half asleep.

Not convinced, I got up and took a look. "The kitchen is flooded!" I called to her. Now fully aroused and not knowing what else to do, she called the fire department and there was a quick and cheerful response.

"Do you have a water key to turn off the water?" a fireman in the yard asked.

Mildred came up with a tiny key she found in a dresser drawer. "Is this it?" she asked. By this time the excitement had attracted a crowd of neighbors in their bedclothes to our front lawn. Now they all laughed. "No, that's not it. A water key is a big thing used to shut the water off, in the main pipe to the house, in the ground."

Someone soon found it, a long iron rod that looked somewhat like a crowbar. The water was turned off and the crisis was over. There is nothing like a pajama party on the lawn at two o'clock in the morning to get acquainted with your new neighbors.

Montgomery, we learned, was a great cotton market, a center for agricultural and livestock trade and in a large dairying section. Its industry was based largely on products made from wood, cotton and cottonseed.

The capitol, on a hill at the end of Dexter Avenue and similar in design to the national Capitol, served as capitol of the Confederacy during the first part of the Civil War. We saw a bronze star on the west portico which marks the spot where Jefferson Davis took the oath of office.

One of the most attractive features of the city to us was the fine old homes set among beautiful gardens along streets shaded by venerable trees that had withstood the march of time. Unfortunately, from an esthetic standpoint, some of these, as in other cities, were being converted to business uses.

The people were generally found to be gracious and friendly. Those who had always lived there were proud of their heritage, but the city was more often spoken of as a "cow town" than as "The Cradle of the Confederacy." I discovered a few people living there that I had known in Albertville and Tuscaloosa.

I bought a new 1941 two-passenger Chevrolet Deluxe coupe from the McGough Chevrolet Company for $857.00.

Insurance for twelve months was $31.50 and the license $12.50. The total cost was $901.00. It was the first car I had owned since leaving Vicksburg. Now we had a way to get to the hospital and other places we wanted to go. One of our first trips was to Albertville.

Mama and Papa were in fairly good health, but she was the more active. He was not able to make house calls any more, but took a short walk every day and would prescribe for a few of his old patients who came to the house to see him.

"We are glad you are back in the state. You have been so far away for so long," he said. He was proud of his children. "What have you got to tell me?" he asked Mildred. While they talked I went to the kitchen and watched Mama do the marvelous things that had always fascinated me as we spoke of things that had happened since I was there, about other members of the family, relatives and friends.

"How long are you going to stay this time?" she wanted to know.

"We have to get back for the opening of the hospital but we are closer now and can see you more often."

Our return to Albertville was sooner than expected. My father died quickly of coronary thrombosis, a condition of which he was conscious. Dr. Isbell, a fellow practitioner and friend of many years who was with him at the end, said, "He diagnosed his condition correctly."

Hard work was the best antidote I knew for sorrow. As before, patients came to the hospital in a never-ending stream. The Surgical Service had been initiated suddenly with an emergency case as operation number one on the first day. I was at home when notified by phone of a man's admission with acute pain in the upper abdomen and rigidity of the abdominal muscles.

I gave the necessary instructions and hurried to the hospital. The patient, Douglas Downey, gave a history of gastric ulcer which evidently had just perforated. Physical examination bore this out and it was corroborated by X-ray. He gave his consent for operation. Orders were given. He was prepared for surgery, abdominal area shaved.

Ann Brooks had the surgical setup ready without delay with basins, instruments, sutures, sponges, gowns, gloves and everything in order. Knowing her capabilities and thoroughness at a time like this was reassuring. The patient was placed on the operating table under the new lights which shone without glare on the abdomen. I hoped that young Dr. Greg Paulus scrubbing with me would be helpful. This was the first of many operations that we would do together.

Sterile drapes with opening at the operative site covered the patient. After a brief wait to allow for complete anesthesia, the anesthetist said, "He's ready." I took the scalpel and made the incision. Our first operation in this brand-new hospital was underway. It was successful and the patient made an uneventful recovery. Thus was the Surgical Service of the Montgomery Veterans Hospital inaugurated.

New experiences, or things done under circumstances not previously met, are apt to be recalled when the usual are forgotten. Each case is of interest at the time, but some more than others. No matter how commonplace a complaint may seem to the doctor, it is probably of great importance to the one making it and could be a matter of life and death.

Gary Melton had been injured in a motorcycle accident and was brought to the hospital unconscious. After complete examinations and consultations, treatment was started with the expectation that consciousness would soon return. But in this we were disappointed as day after day went by. He was given fluids and fed intravenously and his general condition watched carefully.

Surgery in this case was contraindicated, in our opinion, after spinal taps, X-rays and various studies, so other treatment measures were employed. However, we were discouraged after a few weeks of this. His case had attracted much interest among the staff.

"Gary Melton is still unconscious," the nurse would tell me every day when I went to see him. But one morning on entering the ward I heard his nurse exclaim to someone, "He grabbed me! Gary grabbed me when I went to his bed to take his temperature." She sounded excited and happy. He turned his eyes toward me when I went to his bedside, the first sign of his awareness that I had seen. Everyone was elated.

He made steady progress in recovery and eventually was discharged, without any demonstrable residuals of his injury, to return for reexamination later. There was a period of months following his motorcycle ride of which he had no memory, but he and all those who followed the case were happy over the results of the treatment and careful nursing care.

In some cases what was done in a matter of seconds determined what the outcome would be. Chester Hornsby's health was deteriorating rapidly because of a pathological left kidney. A nephrectomy was indicated and he was prepared for surgery. At operation there was a profuse bleeding from an aberrant vessel and the incision was quickly filled with blood. Because of this the urologist was unable to see the structures and stop the hemorrhage by applying a ligature.

"I can't tell where it's coming from," he said.

We brought the bleeding under control with hot packs and pressure and removed the accumulation by suction. The vessel could now be seen. I was able to apply a clamp and succeeded in ligating the short stump. To our relief the field was now dry and our patient safe. The rest of the operation was essentially routine and Chester soon recovered his health.

When Mildred and I had been on the Vancouver harbor wharf during our honeymoon, we had watched the departure of a ship loaded with Canadian soldiers on their way to the war. As the ship moved away we heard one of them say, "Goodbye, Vancouver. God knows when we'll see you again."

Many young British pilots of the Royal Air Force were receiving training in Montgomery before returning to England for duty in the conflict that was expanding to become the second world war. We invited several of them to our home for Sunday dinner, just as numerous other families in the city did.

They talked mainly of their homes and country and of things that to them were new, but not much about their role in the war that they were almost in. Later we often thought of them when reading stories of the Battle of Britain, or listening to the news on radio, and then wondered. These we remembered when Winston Churchill said, "Never have so many owed so much to so few."

I was a captain in the Medical Reserve Pool, although I would have then been a major except for a change in promotion procedures. After my transfer to Montgomery I earned a Certificate of Capacity issued by the Headquarters of the Third Military Area, which stated that I had "satisfactorily completed the required examination and practical test provided for in AR 140-5, and is deemed to have the professional qualifications necessary to perform the duties and to assume the responsibilities of the grade of Major, Medical Corps Reserve." We were not yet in the war but I expected to be called to active duty should the United States become engaged in it.

Mildred was having a little morning sickness but Dr. Dillon, her obstetrician, had assured us that all was well and we enjoyed our walks in the cool of the evening. We did, that is, until the night she said convincingly, "The time has come." I called Dr. Dillon. "Take her to the hospital; I'll meet you there," he advised, very calmly, it seemed to me, anticipating an occurrence of such momentous importance.

It was before dawn on November 10, 1941, when I was waiting, weary but anxious, when the smiling St. Margaret's nurse said to me, "You're the father of a little boy," and I felt the indescribable thrill that only the realization of this gives one.

Another thrilling occasion was the day I brought Mildred and the baby home from the hospital. Now we were three. Dr. Pafford came to visit us. His son and daughter were now in college and with the voice of experience he advised Mildred as to what he thought my attitude toward our son would be. "He will appreciate him more after he learns to walk," was our friend's forecast. To me it did not seem that my appreciation then could have been greater, but the exultation of a new father is tempered by a realization of the responsibilities of parenthood.

Examining patients, treating injuries including burns, lacerations, broken bones, operating for hernias, abdominal and chest diseases and all the other conditions causing suffering and disability that come within the field of a general surgeon filled my days and many nights. Now, however, at the day's end I could be with my little family in our home.

"Dr. Pafford was admitted by the O.D. to the medical section for treatment last night," Miss Brooks said with a look of concern when I arrived at the hospital one morning.

"I'll go and see him. What is wrong?"

"Food poisoning, I think. How are Mrs. Hall and little Edwin? Do you have to walk the floor with him at night?"

"They are both fine and he doesn't disturb me too much. Come and see them whenever you have a chance."

"How do you feel?" I asked Dr. Pafford. He was resting quietly in bed.

"At first I was nauseated and vomited a few times. Now my muscles are painful."

"Do you know what caused it?"

"Saturday night I stopped at that place off the road where

I get something to eat occasionally. They had been cooking pork but were not ready to serve it. I waited a while then told them that it must be cooked by now. The cook said that he was not sure that it was done. I thought it was and ate some. Now I have trichinosis."

"I hope that you didn't get a heavy infection. It's too bad that you got any."

"I did not eat much. My eosinophile count is up. Maybe I'll be all right before long."

The pork that he had eaten must have been heavily parasitized and inadequately cooked. He was receiving treatment but prevention of this disease, I learned, is not something to be forgotten.

Sunday, December 7, 1941, began like most quiet Sundays on North Capitol Street in Montgomery. Edwin, not quite a month old, had been fed and was sleeping peacefully. Mildred and I went into the living room and turned on the radio.

"Pearl Harbor was attacked by the Japanese early this morning," we were astonished to hear. "At 7:55 a.m. more than one hundred fighting planes, dive bombers and torpedo bombers appeared over Hawaii and attacked our largest naval base in the Pacific, the air bases and other facilities around Honolulu. It is known that a number of battleships, cruisers and numerous other vessels of the Pacific Fleet were in the harbor and that many of them were sunk. Most of the planes on the airfields are presumed destroyed.

"Full extent of the damage is unknown at this time but is considerable. It is feared that the number of sailors, soldiers and marines killed may be great. All military leaves in the United States forces everywhere have been cancelled. President Roosevelt is expected to ask Congress to declare war on Japan at the meeting called for tomorrow."

Army Experiences
In Peace And War

Our convoy of thirty-six ships with a battleship and cruiser in front and six slim, gray destroyers slicing the waves around it moved away from the assembly area outside New York harbor early in February, its destination unknown to us. As commander of a medical detachment, I had sealed orders that were not to be opened until we were far at sea.

Several of us, officers of my unit, standing on the deck of our transport gazed at the remarkable scene all around us. The ships—some near, others distant, all steaming at about the same speed as had been ordered, each throwing up spray—were now out in the Atlantic and all headed in the same direction.

A few airplanes flying over us that had covered our departure and accompanied, as far as they could, the great aggregation of vessels loaded with many thousands of people in uniform had turned back toward land. The next craft we saw might be enemy aircraft or submarines.

"We seem to be going southeast. Maybe we'll go through the Panama Canal," Captain Burk said. He was our orthopedist.

"You can't tell," said Buchignani, the otolaryngologist from Memphis. "We could turn north and go to England. The convoy has to be evasive to dodge submarines."

These medical officers I had known only a matter of months, but I knew them better than people I had been acquainted with for many years, having been with them nearly twenty-four hours every day since the army had thrown us together. Some day I would write a true story of our experiences but not always give their real names or outfits.

War had been declared on December 8, 1941, only one

person voting against the declaration, Congresswoman Jeannette Rankin. I had been ordered to active duty effective May 12, 1942, to the 82nd Infantry Division, Camp Claiborne, Louisiana, to rank from that date. The fact that I had been a captain for the required number of years and had a certificate from the adjutant general stating I had been examined, tested and deemed qualified for the grade of major counted for nothing as the rules had been changed. I was in the army.

This, however, was not my first army service and it recalled former tours of duty. Besides the short periods of active duty for training, I had served as a Medical Reserve army officer with the Civilian Conservation Corps (C.C.C.) for nine months during the Depression, assigned to the Tenth Medical Regiment as a first lieutenant and to Headquarters District "D," C.C.C., Fort McClellan, Alabama. I had practiced medicine in the woods part of this time.

The Civilian Conservation Corps was an agency set up as part of an emergency program by the government to hire unemployed young men for such work as fighting forest fires, planting trees, building dams and bridges. Over two million men served in it. The army was called upon to provide organization, supplies and medical attention.

The C.C.C. camps in the vicinities of Oxford, Heflin and Munford, Alabama, had tent dispensaries, in which were kept a few common medicines, antiseptics and dressing materials, with a man in charge who could give first aid. The Fort McClellan Hospital, where I had been quartered temporarily, gave surgical and medical treatment to those in the corps requiring hospitalization as well as to the regular army troops stationed at this post.

In addition to my duties in the hospital, I had conducted regular sick calls at the camps to which I was taken by an army driver, Sergeant Buckrun, in a Plymouth. He wasted no time on the road and apparently thought that we should pass every car ahead of us.

"Sergeant Buckrun used to drive the school bus but was taken off because he drove too fast," Private Unsur, an orderly in the hospital, confided. "The parents complained that he was too reckless."

We were slightly behind schedule once when on our way to the Thursday morning sick call at Munford. The road was curvy and narrow. We got behind a truck, the driver of which would

242

not let us pass, although several attempts were made over a distance of miles. Finally we reached a village where the road widened. Sergeant Buckrun got in front of the truck, blocked it and jumped from the Plymouth saying, "I'm going to bawl them out." From the way he did this, I expected a fight, but the two burly men in the truck were surprisingly meek and stayed where they were.

The sergeant became quieter and asked them, "What's the matter with you dummies—holding up an army vehicle? I've got a doctor here who is trying to get to some sick people." We got there on time.

One unusually cold morning after a snow the road was slick with ice. Where it made a right turn my driver rotated the steering wheel that way but the car continued in the same direction that it had been going, sliding on the icy surface. Some washerwomen with big bundles of clothes balanced on their heads who happened to be walking nearby became frightened when they saw the car, out of control, coming toward them and began to run. One of them, Ambrosia Wilcox, fell in a ditch and received a minor leg abrasion. Her claim for damages necessitated reports of the accident and hearings at headquarters before there was a settlement.

"Tell us just what happened," the claims officer asked her.

"I was jest walkin' along, mindin' my own bizness, when I see this car come aslidin' at me. It look like it gonna run me down so I try to git out of the way; then I fell in the ditch and skinned my leg."

She was given sympathetic treatment and compensated. Luckily no serious injury or damage resulted from our failure to make the turn on that ice-covered road, but this was not the last accident that Sergeant Buckrun had to report.

"The lieutanant is needed in the delivery room. Mrs. Harmon's baby is coming. The nurse said that it's nearly here," Private Unsur informed me while I was eating breakfast. His expression suggested that haste was indicated and I did not delay. This was the first time in years that I had been called upon to attend a patient at childbirth.

The delivery in this case was uncomplicated. Mrs. Harmon and the baby were in satisfactory condition and in answer to her question, "Is the baby all right?" I had the pleasure of telling her, "Your baby boy seems to be all right in every way." It was a happy way to start the day.

243

Army posts in peacetime were supposed to be quiet and the duties monotonous, I had understood. But the presence of hundreds of young civilians at this post made it different. Many of the boys were away from home for the first time and bringing them together in large numbers had resulted in a great many cases of contagious diseases, too many to be treated in the hospital itself. There was a large tent for mumps patients, others for measles, whooping cough and even one for chicken pox.

Major Hendricks, in the regular army medical corps, had become accustomed to functioning in a routine manner. Sergeant Kelly, who had been with him since they had been stationed in the Philippines together many years before, prepared the reports which the major signed when he appeared at his office about ten o'clock each morning. One of Kelly's other duties was to supervise the activities of certain post hospital enlisted men, corporals and privates. At times when on night duty he appeared to be uneasy.

"Kelly is often jittery," Nurse Ramsey divulged in a moment of quiet relaxation. "He has a drinking problem but Major Hendricks looks out for him and, after all, the major is the commanding officer of the hospital now."

The commanding officer of the Civilian Conservation Corps District was Lieutenant Colonel Michie, a cool, considerate, career officer who endeavored to make the program effective for the good of the country and those who were enrolled in it. He was interested in how the young men employed their time while not working as well as when at their work.

"The boys from the New York area like to get up plays and act on the stage. Those from this part of the country enjoy sports and would rather play ball than play act," he said smiling.

"A good surgeon can do an operation with only a knife, a few forceps and suturing material," he said when we were discussing the first-aid equipment available in the camps.

The commanding officer of the fort and the Coast Artillery (A.A.) stationed there was Lieutenant Colonel Smith, a regular officer and gentleman to whom I paid my respects soon after my arrival by visiting him and his gracious lady in their pleasant home. He did not interfere in purely professional matters inside the hospital, but one day I received a phone call from him.

After a few pleasantries, Colonel Smith said, "We have two

Irish setters that are very valuable. The family is fond of them. Would you mind looking at them?"

"I've never treated dogs but will be glad to see them and will be there soon."

They were handsome animals with excellent form and luxurious, rich, reddish hair but were evidently not feeling well. One would not stand when we entered the basement where they were.

"I wouldn't want anything to happen to them. They really belong to my son. He is at West Point now. They have not seemed just right after getting wet and cold the other day."

Colonel Smith said that he was keeping them in a dry, comfortable place, letting them rest, giving them water and food as wanted and using medicine as advised by a veterinarian. I suggested that he continue these measures and hoped that the setters would recover. Fortunately for them and everyone concerned they did. My practice was varied, to say the least.

Once each month the troops were given a "short-arm inspection," a euphemism for an examination for venereal disease. The men of a unit or barracks would stand in line, unclothed, and one at a time would be examined. The genitalia and body orifices would be inspected and if a lesion or discharge was found, laboratory tests were made. Records would be kept by the officer or noncommissioned officer in charge of each group. Those found to have syphilis, gonorrhea or other disease were given treatment.

At the routine monthly inspection we looked for signs of any contagious diseases, uncleanliness or presence of vermin such as pediculi, or lice. Skin diseases or other abnormalities were often discovered that would not have been disclosed otherwise.

The hospital was not equipped to treat insane patients but from time to time there would be one or two with mental disorders on the wards, for short periods, who required special attention while awaiting appropriate disposition. Duncan Wooley was such a case.

"Last night I was lying on my bunk and felt something poking me from below. I looked and there was Duncan lying on the floor on his back under my bed and punching the mattress with his toes," the young ward man, Cpl. Barry Keith, said one morning.

The next day Corporal Keith came to my office and said

excitedly, "Duncan has a knife with a long blade. I don't know where he got it but he acts like he is going to cut somebody."

When I got to the section I saw Duncan, in a room at the far end, coming toward the entrance to the main part of the ward holding the knife menacingly before him, a maniacal expression clouding his face. I had seen such weapons wielded before but as a spectator. This was different. The uneasy patients in the two long rows of beds on this ward could only watch. There was no time for contemplation.

I reached the entrance as the mentally disturbed young man, now dangerous, came through. As the knife approached, I stepped aside, grasped the wrist and gave it a quick twist. His hand opened and the knife clattered on the floor to end that moment of crisis.

Corporal Barry, in telling someone of the incident several days later, said, "Lieutenant Hall was not a bit scared of the crazy man." That just goes to show how difficult it is to read another person's mind.

The first-aid men in the camps had learned certain procedures such as taking temperatures, cleansing wounds, use of antiseptics, pressure control of bleeding and application of dressings. On visits I would see those with complaints, dress wounds, determine if any needed to be hospitalized, make a sanitary inspection and check medical supplies.

A few narcotics for emergencies were kept locked in camp dispensaries, with the key kept by a responsible person. An accounting was made regularly. I counted the pills at least once monthly in each container to be sure none was missing and made a record of the count.

"Make a count of the narcotics on hand at Oxford while you are there," Major Hendricks said to me one morning just before I left for that camp.

"I counted them yesterday after the sick call," I said, feeling pleased that this had already been accomplished.

Major Hendrick's face grew redder than usual and his voice rose. "Lieutenant Hall, you will make the count today!" he ordered, with emphasis on the word "will." I did. The results were the same as on the day before. Apparently I was not supposed to reason why, only to say "yes, sir" when given a lawful order.

One unusual assignment given me was to locate a young man who was absent without official leave and to return him to

Ft. McClellan if physically able to travel. Another officer and I went to his rustic backwoods home by automobile over country roads, uncertain that we could find him there, or anywhere, or how he would react if we did.

"We came for Willis. Where is he?" I asked his father.

"He's in the woods back of the house," he said, apparently thinking it best to cooperate. Willis offered no resistance, to our relief, and rode back with us quietly.

The main provision for social life on the post was the officer's club where occasional parties were held to which Anniston girls were invited. Here I became acquainted with officers of the artillery regiment.

"Were you at the Point?" Capt. Brierly asked me, between sips from the drink held in his hand, referring to the United States Military Academy on the Hudson River.

"No, I'm a doctor and graduated at Tulane."

"I was at the Point, Class of...," one of the other officers said to him enthusiastically and, under the volley of their ardent questions and answers to each other, I retreated.

I slept in the bachelor officer's quarters when not on duty in the hospital; that is, I tried to sleep there. Usually there were three others in the room, officers stationed there or visitors, mostly of the air corps, but an assortment from the infantry and other branches of the service. The Officer of the Day, together with those in transit coming and going, kept the light on most of the night. This was not conducive to excess energy and exuberance during waking hours.

Saddle horses were available on the post. Captain Woodson, an Anniston surgeon, and I went riding a time or two. The horses were spirited only when going toward the post. I had a few dates with the sister-in-law of a sergeant, unofficially, but hospital duties and taking care of the sick and injured in several camps took most of my time.

Sergeant Buckrun and I were returning late in the morning from the Heflin C.C.C. camp over a graveled road which was firmly packed in the center so that we could travel at a speed which would allow us to get back to the hospital by noon. There had been an unusually large number at sick call that morning.

The work done by the boys in the civilian corps on the post and in the outlying areas was sometimes arduous, especially for those unaccustomed to physical labor such as cutting trees and building roadways. Therefore, many of them often tried sick call to delay going out with a work detail or maybe be excused from work to enjoy bunk comfort while the others labored. The need to discourage this natural tendency increased as admonition did not seem to be an effective remedy.

"Sore throat" was a common complaint. This was good for a few hours of respite even if not found justified when the doctor took the temperature and examined the man. The pharmacist provided him with throat medicine which, although indicated, had a terrible taste. Even this was welcomed by the chronic complainers. The taste was so bad that they felt sure it must be good for them. Anyway, the sick call had taken a long time.

We were about halfway on the return trip from Heflin when we overtook a car that was traveling slower than Sergeant Buckrun, even when not in a hurry. He sounded his horn and without hesitating pulled left to pass. The driver in front of us pulled over to the right but not very much.

The two cars came parallel. Then we went ahead and my driver was turning back to the right when I heard the gravel rattle under our car, then the sound of sliding. Sensing the car turning and the road surface coming closer, I grasped the instrument panel with one hand, the seat with the other and instinctively tried to brace myself.

Our car's left side struck the road first with a bang, rolled completely over so quickly that I had the sensation of being whirled, and repeated this twice before coming to rest. The other car had stopped at some distance back. The man in it got out, walked toward us alarmed, and asked, "Are you hurt?"

"Not much, I guess; how about you, Sergeant?" I answered.

"My left knee and leg got bumped but I can walk so don't think I broke any bones," he said, looking at his leg, then over the car, which was battered and scratched. "Looks like I can drive it in if we can pull this fender off the wheel." Being able to hold onto the steering wheel had apparently minimized his injuries.

The man from the car we were passing stood looking amazed at us and our sturdy but blemished vehicle, shaking his head and making clucking noises. "You rolled over three times!" he exclaimed.

I noticed some blood on my right hand and that a little

knuckle skin was missing. On top of my head was a tender lump and small scalp laceration. There was soreness of my neck and lower back which persisted for several days.

Major Hendricks did not seem particularly disturbed when I informed him of the accident on arriving at the post hospital.

"I want you to go to Munford this afternoon. They are expecting you to be there for sick call. You had better leave as soon as you have eaten lunch. Another car will be ready for you."

Several thousand young men had been processed at Ft. McClellan, given physical examinations and inoculations, outfitted and assigned to the various work camps. The ward tents for contagious diseases had been gradually emptied as the patients in them recovered. Then eventually I was relieved of my duties at the fort and ordered to "—proceed without delay to Camp P-62, Bessemer, Alabama, reporting on arrival thereat to the Commanding Officer, Company 487—."

The camp was in a large tract of land covered mostly with a heavy growth of pine and maintained as a national forest. The main C.C.C. work was in the prevention and extinguishing of forest fires. Whenever there was a large fire with danger of it getting out of control, additional men in the area were employed to help fight it. As this was during the Depression when jobs were scarce, it was suspected that in some instances fires were started by incendiaries, although there was no proof of this.

Captain Allen of the U.S. Army was the commanding officer and Lieutenant Baugh his assistant. Besides the C.C.C. boys, there were about a half dozen foremen who had some experience in forestry. Tents in neat rows furnished the only cover. My tent was near the dispensary or medical tent. Except for emergencies there was not much to disturb my sleep in the dark, quiet, pine-scented forest in contrast to the B. O. Q. situation at McClellan.

The officers and foremen ate together at a long canvas-sheltered table under the trees. I never had witnessed such voracious appetites as these woodsmen displayed, not even among farmers, miners and others who expend considerable energy. The camp was a good customer for the Bessemer butcher and baker.

People in town seemed to appreciate the business stimulation provided by the project. For whatever reason, they were hospitable and kind to us. I went to a movie and the manager introduced himself. "Come any time you like and there will be no charge," he said. The owner of a recreation spot where weekly dances were given during the summer not only invited me to attend them free but the bouncer came for me as I did not have a car; neither did I have Sergeant Buckrun to drive for me.

An important part of the conservation work was cutting fire lanes through the forest to provide a passageway for equipment, as well as a break or space at which a forest fire might be stopped. Because of these it was possible to confine a conflagration to a relatively small area that would otherwise have spread widely, destroying the timber and wildlife on hundreds of acres.

Some natural resources and improvements in public lands that we enjoy today exist because of what was accomplished by the C.C.C. boys while benefitting themselves and their families, who received a part of the wages that they earned. Many of these boys, especially those reared in cities, were awkward at first in working with unfamiliar tools such as saws, axes, picks and shovels.

Cuts, scratches, bruises and blisters were common. Cases of poison ivy and "athlete's foot" were numerous. One boy was bitten by a poisonous snake. He recovered with treatment, which included the use of antivenin. Thereafter he was known to his fellows by a nickname and such a call as this might be heard, "Hey, 'Snakebite,' let's go play baseball!"

A diversion for me here, as in the mountains of West Virginia and other places, was to take a walk. Too, I usually had a daily workout on a punching bag which hung in the open air. The other officers and I bought sturdy canvas camp chairs and at the day's end, when not busy, we would sit in front of the headquarter's tent and talk.

Lieutenant Baugh's wife, Margery, was staying in Bessemer and he generally spent part of the evening with her, although he slept in camp. "We are expecting the boy in about six weeks," he said. He had started his active duty as a reserve officer but wished to become a regular and remain in the army.

Captain Allen's wife had remained in their home while he was temporarily assigned to duty with the C.C.C. He spoke of his experiences in other assignments.

"Bea cried when I was transferred from Hawaii because she liked it so well. I was R.O.T.C. instructor and we were there for seven years. In the islands you find a mixture of many races—Orientals, Polynesians, Caucasians, not many pure Hawaiians. Among my students more were of Japanese ancestry than any other. It sounded strange to me when I heard those kids say such things as 'When our forefathers landed at Plymouth Rock.'"

Mosquito control was one of our projects that summer. We made a search for possible breeding places in the vicinity of the camp. Ponds or pools of water in ditches or other places were drained or covered with an oil. At some farmhouses we found barrels of rainwater in which swam enough larvae or wigglers to produce swarms of mosquitoes. These were emptied, buckets turned upside down and cans crushed so that they could not hold water in which the mosquitoes could lay eggs. The campaign was so successful that we had no cases of malaria, nor were we annoyed by the pests. Also benefitted were the people in the communities around us.

Lieutenant Baugh received a telephone call one day. "I have to go into town and see Marg," he said and left at once, appearing concerned. We did not detain him but wondered what might be wrong. He was an independent kind of man. We felt, however, that he would let us know if we could help him.

Townspeople, except for a few men who came on business matters, were not often seen in camp. Perhaps they did not wish to interfere with our work. The camp was a busy place but clean and orderly. During the day while the men were working in the woods, it was rather quiet. Occasionally there was a little grumbling concerning certain assignments but I did not hear much of this.

Baugh was haggard the next time I saw him after the telephone call. "The baby was born dead or died soon after birth," he said quietly and bit his lip. "The doctor says that Marg is all right. We will have the funeral tomorrow. I've talked with the priest."

"I am sorry," was about all that I could think of to say at the time. Words seem so inadequate in some situations. This sadness had followed a relatively tranquil summer that passed without much disturbance except when, at the end of a long dry period, the lookout man saw smoke at one point in the vast forest.

The fire alarm was sounded and one could detect a faint odor of burning pine. All hands rushed to keep the fire confined and on the ground, as usual, while dreading that it would get out of control. Flames in a crackling line, fanned by the wind, rose high and raced forward, leaping from one treetop to another to advance as a roaring wall of fire consuming the virgin timber, throwing showers of sparks and intense heat ahead, leaving black trunks, ashes and suffocating smoke behind.

The fighters took advantage of space afforded by one of the lanes that had been cut through the forest. At the edge of this lane, between it and the advancing flames, they started a small backfire that could be controlled in order to obtain a bare gap of sufficient width to eliminate any danger of the fire leaping over it. With this and other measures, the fire was extinguished without much loss. Rain which fell the next day was welcomed.

"They finally found out at Ft. McClellan that you are a qualified surgeon and you are needed there," Captain Allen informed me when I went to the commanding officer's tent on a November day after sick call was completed. "Here are your orders."

My orders stated that I was relieved from duty at the Bessemer camp, that I was to proceed to Ft. McClellan and report on arrival to the surgeon, District "D," for duty. A medical officer to replace me in the camp was expected shortly. In the meantime I got my property ready to transfer to him and checked it against the inventory to be certain that all was in order for my departure.

The day I left, all of the men in camp lined up in military formation in front of the company headquarters area to bid me farewell. Their spokesman presented me with a leather punching bag and striking gloves that they had bought and made a little speech. Seldom have I been touched as I was by this gesture of appreciation. Back at the fort my assignment in the post hospital was equivalent to that of house surgeon in a civilian hospital and my duties similar, in a general way, to those I had in the larger Memphis Veterans Hospital to which I expected to return.

Major Hendricks seemed pleased to see me back and said, "This is a good chance for you to get in the regular army. You could get commissioned as a regular and have a fine career in the service."

"I'll think about it," I parried, not convinced of the wisdom of his advice.

Sergeant Buckrun was standing by a car in front of the hospital and saluted when I came out. I returned his salute and said, "I won't be going to the camps with you any more, it seems, but will treat the boys that you bring in. Had any accidents lately?"

"No, but I'm apt to. The cars are too top-heavy and flip over sometimes. I finally got through making reports about the one when we rolled over three times on that loose gravel."

"Better take it easy and slow down for the curves. You might not be so lucky next time."

A soldier admitted to the hospital had been injured in an unusual way. He was walking along an Anniston street when some skylarkers in a car passed by. One of them shot a pistol. The bullet hit the sidewalk, ricocheted, struck him in the abdomen and passed through several loops of intestine. Many memories of calamitous incidents mercifully fade with the passage of time while pleasant ones persist. The events of one of my nights at this post are now recalled.

Corporal Keith came to me one night and in a tone of urgency said, "Patient Blank has disappeared. He had been acting strange and was admitted for examination and observation. We've been watching him but he got away when Sergeant Kelly was off the floor for a little while."

"Have you looked in all the rooms and on the other floors?"

"Yes, even on the grounds around the hospital."

A patient on the ward said, "I saw Blank go out the window in his bathrobe right after Sergeant Kelly left the ward. He didn't say anything to anybody and took nothing with him."

Major Hendricks was notified and he called Colonel Smith to tell him what had happened. Approximately a hundred men participated in a search for the missing patient that lasted most of the night and covered all parts of the reservation including the barracks, parade ground, motor pool, sports field, ranges, and wooded areas without success.

The men were sent in small details in every direction in the hunt, which extended beyond the reservation while hours of discouragement made their task seem hopeless. They appeared more apprehensive the longer they searched for the man considered by them as an escaped person who could be violent if encountered.

"He must be tricky," "I wonder where he's hiding," "We

had better stay close together," "Don't try to take him by yourself," and "He might be dangerous" were comments of some of the soldiers who feared the unknown more than an enemy or dangers they understood. They had heard stories of the prodigious powers of maniacs or insane persons. They and the alerted guards on duty became weary and more jittery as the night wore on.

The patient most certainly was unhappy in the hospital and now somewhere outside, all alone, he must be in the depths of melancholia. I could perhaps help him as despondent people in Gallinger had been helped or at least persuade him to return to the hospital with me. So I went by myself to look for him, trying to reason where one in his state of mind might go in an attempt to escape and hide.

Some buildings in a gloomy area in the vicinity of the hospital that had been bypassed by the search parties appeared to be the logical place to start. I could see nothing in the darkness on a general inspection tour and was approaching one of the buildings when suddenly I heard a sharp command, "Halt!"

I stopped but could see nothing because it was so dark in the shadow of the structure. "Advance!" I was ordered and took a few steps, then stood still at "Halt!" When this was repeated, I decided that it might be best to say something, considering the risk in silence. It was now evident that I was being challenged by a frightened sentry, who was unable to identify me.

"I am Lieutenant Hall," this uneasy lieutenant stated, trying not to startle him.

"Oh, I thought that you were the crazy man, sir," said a quavering voice. I could now see that he was a pale young recruit with a tremulous finger on the trigger of a rifle pointing toward me.

We failed to find the missing patient, although many trained soldiers searched methodically and calmly throughout most of the night, returning to their barracks only when nearly exhausted. I finally went to bed but had not been there long when Corporal Keith awakened me.

"Blank was found and they want you to see him before he is brought in," the capable corporal said and told me more as I prepared to go. "A little girl found him in the woods back of the farmhouse where she went to play early this morning."

I went to the small farm, which was not far away, with several other officers of the fort. The farmer was waiting for us.

"Come with me," he said quietly and walked about fifty yards behind the little home. It was my duty to pronounce patient Blank dead.

The body, covered by hospital garb, was hanging from the limb of a tree by a clothesline rope which was embedded deeply in the neck. The face was puffy and purplish, the tongue swollen and protruding and the lifeless arms hung by his side. Near his feet was an overturned bucket upon which he had apparently stood and then kicked out from under himself.

Fort McClellan I would like to remember as the site of parades by splendid military units with band playing and flags flying, where much worthwhile was accomplished and impressive ceremonies witnessed. I saw many young men reclaimed to health and productive lives there, but the tragedy of one called Blank cannot be forgotten.

In the spring Veterans Administration appropriations made it possible for the Veterans Hospital in Memphis to recall me, so my extended tour of active duty in the army was terminated, although I was subject to recall in case of a national emergency. Leaving Ft. McClellan was rather informal as was my return to the surgical service that I had left in the V.A. hospital. A letter from Colonel Smith stated: "I regretted not seeing you before your departure to express my appreciation of your excellent work on C.C.C. duty. Wishing you continued success...."

My next extended tour of active army duty was during World War II, starting soon after the declaration of war. My first assignment was to Company "D," 307th Medical Battalion, 82nd Division, which was then at Camp Claiborne, Louisiana. It was commanded by Omar N. Bradley, who was then a major general but eventually became General of the Army and chairman of the Joint Chiefs of Staff. He was in command of the United States Ground Forces for the invasion of France.

Sergeant Alvin C. York of Tennessee, outstanding soldier of World War I, was with the 82nd Infantry Division and single-handedly killed about twenty Germans with a rifle and pistol and forced 132 others to surrender. This deed was called by Marshal Foch "the greatest thing accomplished by any private soldier of all the armies of Europe." Sergeant York visited the division when it was at Camp Claiborne early in World War II.

"Your experience and maturity qualifies you for more than a company assignment—regimental surgeon at division headquarters, perhaps," I was advised shortly after reporting for duty. My next orders relieved me from duty with the 307th Medical Battalion and assigned me to the 327th Infantry of the 82nd Division, which later would be airborne. On the uniform shoulder patch were the letters "AA," insignia for "All American."

Training included qualifying on the obstacle course, traversing it in a specified number of minutes going up and down, over, under and through a variety of obstacles while having thoughts concerning the diabolical cunning of the one who devised the course to test strength, agility, skill, endurance and timing. Such things as jumping and climbing walls did not bother me much but a wide, deep ditch required a running jump off gravel-covered boards at its edge. Later I recalled how treacherous loose gravel can be.

A broad creek that had to be crossed by swinging on a long manila rope was the feature that created the most interest. "The general got dunked here when he tried it," an instructor said. "The trick is to get a good swing across and then let go of the rope quickly, as soon as your feet hit the ground on the other side. If you hold on too long, you'll swing back and may get wet." I was lucky.

Before leaving Montgomery to report for army duty, I had received this information from Camp Caliborne: "No quarters for officer's families are available on this Post. Living quarters could probably be obtained in Alexandria, Louisiana, or other nearby communities, although these communities are very crowded."

Mildred came to Alexandria, which is on the Red River about two hundred miles north of New Orleans. During the day while I was at camp, she tried to find a place for us. When she entered the yard of one home, a pet bear greeted her. "I couldn't believe my eyes when I saw it coming toward me," she related that night. Finally she found a small garage apartment in the back yard of the home of a woman whose husband was serving a prison term. The space over her automobiles had been partitioned into three little apartments, which she quickly rented. They were hot but an electric fan that we bought helped us sleep.

We were about twenty-five miles from where I had to be present for reveille each morning before daybreak, which meant getting out of bed a few hours earlier than customary to be on time for the roll call by flashlight. We did not know how long we could be together before I would be ordered overseas, so we made the best of the situation.

"Today I drove across the river to Pineville," Mildred told me one night. "Coming back, the traffic was backed up at the bridge as one slow car at a time crossed it. After I got back on this side I saw that the river was so high that muddy water was up to the bridge."

My next assignment was to LaGarde General Hospital in New Orleans. The large hospital was housed in rows of small wooden buildings connected by ramps and was built in the manner of temporary construction in those days. I was placed in the Medical Department Replacement Pool along with many other doctors who were being readied for war service. On reporting I was sent to a surgical ward directed by a young Major Gregg, who had come from a residency to volunteer before those in the reserves had been ordered to active duty. By then I had learned that rank was based on the day active duty began and not on previous training, experience or the date when commissioned.

"Just stay out of the way," was the only instruction that Major Gregg gave when informed that I had been assigned to his service for training. Thus were my duties defined. I went to an office between the main ward room and the entrance to the building and, together with some other newly arrived medical officers, studied records and blank forms used by this hospital.

"Were you ordered to active duty from the reserves?" Lieutenant Burnham asked me.

"Yes. How about you?"

"I was, too. That's why I'm a lieutenant instead of a major. I'm a psychiatrist and was at St. Elizabeth's Hospital in Washington. Five of us about the same age, with the same education, training and experience and doing similar work, came on army duty together. I was the only one with a reserve commission. All of the other four were commissioned as majors."

"Rank among medical officers is like honor among whores," said Captain Buck. "We're all just doctors in uniform, as I see it."

"Those with more rank usually become less as doctors," was Burnham's comment.

"By the way, you used to be in the Memphis Veterans Hospital, didn't you, and some were furloughed without pay?" Buck asked as I nodded. "Well," he continued, "after you were recalled, I ran into Dr. Mulenberg, who had been furloughed from another veterans hospital and was sore as hell because you were recalled and he wasn't. Guess who is chief of the Surgical Service in LaGarde. Right, Colonel Mulenberg." I had already reported to him "for training."

"Promotions have been frozen for us in the replacement pool. They say that there is not much chance of being promoted before we get overseas anyhow," Burnham said. "Mulenberg will be the one who will grade us on efficiency reports."

The assignments to LaGarde were regarded as temporary for most of us but some saw opportunities to get experience they could not get in a civilian hospital and would try to remain. For me the surgery was largely of the kind in which I already had considerable experience.

My transfer from Camp Claiborne to the hospital on Lake Pontchartrain was the first of changes that enabled me to work in many kinds of situations that the war presented in the infantry, a named general hospital, station hospital, numbered general hospital, dispensary, field and evacuation hospitals, on land, sea and even in the air at times.

At LaGarde we saw patients, learned military procedures, attended staff meetings, served on boards and incidentally made friendships, some of which would endure through the war and beyond. It was here that I met Roy O. Yeatts, a general practitioner in civilian life, who was born in Virginia, educated in California, served on Indian reservations and just before entering the army was a Seventh Day Adventist missionary to New Orleans.

One board of three officers to which I was appointed was ordered "...to meet at this general hospital, as soon as practicable to investigate the circumstances and report the facts leading up to and connected with the injuries sustained by Private Buster J. Reilly...New Orleans Army Air Base, New Orleans, Louisiana, and determine as a result of such investigation whether the injuries were incurred in line of duty or whether or not the result of soldier's misconduct." This is an example of a way in which our time was often employed. It involved, in this instance, recording the details of a fight in which Private Reilly had participated and making a decision, the most difficult part of the order.

Mildred found an apartment for us as she had done in Alexandria, but this one was more spacious and, moreover, was attractive. We had the first floor of a home on Elba Street that had originally been built by a contractor for his own use, and beautiful parts and materials obtained from demolished mansions had been used in its construction. Our back door opened into a pretty garden in which we enjoyed sitting when we could be together.

Our temporary home was a restful place of beauty. I looked forward to returning to it at the end of each day. But it was here that a cloud of unhappiness would shadow our little family.

Once when Mildred went downtown to do some shopping, I stayed at home with Edwin. I took him outside, let him pull some peach tree leaves for amusement and then put him on the living room floor. After a time he discovered that he could move himself forward and soon was gleefully crawling across the floor, even to the fireplace.

"Why is he so dirty?" Mildred said in consternation when she returned.

"He learned to crawl while you were gone," I proudly informed her and she was pleased to witness a brief demonstration of his new skill before giving him a bath.

"Edwin has a diarrhea," Mildred said somberly when I came home one day. "His bowels moved more than usual and too loose. I'm afraid he is sick."

"Maybe it's from a change in food or water," I said in a half-hearted attempt to reassure her, "but if he is not better tomorrow we should get a pediatrician to see him." It was evident that he did not feel well and we gave him water that had been boiled. We were thinking of the possibility of dysentery, a disease of babies that was often fatal.

The pediatrician prescribed, among other things, a banana diet. Because of the submarine warfare which had resulted in the loss of many ships, bananas were scarce even in New Orleans, the nation's main banana port. So Mildred and I hunted over the city to buy the few that were available. We also bought canned bananas for our baby son, who continued to have too-frequent bowel movements and watery stools. Often, even before finishing a feeding, he would have cramps and his face would turn red as he strained. As his illness persisted, our concern for him grew.

An alternative to the therapeutic measures being employed was a period of starvation to eliminate the materials in the intestine on which the infection subsisted. However, the pediatrician regarded this as drastic and was dubious of the consequences in a child already weakened. How long an infant could survive with dysentery had to be weighed against the chances for survival with extreme treatment methods.

Days and nights passed slowly. For a while it seemed that Edwin was getting no worse. We watched his temperature, respirations, heart rate and movements. Mildred proved to be an excellent nurse for him. We felt encouraged, but then came a relapse and previous episodes of diarrhea were repeated.

The resources for combatting such infections were limited before the war, which brought improvements in treatment techniques and in the availability of effective antibiotics. This would benefit sick babies in future years. Edwin and we struggled along without these benefits. Eventually his defenses prevailed and he recovered, for which we were more than thankful in that summer which, for us as well as the country, was so eventful.

In August I was ordered with many others in the pool to duty with a five-hundred-bed numbered station hospital at Fort Rucker, Alabama. Here, at least, were a number of medical officers that I had known at LaGarde, Capt. Roy O. Yeatts among them.

Mildred and I, again looking for rooms to rent, explored the area, visiting Dothan, Dalesville, Ariton, Brundige and other nearby towns. In Enterprise we saw an unusual memorial, unique in that it is dedicated to an insect. On the Boll Weevil Monument are carved the words, "In profound appreciation of the boll weevil and what it has done to herald prosperity." This insect was so honored in 1910 because the severe damage it inflicted on the area's cotton crop contributed to diversification of agriculture, including the cultivation of peanuts.

We found rooms in an Ozark home, not in the henhouse which was converted into living quarters and rented to people anxious to be within commuting distance of the fort. I managed to buy a truckload of coal from the quartermaster for our open fireplace so that we could be fairly comfortable when cold weather came.

Edwin learned to walk in Ozark. One day while standing in the kitchen holding onto a cabinet, he let go and toddled to the table. Soon he was taking walks with me and quickly was adept at finding interesting objects, such as pecans, on the ground. When we went to the 81st "Wildcat" Division Parade, however, he was content to watch it from the vantage point of Dr.

Yeatt's shoulder. Before long he was talking and would greet me with cries of "Daddy!" when I returned home from Ft. Rucker at night.

My days were occupied with things that soldiers do such as drilling, hiking and becoming familiar with the station hospital and equipment and army ways. I was ordered to be president of a Special Court Martial Board of six officers "appointed for trial of such persons as may properly be brought before it." This duty was among the more disagreeable ones that came my way. One of the first cases with which we had to deal was that of a young enlisted man of independent nature whom we found guilty of refusing to obey a nurse's order.

Some of the doctors who had been ordered to the numbered station hospital for training until the time it would be sent overseas had not had much previous contact with the army. Military courtesies and chain of command, saluting, standing at attention, speaking to another doctor in the third person and other formalities seemed foreign to these matured individuals. However, most of them adjusted to the regimentation with only a normal amount of grumbling.

"It gripes me to have to take orders from a young squirt who was in high school when I was practicing medicine, just because he happened to go on army duty a few days before me," Captain Wolcott said between drawn lips. "I have to get his approval for what I do even though he is my junior professionally."

"Just try to rise above it," Lieutenant Cave said, "and remember that this won't last always. It's time for calisthenics; we'd better get over there."

Lieutenant Colonel Seward, our commanding officer, was striving conscientiously to get the hospital and all officers and men ready for whatever overseas duty might be given us. Medical Administrative Corps officers had been assigned to the unit but no nurses as yet. I was the senior surgeon on the professional staff at the time.

"You deserve a promotion," Colonel Seward said one day after a training session in surgical service organization and procedures. "Doctors with less training and experience than you who do not have reserve commissions come in as majors. The 'Big Brass' say that this is not discrimination against reserve officers, that nothing is taken from them, that they have to offer higher grades to those over which they have no control in order to get volunteers.

"The reservists are discriminated against because consistently they are not allowed to take advantage of the better opportunities offered to professional men not handicapped by already being subject to active duty. In general, the practical effect of this is that doctors who were in the reserves before the war are now serving in relatively lower grades. It is ironical that those who were not are being rewarded."

"I have a certificate which states that I am qualified for the grade of major but promotions were frozen," I told him. When this certificate should have been of significance the rules had been changed.

Colonel Seward recommended me for promotion and forwarded the papers with endorsements through channels, but because of the regulations and restrictions in effect, under the existing circumstances, final approval was not obtained. Events that followed did not improve the situation for me and my fellow officers from LaGarde in respect to prospects for advancement in grade.

"Familiarity breeds contempt, they say, and I'm learning more about doctors than I ever knew before," said Warrant Officer Boddeau, talking to a few of us in the barracks after retreat. "I always looked up to the doctors in our town, especially old Dr. Monroe who always treated our family. Now I'm getting a closer look in a different light."

"We're just like other people, a mixture of good and bad," he was reminded.

Living at close quarters with men from a variety of environments and pursuits enabled us to hear some new viewpoints and led to a better understanding of those with whom we worked, but in some instances perhaps we were left more confused. Chaplains, for example, were often puzzling. Certain ones seemed to strive strenuously to be recognized as good sports, known more for broadmindedness than for piety or other qualities usually associated with men of God. Maybe these thought they could do more for the morale of those who looked to them for guidance and inspiration by being "one of the boys."

"What do you think of the chaplains since you have been around them so much every day?" Stacey was asked.

"I respect what they are supposed to represent but don't have any reverence for some reverends, so-called, that I've seen. I'm not talking about all of them."

The comments were recalled when on our next hike Chaplain Shaughnessy was saying to us, "I heard a funny story at the club last night," and Lieutenant Cave called out, "Keep it clean, Chaplain."

One of the important lessons learned in the war was to live in some degree of harmony with an aggregation of men with various characteristics, habits, ideals and ambitions, taken away from their civilian lives and homes and put under army regulations and conditions. Most were able to function satisfactorily, but there were those for whom discipline seemed difficult and rules challenging.

The barracks were off-limits to females. So when Chaplain Shaughnessy entertained in his quarters an officer and girls who visited him one night, the news of it spread. This resulted in an investigation and a hearing over which Colonel Sullivan presided.

"After all, it was against regulations and could not be ignored," Lieutenant Cave commented. "I couldn't have got away with it."

"It will be interesting to hear what they do," was Stacey's comment.

The hearing, being the first one in our organization that attracted much attention, was a popular subject of conversation, particularly since it involved an officer who was not only well known to us but had been regarded as one designated as our spiritual adviser. It would not be the last episode to disturb the serenity of this outfit, of which monotony was not a characteristic. Uninterrupted tranquility, however, would have been unnatural under the circumstances.

Chaplain Shaughnessy was transferred to a unit on another post, left quietly and was heard of no more. He probably adjusted. Many people observed general standards of conduct to which they were accustomed back in their hometowns; others apparently did not.

"Army living strengthens the character of some and weakens others," was Lieutenant Cave's sage observation. He appeared thoughtful. "But you don't have to change."

"The army claims that it builds men, but I wonder," said Stacey.

Barracks conversation was usually light, but it sometimes took a serious turn. After mail call you could pick those in the crowd who were disappointed in not receiving a letter. The cheerful ones you assumed were pleased with what they read and those who had received unpleasant news betrayed it usually by the expressions of worry they wore, rather than by sharing it.

"I don't see why we could not have stayed at home with our practice until they needed us overseas in a hospital already set up. The doctor that I left my patients with is overworked already. We're not needed in the post hospital here; they are using only some of our enlisted men," Captain Wolcott complained. "I learned how to salute in R.O.T.C."

We did not know what or where our mission would be, so our training was extensive. It included physical conditioning, marching with field packs and gas masks and strenuous as well as the usual setting-up exercises. Our muscles, at least, were being strengthened. Going along a country road at route step on a clear, cool day might produce a few blisters but was relatively pleasant for those accustomed to taking long walks. Occasionally the ambulance or a jeep would pick up one who had to drop out for some reason, such as heatstroke in August.

"Getting pneumonia or something won't make us healthier or more fit," Captain Wolcott remarked after a double-time march in the rain on a wintry day.

"Would you like to go to the quartermaster's warehouse with me?" Colonel Seward asked during an intermission in the schedule.

"Yes, I'd like to see what is in it."

On the way there he said, "The rainfall in this area is about the heaviest in the country, especially in the winter months, and the mud around our barracks is getting sloppy. We have lumber for more boardwalks but need some nails."

"I'd like to see some nails," he said to the man in charge of the warehouse stores and was shown many kegs of them in various sizes.

"Good, now I'll make the requisition for what we need."

While there we looked at other supplies such as equipment, tools and various kinds of hardware. Outside again, the colonel said, "If I had sent the requisition through channels without checking first, the chances are I would have been told that the nails I wanted were not in stock."

On the way back to his office, Colonel Seward spoke of our hospital in the making and confided, "According to the grapevine, another five-hundred-bed station hospital will be combined with ours before we go overseas to make a thousand-bed one. The officers of the other station hospital are expected in here soon. If they were activated before ours they will out-rank us and get the higher slots. One consolation is if you remain a captain you can continue in professional work as a surgeon and not be tied up with administrative duties.

"We all realize that promotions depend upon being at the right place at the right time."

We heard many guesses and rumors as to the future of our unit and its personnel and when we might leave the states. All movements were kept secret. In the meantime, preparations went ahead and one of the activities was close-order drill.

Captain Wolcott was drilling the enlisted men one morning under the observation of Colonel Seward and executing movements such as column right, right front into line, right by twos and so on. His "March!" and "Halt!" commands were loud and clear and the drill period was going well until he gave the command, "To the rear, march!" Then there was confusion.

Colonel Seward stepped forward and advised the captain that he had given the "march" order on the wrong foot. "One more step is taken after the final word of the order," he stated. Then he relieved Captain Wolcott and assigned another officer to be drill instructor. Captain Wolcott was obviously chagrined and left the field.

"I've made a formal complaint at headquarters against Colonel Seward for reprimanding me in front of the men," Wolcott informed us at noon. "I would not want to go overseas with him. The chaplain did nothing wrong but he went against regulations and was transferred. What the colonel did to me was not according to regulations. Maybe we can get rid of him."

An investigation and taking the testimony of witnesses as to what occurred on the drill field seemed to be inevitable. This placed Wolcott's officer friends in the uncomfortable position of having to testify in a matter that could be detrimental not only to the principals involved but also to the organization of which each of us was a part. Not only was Seward our commanding officer but I considered him to be a friend and regretted the necessity of having to appear at a hearing and state what was seen and heard.

My fellow officers who participated in this affair shared my feelings, I think. But close on its heels was another event that engaged our attention. Before we learned of the action taken in the Wolcott-versus-Seward case, the personnel of the five-hundred-bed station hospital to be combined with ours arrived under the command of Lieutenant Colonel Gross, who was made commanding officer of the resulting numbered hospital which now boasted, on paper, one thousand beds.

Colonel Seward was transferred to another post to assume command of a medical unit being trained there for foreign service. The next time I heard of him he was commanding a unit in England. As he had forewarned, the officers in the hospital unit joined to ours had been on active duty a little longer than we had. Doctors in it were recent graduates who had served internships but as they were not established in practice or in positions from which they could not be spared, they had entered military service early; consequently they outranked us. Even so, there were things for which I could be thankful.

Mildred and Edwin were fairly comfortable in Ozark and I could still be with them at night. Our little son was growing and learning new tricks and Mildred was perfecting her tactics in combatting pests such as ingenious cockroaches. The big, open fire contributed to the warmth and cheerfulness of my reception after the day's work was done.

Captain and Mrs. Barnett had rooms in Ariton and we visited with them when time permitted. Just before Thanksgiving we rode to a turkey farm and selected a plump gobbler for our feast. On the holiday, Barnett and I took the bird to a chopping block in the backyard and finally did what was necessary, ignoring the critical remarks of our spouses concerning our technique.

"You must be chicken-hearted," one of them chided.

"Well, the fowl deed is done, anyway," we admitted.

Then came the scalding, plucking, cleaning, roasting and all the other things that went into the preparation of this special dinner. To it we invited a few of the leaner bachelors from camp.

"Now, we'll see how a surgeon operates," someone said when all was ready and thanks had been given. "Scalpel."

Day after day of uncertainty passed with nothing to satisfy our curiosity as to where we would be next. Then came Christmas. We had a small, brightly decorated tree in the living room of our temporary home in Ozark and, outside the window, two large japonica bushes were filled with red blooms. With assistance, Edwin for the first time opened his presents, but he

266

seemed to be more interested in the colorful wrappings than their contents, having fun playing with the red-and-green paper and ribbons. The Barnetts and a few other new friends ate dinner with us and we looked forward to the new year with hope.

Each of the barracks at Camp Rucker had a little Christmas tree and decorations and special dinners were served in the mess halls in observation of the day. For many, however, these evidences of recognition of the joyful season were reminders that they were away from home, family and old friends.

"I heard that the station hospital training at Rucker will be leaving soon," Mrs. Barnett heard a woman shopper say in an Ozark store one January day.

"Where did you hear that?" she was asked.

"My husband works for the railroad and is helping in getting all the cars together and ready. He thinks that they are going to Camp Kilmer, New Jersey, but can't be sure, of course."

Our orders to move came ten days later. Even then we were not informed of our destination. The hour for separation that we dreaded had arrived. Mildred came to the departure area with Edwin to see me off, but we had only a few minutes together before the time for entraining came, suddenly it seemed. Edwin seemed to realize that on this occasion my leaving was different than usual and cried. I would not see them again for nearly three years.

On the train my reverie was disturbed by attention to duties that had been given to me relating to the safety, conduct and comfort of the detachment and being certain that all arrived. There were no mishaps on the long trip and no one left at stops on the way. Most were jovial, apparently relieved that the period of waiting in training at Rucker was over. On arrival at Camp Kilmer, however, we were restricted to the hospital area inside this camp which was named for the poet Joyce Kilmer, author of "Trees," who was killed in World War I.

We were not allowed to communicate with the outside. One of the enlisted men could see his home beyond the wire fence. There was an officers' call at 0800 each morning and orders were given for the day's activities. The wife of one of our officers managed to get inside the camp and see him briefly by posing as a member of a U.S.O. troupe admitted to entertain the troops.

I learned much later that Mildred, with Mrs. Barnett and

Edwin, had driven to Newark, New Jersey, and gotten a room in the Robert Trent Hotel. Because of the security regulations in effect, however, they could learn nothing concerning us and left in a day or two without being able to talk to us, even by telephone. Mrs. Barnett returned to her home in Indiana. Mildred and Edwin went to Albertville to live with my mother until my return.

Our training continued at Kilmer while waiting to be shipped somewhere overseas. We had no idea where we would be sent or whether it would be to a hot or cold climate. One night we were ordered on a hike carrying bedding rolls, a full pack and wearing gas masks in a snowstorm. We passed some soldiers and I heard one of them say, "That must be a tough infantry outfit."

Rubber galoshes were bought by some of the officers, but we were not allowed to wear them at formations because the enlisted men did not have any. "They are not part of the uniform and should not be worn if not available to all the men," our commanding officer stated.

Captain Jones, our surgeon of highest rank by the army's method of ranking and one of the young officers in the unit recently joined with ours, said proudly, "I've had no postgraduate courses or residency. All I have is my M. D. degree and a year of internship."

"Some of us have more than that," Lieutenant Cave remarked. "I think one or two are Fellows of the American College of Surgeons. There is the right way and the wrong way and the army way of doing things. You will be a major soon, no doubt."

"Doing major surgery is what I'm looking forward to. I saw a spinal injury in the post hospital that I'd like to operate on," Captain Jones said. It was evident that he was not hampered by any inhibitions or restrained by lessons that could be learned only from experiences through which he had not lived.

"Fools rush in where angels fear to tread," said Captain Wolcott. "Have you ever done a laminectomy?"

"No, but there is a first time for everything."

"I hope that I'm not the first one that you do it to," Lieutenant Weems, one of the medical administrative officers, contributed to the conversation.

"We are glad to have you administrative officers with us. Now maybe the doctors can doctor and I won't have to be the transportation officer any more and can get rid of the motor pool," Lieutenant Cave said.

Major Groen, who was a mature surgeon on a medical school faculty, and a complement of nurses were assigned to our hospital while we were at Camp Kilmer. This gave us the personnel required to operate a station hospital that could accommodate a thousand patients and we were near a port of embarkation. Movement to a foreign location seemed imminent.

Major Groen, ostensibly assigned to us to be chief of the Surgical Service, was middle-aged, of medium height, balding with graying temples and agressively competitive. He apparently was lacking in assurance. A method of boosting himself was by trying to reduce the self-esteem of those working with him rather than encouraging or helping them.

"If I had gone into my family's clothing business, I could be lying on the sand at Miami Beach now instead of being in this miserable place," was one of his first assertions. "We usually are there for part of the winter if we don't go abroad. I hope that we have some decent equipment to work with when we get set up. We had the best in our hospital. How long do you keep your patients in bed after operations? We've been getting good results and less complications with early ambulation, usually getting abdominal cases, appendectomies, hernias, up within twenty-four hours."

"We couldn't get all of our orthopedic cases on their feet that soon, but we've been getting them up as soon as we thought it was safe," Captain Burk said.

"They're safer up than in bed," said the major and discontinued the discussion.

The officers of our hospital, nurses included, were divided into two detachments in preparation for sailing to our destination overseas in different ships. The purpose of this was to have enough of the staff left to establish a hospital in case one of the vessels was sunk on the way.

Orders issued on the day before we left Camp Kilmer stated that "the officers of NY 10 will fall in formation in front of Building No. 760 at 8:45 a.m. and pass to the command of Captain Hall, M.C. They will remain in front of building No. 760 until marched to the train in military formation." The train would take us to the wharf where the U.S. Army Transport *H. F. Alexander* was waiting. For a while, at least, we would be separated from our friends and associates of the other group.

269

About forty nurses and male officers of my command gathered inside the building, out of the early-morning cold, before the formation on that February day we went to war, each with the baggage to be carried on board ship. Colonel Gross gave a brief talk in which he said, "No use in worrying. If a bullet has your name on it you will be hit; if not, you're safe."

A few nurses, while waiting for the "Fall Out" order, began to hum, then sing popular tunes, and everyone joined in. Just before we left, the building resounded with "Roll out the barrel—we'll have a barrel of fun."

What was on the minds of those about to embark on the greatest adventure in the lives of most of them would be difficult to say. Before the singing started, many appeared to be deep in thought, but I was busy with my duties.

The most excitement that I had experienced at Kilmer was when our barracks was on fire. While reading on the second floor, I suddenly heard a crackling noise and saw a sheet of flames coming up the stairwell. Those who had been playing cards in the room beyond had their hair singed when they ran by it to reach the fire escape. The fire, which had been started by a plumber's torch, was extinguished but the wooden building was so damaged that we had to move into another one. Now we were poised to participate in the greatest of war's conflagrations in world history.

World War II
In North Africa

"We are going to North Africa" was repeated in an air of excitement all over our crowded transport when this became official. Then, in an area of the vast ocean where no ship outside the convoy was expected, we got the ominous word, "Suspicious-looking object has been sighted just north of our course." After a few long minutes of suspense, it was identified as a small vessel. The significance of it was uncertain at the time.

The vessel seen might be only a fishing boat as its external appearance suggested, but there was a chance that it was spying on our ships for submarines lurking in these waters. So our convoy changed direction. By zigzagging we hoped to elude them. However, by doing this it would take much longer to cross the Atlantic, thus increasing the number of days that we would be exposed to the danger of attack.

Each transport ship, for its defense from sea or aircraft, had a limited amount of armament and artillerymen to man the guns which varied in kind, caliber and number, depending on the vessel's size. We had some three-inch and four-inch guns which were fired during drills and I was reminded of my R.O.T.C. summer training at Fortress Monroe, Virginia.

The medical officers were "—assigned to sick bay areas for the duration of the voyage for the purpose of conducting daily sick call for the troops at 0900 and at 1800 hours." My area was "D" Deck, Compartments 2 and 3. We also received these orders: "The following named Medical Officers are hereby assigned to the Battle Stations as indicated opposite their names and will report to these stations at the alarm indicating an alert." My battle station was "Forward of Stack on Boat Deck Starboard Side."

Our transport, the *H. F. Alexander*, when built as a commercial ocean liner had been designed to carry three hundred passengers, but on that February crossing there were about three thousand people on board. Extra bunks had been installed in tiers on the walls of the rooms and many soldiers slept on the decks. Water was limited. Each morning we could get our canteens filled, one per person, for our needs during the day. We were careful not to waste any.

"We have three rows of bunks on each wall in our stateroom," Boddeau said one day as some of us watched the ships and waves. "A chaplain in there sleeps in a lower bunk. One of the guys sleeping in a bunk over him has been stepping on him when he climbs up. Last night he stepped on his face and that chaplain really cussed him out."

Blackout was in effect at night. No light was permissible, not even a cigarette, that could be seen outside the ship. One night we heard a strong voice coming over a loud speaker ordering us to "put out that light or we'll shoot it out!" Someone had failed to cover a porthole and the light shining through it had attracted the attention of one of our destroyers. It speedily came alongside and gave the order, which was quickly executed. The offense was not repeated.

I called a meeting on deck one sunny day for all the members of my detachment so that we could get acquainted and to give them what information and advice I had for them. We were to land at Oran, Algeria, where there would be trucks to take us to the camp area outside the city. There we would be joined later by the rest of our hospital personnel in a day or two, according to plan. As they were on a larger ship further back in the convoy, we would reach port first if all went well.

"We are on the decoy boat," Captain Wolcott asserted. "It is expected to be hit by the torpedoes in case of attack so that the detachment with Colonel Gross won't be sunk and can still set up the hospital. You can see that their transport is in a better-protected position in the convoy."

"I'm not sure about that," said Lieutenant Cave. "They are a bigger target than we are."

After that meeting our transport was referred to, more or less facetiously, as "The Decoy" and a few of the nurses began to "pair off" with certain male officers. Early each morning

Captain Wolcott would appear on deck at the ship's bow, usually with several other officers in tow, and, in the pose of an admiral surveying his fleet, would say, "I'm making my inspection. It makes me feel better to see my battleship and cruiser leading the way out there."

The morale of my detachment was excellent under the circumstances. Life on board the transport was rather informal. There was much joking, but underneath it all there was an awareness of the serious nature of our mission and no illusion as to the situation where we were going. Daily bulletins of the fighting were received.

"You are going to have to learn to cut their guts out!" Colonel Donelly, the transport commander, said at a meeting he called. "Our forces retreated eighty kilometers yesterday in the face of an attack by Rommel's Africa Korps. That is understandable; our young men were reared to be kind and gentle. They will have to get tough."

We were given little booklets on North Africa which advised us concerning the people, their customs and how we should conduct ourselves when with them. It contained lists of useful words and phrases in their language. We were instructed to respect the women and their veils and that it would be dangerous to do otherwise. It informed us that when two Arabs are seen walking along a street holding hands, it does not have the same connotation that this would have in the United States.

The sea was not especially rough and the scene was relatively peaceful and quiet one day as our big convoy ploughed through the waves. Then the alert alarm was sounded. We rushed expectantly to our battle stations, not knowing if it would be the usual drill or was in response to enemy action. The rapid fire of our guns sounded somewhat like the firecrackers at Christmas time, or on the Fourth of July, back home except on a greater scale. The reverberations over the water crackled a little differently from those heard on land during summer training but not as loudly as the railway guns at Fort Eustice.

The signal to return to quarters was eventually given. We were not informed as to whether enemy craft had been sighted. If so, our naval escort must have dissuaded them from attacking the heavily laden transports now approaching the North African coast.

Corvettes of the British Navy, appearing as we neared

Morocco, tackled the task of protecting the convoy the rest of the way. They would accompany the transports through the Strait of Gibraltar and in the Mediterranean to Oran, where it would be more unsafe for larger naval vessels. The battleship, cruiser and destroyers that crossed the Atlantic with us had turned back, their mission accomplished.

The corvettes, smaller than destroyers and only lightly armored, were highly maneuverable escort vessels, armed with antisubmarine and antiaircraft guns. Their crews, consisting of relatively few men, earned our esteem by their alertness, skill and daring. These little boats were continually dashing around the big transports, being able to change direction or turn around quickly. Their presence made the constant threat of enemy action seem less hazardous to us who now felt more exposed.

The Rock of Gibraltar stood out in bold relief as we sailed by it. I recalled the last occasion that I had seen it when, in a time of peace, as a ship's surgeon and in the company of Martin and Osa Johnson, I had looked upon it as one of nature's wonders. Now I wondered about the armament on it and thought of the phrase, "As strong as the Rock of Gibraltar."

A merchant seaman talked with us as we watched. "You'll be landing soon," he said and then added, "I'm glad it's not me. We're lucky that there was no attack on the way over. But our wages are very good. We get extra pay on these crossings because of the greater risk."

The members of my detachment were assembled with their gear when our transport docked. We awaited our turn to go on shore impatiently, so the delay seemed long. Thousands were being unloaded and the dock areas bustled with activity. At last we were on North African soil. We climbed into the trucks to which we were directed and rode through the streets and countryside to our space on Goat Hill, which was already dotted with scores of tents in rows.

Winter nights in North Africa are cold and we arrived during the rainy season. Wall tents had been provided for temporary shelter until we could set up our own, which would be a pup tent for each person. I went to the supply officer of an established unit near us and asked, "Can we borrow a blanket for each one of us? Until our supplies come, all we have are those in our bedding rolls."

"It gets colder here than you'd think. I'd better let you have three each; two should be put under you, where most of the cold comes from, and the other one over."

I am still grateful to this considerate American who, no doubt, had been reared to be kind, but I learned that his helpfulness was not atypical. Perhaps danger and unaccustomed hardships that, more or less, became common over there contributed to the attitude he exemplified.

Blackout, first experienced on shipboard, was enforced while we were in the Goat Hill camp and thereafter during the war. A candle or flashlight could be used inside a tent but the flaps had to be kept closed.

Army trucks bringing the rest of our hospital staff from the port of Oran, the detachment that had been on another ship, rolled to a stop in front of our headquarters tent one afternoon. Seeing those from whom we had been separated on the long, perilous voyage broke the tension that was natural under the circumstances. They were given a rousing welcome and asked questions such as "Hi, George! Where have you been?" and "What took you, Joe, did a sub get you?"

Colonel Gross gave a stern lecture at officer's call early the next morning. "You should have been in military formation and standing at attention when we appeared yesterday. I've been with some tough outfits. I was with Pershing on the Mexican border. This will be a disciplined organization and military courtesies will always be observed."

With this matter off his chest and as someone whispered something about "chicken" under his breath, the colonel continued, "We have a shortage of toilet paper just now, so when you go to the latrine of that General Hospital on the hill opposite us, you might bring back a little of their paper in your pocket."

After the meeting, Captain Wolcott and a few others, remembering what happened to Colonel Seward, were quietly singing a popular song written about the defeat of Germany in World War I, "We Did It Before and We'll Do It Again." Colonel Gross was destined to be replaced.

The following day, Lieutenant Weems was seen returning from the opposite hill, where the General Hospital was bivouacked, carrying a carton containing twenty-four rolls of toilet paper. "I thought that if I'm going to steal I might as well get enough to make it worthwhile," he said.

We slept in pup tents but did whatever we could to make them livable. Some of the soldiers who were on duty there for long periods had dug little caves in the hillside and in them had put many items that had been scrounged for comfort, such as floor boards, mats, shelves, shaving mirror and basin.

Captain Barnett and I decided that it would be an advantage to combine our two tents. We dug out a space the length of the two tents, with three different, smooth levels: the top one for our bedding rolls head to foot, the next one to stand on and the bottom one for water seepage. As it was the rainy season, almost any time that we touched the canvas above us a leak started at that point. A trench was dug around the tents to drain off the surface water to keep it from running into our canvas bedding rolls in which we were strapped at night.

I got into the habit of sleeping on my back, arms at my side, as turning over under the circumstances was difficult. It would not have been pleasant for anyone suffering from claustrophobia. At first, field mice that sought shelter in my tent disturbed me by running around my head and I put a few boards on edge around that end of my bedding to detour the little rascally rodents. But eventually I became used to them. It was reported that snakes crawled into a few of the tents. One morning I overheard, "An Arab shot last night was trying to steal a soldier's uniform as he slept."

When I took my bedding roll off the ground the day we left Goat Hill, I found that the area under it was honeycombed with the burrows and nests of field mice that had made their homes under me where it was relatively warm and dry. Perhaps the arrangement was mutually advantageous, an instance of cooperation between man and nature.

The North African flies were numerous, maneuvered in intricate formations and were more persistent than the North American ones. Threatening them was not enough to discourage them. They must have had military training. After they landed, it was almost necessary to brush them off.

Our drinking water, always chlorinated, we got from large, canvas Lister bags hung on wooden tripods. We ate C-rations from cans, either hot or cold depending on the situation and provisions for heating, usually in the open. When it rained the food became diluted.

One night nearly everyone had diarrhea at about the same time, which was near 1 a.m. To get to the latrine a hundred yards away on the hill beyond the big ditch, some sufferers had to hurry to avoid being late for the rally. On the way back they would meet their replacements. It was a day or two before we felt like laughing over our nocturnal excursions.

Shower baths installed on Goat Hill had canvas walls around them but were not covered, so in order to see while taking a shower, one had to go there during the daytime. We appreciated the opportunity and whenever there took advantage of it to wash our clothes at the same time.

We learned of enemy air attacks occasionally and looked carefully whenever an airplane approached to see what kind it was, whether it was one of ours or bore the swastika or cross of the German Luftwaffe, a Junkers Stuka, perhaps. Ground fighting was to our east. We heard rumors of what was happening and of plans for the use of our hospital. We were hungry for reliable news.

"A plane is coming this way from the north," I heard Lieutenant Cave say. Visibility was good.

"It must be a small German bomber, coming from that direction," said Captain Jones. "Maybe we had better take cover." I went outside to look.

"No, the shape is not right," Lieutenant Cave said, "and now I can see a star on it. It's one of ours."

The plane flew so low over our area that we could see the pilot clearly. He circled, returned and this time dropped a tiny parachute with a white object fastened below.

"That must be a message. The Germans may be advancing toward us," Captain Jones said, and there was increasing excitement in the crowd that had gathered.

"I'll get it!" Lieutenant Weems said. He and Stacey ran toward the place where the parachute was floating down and quickly returned with it and a piece of paper attached.

The parachute was made of a handkerchief. A string from each knotted corner was tied to one metal weight to bring it down. On the note was written: "You nurses had better put a cover over your shower unless you don't mind the observation planes. Observer."

Sidi-bel-Abbes, headquarters for the French Foreign Legion, one of the world's most colorful fighting forces, was to our south. While in Algeria we talked with legionnaires of various nationalities who greatly admired General Charles de Gaulle, leader of the Free French. They felt that he deserved more recognition by the Allies than he had been accorded. "He is a great man and could do much for our cause," they said.

"Last night I met with two French officials concerning a location for our hospital," Colonel Gross confided to us at a regular morning meeting. "We talked a long time. With the bottle of wine I bought for them, I think that I got a good place."

"The chances are that the Frenchmen took him," Captain Wolcott murmured as we left this meeting. "We'll see."

"Anyway I'll be glad to get to work," Captain Burk said. "I'm tired of waiting."

We left the Goat Hill camp by truck convoy, traveling eastward on the road known as "Messerschmidt Lane" because the vehicles on it had been strafed so many times by the German planes.

"I'm riding in the command car with Colonel Gross," Major Groen informed us. The rest of us climbed into the rear ends of the canvas-covered trucks, over the tailgates. We sat on the wooden benches that turned up on each side and extended the length of the truck body. A manned machine gun was mounted above the cab on each truck.

Our road ran north of the Atlas Mountains, south of which is the desert. Through the opening in the back of the truck we could see some barren land. However, as we were not far from the sea in a strip where there was rainfall, we saw fields of grain, orchards and grazing lands on which were small herds of goats, each under the watchful eye of someone, often a small boy in ragged clothes. We went through some narrow village streets under the gaze of many Arabs in their characteristic robes, the women heavily veiled, and a few French people in European dress.

This trip was similar to others we took while going across Algeria and Tunisia. There were not many civilian automobiles or trucks and these used charcoal for fuel. We saw many donkeys used as beasts of burden and frequently passed camels, often in caravans, and occasionally a beautiful Arabian horse.

"We have to be careful and not hit a camel," our truck driver said. "They charge our government more for a camel than they do for a person. A horse is more expensive still."

Whenever night fell we would encamp and be given rations. A temporary latrine consisting of a slit trench would be dug and filled in again when we left. All trash would be picked up before leaving so that the area would be at least as clean as it was before our arrival.

Our hospital was set up for the first time in the French—

278

Arab village of St. Arnaud. The theater and adjacent buildings were altered so that our patients, equipment and supplies could be accommodated. These alterations were done by a British unit already in the area. Being unaccustomed to the English tea-time customs or even to coffee breaks, our doctors, wishing to get started at taking care of the sick and wounded, watched impatiently as the workmen stopped work at mid-morning and again in the middle of the afternoon to have tea.

Artillery guns pulled by army trucks in long convoys rolled by on their way to the fighting lines. Traffic on the main road near which we were camped was mostly that of military vehicles rumbling eastward. The words of the army song, "As those caissons go rolling along," came alive.

The opening of the hospital was an important event for us; we had long looked forward to this day. Among the first patients were Englishmen, black men from the French African colonies with tribal scars on their faces and Indians wearing turbans. Watching through the wire fence were our neighbors, the Arabs, who were filled with curiosity.

Along with their professional duties the doctors were given additional assignments with the establishment of the hospital. I was appointed president of a Special Courts Martial Board of seven officers, was in charge of one of the three officer groups named to oversee the observance of camp restrictions and was a member of a council "...appointed for the purpose of auditing the Post Exchange funds and establishing the policies under which the Post Exchange will function."

Thus our mail was censored with me in charge of one of the large groups appointed as a censoring board for the hospital. Reading the letters written to the people at home and deleting those parts giving information not permissible under the rules was enlightening but not a pleasant duty. We were not permitted to reveal the part of the world in which we were located. Hints such as "I heard hyenas last night" were deleted as this indicated that the location was Africa.

Lieutenant Colonel Boyle, our new commanding officer, was a typical physician turned into an official in the army whose title made his opinions potent. His better qualities, his earthy sense of humor and gallantry toward the nurses, for example, were not always appreciated by the rank and file.

Roy Yeatts saw one of the enlisted men, apparently ill, on the ground in our area. He questioned him and was assisting him to the hospital when confronted by Colonel Boyle who said, "Captain Yeatts, you should not baby the men."

"He is sick, Colonel. I was helping him get to the hospital," Dr. Yeatts explained.

"Then let him ask for treatment in the usual way. You have plenty to do without going out looking for patients."

When not busy in the hospital, Yeatts tried to help sick people wherever he found them, whether they were in the army or natives in our vicinity as we moved across North Africa. Many of the inhabitants, it seemed, did not get adequate medical attention. We frequently noticed people, especially children, with eye diseases—even blindness—that could have been prevented or cured. Many of them suffered from malnutrition. Whenever any of us took a jeep trip into the country and stopped in some place to eat lunch where there was no one in sight, we would soon be surrounded by a ring of hungry-looking people and would lose our appetites. Children often asked for chocolate, giving it the French pronunciation.

Children frequently followed us when we went hiking or to drill. Sometimes they would have a formation of their own in the rear and, for fun, executed the commands in their own way. Often they were undernourished and inadequately dressed. One often thought of them, as well as of the sick and wounded, before going to sleep.

Walking alone on an exploration excursion, I followed a dirt road that was little more than a path through the almost barren hills where few people were seen. No enemies were thought to be in the area. I came upon the marble remains of an ancient Roman bath gleaming at the bottom of a hill and felt rewarded in my search for the unusual.

Suddenly a man appeared at the summit of the elevation beyond the ruins. He rushed down the hillside toward me, angrily shouting what seemed to be imprecations. His threatening attitude suggested that I was unwelcome there. Not looking for additional troubles in a foreign land, I took the hint.

I took another walk at the first chance and, because of interest, hesitated in front of the rural home of an Arab, comparing it perhaps with those in my homeland, when three or four men walked toward me. Although a bit apprehensive, I stopped. They appeared to be friendly, almost smiling, so I shook hands with them. Then each one touched his hand to his lips. I thought they wanted cigarettes. By words and sign language they were made to understand that I had none and did not smoke. The hospitable, dignified men informed me that they did not smoke either and did not want any cigarettes. We could communicate to some extent in French and they seemed pleased with my comments in reference to their farm. I felt somewhat embarrassed on learning that touching their hand, the one I had shaken, to their lips was a gesture of courtesy extended to me as a friend.

A wealthy Arab invited several of us doctors to have dinner with him at his home in the country. Although Algeria was under French rule then, he was the head man in that area and was recognized and respected by the French government and by the natives as a sheik.

The meal was served by men. It consisted of a thick soup; mutton, lamb and vegetable dishes, including artichokes; cous cous made from unripe wheat with a delicious sauce and, for dessert, sweets and fruit. No alcoholic beverages were served.

His women remained in the kitchen or their quarters and were not seen at all except veiled and at a distance when, with pride, he showed us his handsome Arabian horses and other livestock after our lavish dinner. The day was quite different from those we usually experienced.

The French people let us know that they did not particularly like for us to fraternize with the Arabs, which they seemed to think constituted a threat to their position. In the towns there was generally a group of enclosed buildings for the French officials and gendarmes assigned to the particular area.

Many nomadic families roamed over North Africa. They usually had a few goats, donkeys and a camel or two. After the wheat had been harvested they were allowed to glean the fields to pick up the straw and grain left by the reapers. They lived in tents and did not remain in one place very long.

"A nomad family out in the field was strafed just a while ago," Stacey told us.

"Who did it and why?" we asked.

"It was a small plane, R.A.F. Spitfire, I think, not one of ours. Nobody knows why—maybe just a crazy pilot wanting to shoot up a tent, one of those things that happens sometimes for no logical reason." We heard no more about it.

Once when taking a walk I passed a family of nomads. The man and woman, with a child or two, were outside the tent and she was cooking a meal over an open fire with a pot hanging over it on a tripod. A camel and a few other animals were tethered nearby. Their big dog, with hair raised and vicious, throaty sounds, came charging toward me. The man rushed after the dog, calling to it, and fortunately it stopped before reaching me.

Our administrative officer in charge of supplies, Barry Smiles, had a large white dog that stayed in the supply tent most of the time. Later he acquired a monkey that he named "Doc." It liked to ride the dog and otherwise entertain Smiles and others. It came to be the mascot and was taken along whenever the hospital moved. Once when we moved to a new place by train a young Arab boy we had befriended, a waif without a known family, went with us.

Patients in our hospital were mostly from the air corps at first. From fields in our vicinity they made bombing raids, usually on targets in Europe and especially those in Italy and Germany. We were getting almost as many road accident cases as battle casualties.

We saw planes leave in formations on missions nearly every day and became acquainted with many of the pilots, who came to the hospital to see the nurses if for no other reason. A few of them agreed to let some of the doctors go with them on a raid over Sicily. These bombers flew into intense anti-aircraft fire in the Palermo area. Flak was thick all around. Dr. Wolcott stooped to pick up something as he was struck by one of the missiles that banged into the plane; otherwise, his injuries might have been worse. He was struck across the buttocks.

The doctors had not been officially authorized to go on raids so our executive officers were in a dilemma and considered reporting Wolcott's wounds as resulting from an accident on the hospital grounds. Eventually, after much deliberation, it was decided that he was on the bomber as a medical observer and to treat casualties; doctors should know the conditions to which pilots are subjected in warfare. Wolcott was awarded the Purple Heart but because of the location of his wound, some wag said, "The wrong part of his anatomy was named in the award."

Another instance in which a question was raised as to eligibility for the Purple Heart award was when Private Ruston was injured as the result of tripping on a tent peg while running during an air raid. "It was due to enemy action," one officer said. "It was his carelessness," thought another.

Marion Malone, one of our nurses, had a date with a pilot for Saturday. They planned to enjoy a rare respite from the war at a club that special evening. He had an early-morning mission to knock out an oil refinery that was supplying fuel for enemy machines, tanks, submarines, fighter planes and bombers.

Heavy anti-aircraft fire was encountered and his Flying Fortress was struck. He was fatally injured, being dead on arrival at the hospital. His body was placed in the temporary morgue, an attended tent. To it Marion Malone went that Saturday evening. The war had added personal grief to her sorrow for its victims all around us.

I felt that we had been in North Africa for a long time when at the end of three months, while talking with a British Eighth Army soldier, I learned that he had been away from home for three years. My arrival in Algeria was comparatively recent, but I was becoming accustomed to walking past a huge bomb explosion crater, a camel livery stable, open-air barbers, scribes sitting on the sidewalk writing letters for people unable to write and other sights that seemed strange at first.

Paratroop patients from the 82nd Airborne, my old division from Camp Claiborne, Louisiana, told me of some of their experiences. On one occasion when they jumped, a strong wind struck the troops and their parachutes as they descended, causing them to strike the hard ground with such terrific force that about seventy-five of them received wounds, sprains, broken bones and other injuries.

Our guards around the camp area were sometimes quick to fire at a suspicious person advancing in the dark. Almost asleep one night, I heard a rifle shot and the whistle of the bullet, too close for comfort. The next morning Stacey told me, "When I came in last night, I saw the guard raise his rifle and aim it at me. I fell to the ground just as he fired and the bullet went over me." One of our nurses was shot through the hand by a guard who fired at the vehicle in which she was riding when it did not stop at his post.

Ward, one of the dentists, and I were standing near the hospital at lunch time when we heard a loud explosion. Then we saw, a few miles away in that direction, a great cloud of smoke mushrooming upward.

"We'll be getting patients from there in a little while," I predicted.

The first ones were there in about half an hour. Twenty-six were dead on arrival or died shortly thereafter, but over a hundred survived. An effort was made to treat first those most seriously injured who could be saved. One soldier that I saw there on the ground, propped against a wall, was obviously in an extremely critical condition. I went to him and knelt down. His abdomen had been torn open and his intestines were outside. This young man seemed to realize that he was dying.

He said with his last breath, "I don't want to die. I want to see my mama." That was not possible as death came quickly.

The catastrophe that had caused all these casualties was the explosion of a trainload of bombs. We did not learn how it happened. Fragments of the train and rails were thrown over a wide area of the countryside by the enormous force. I talked with some of the men who had gathered bodies and pieces of bodies of those who had been killed which were found in the railway area or where blown some distance away.

"Some of them were so mangled and burned and in such small fragments that they could not be identified. Lots of them you could not tell if they were black or white," one of the men said.

We tried to see regions and things of interest as our hospital moved from place to place across North Africa—the coast, mountains, desert, Roman ruins, cities and people. On rare occasions we could get a ride but usually walked and a few times ran. I saw odd combinations of draft animals. A cow and a donkey or a camel and a horse or oxen might be seen hitched to a cart or wagon and pulling a load. Camel caravans were often seen.

A man riding a donkey, followed at a respectful distance by his wife, was frequently seen. But in areas where there were land mines that might be detonated by man or beast, it was said that a man would let his wife walk ahead of him. I did not verify the latter.

The first time I saw a camel being used to pull a plow was at a distance. I asked the jeep driver to wait for me as I walked across the field to see it closely and take a picture. Then, riding further down this road, I discovered that in nearly every field there was a camel pulling a plow, often near the road.

Yeatts and I walked to a British radar station one day and talked to the man attending it. Leaving there, we were about halfway across the open space in front of it when the man called to us, "Hey, there! I forgot to tell you that the field you are in is mined!" We tiptoed out with care and fortunately did not explode any of the mines.

We were walking along the beach one day and I heard something strike the sand with a thud near us. We stopped, looked around and saw nothing to account for the sound.

"Maybe it was a big bug that fell," I said.

We walked a little further and heard the whining whistle of a missile and another thud, then another. We ran and got behind a sand dune, lay there a while, heard nothing, got up and again heard' bullets whistle close by. We ran to the next dune and waited. Every time we exposed ourselves this was repeated until finally we got off the beach. We never knew where the bullets were coming from but counted ourselves lucky and stayed closer to camp thereafter.

Towns that we had opportunities to see included Orleansville, Bougie, Philippville, Setif, Constantine, Bone, Sousse, Sfax and many other small old walled Arab—Berber communities along the way. I visited the Roman ruins of Djemila and was amazed, on reaching the crest of one of the barren hills surrounding it, to see parts of many great buildings of this ancient city still standing in marble grandeur. There stood the Great Temple, Arch of the Grand Cardo, the Arch of Triumph of Caracalle, remains of the Forum, Market Place, Bath and other structures, paved streets and chariot marks. Donkeys and goats wandered among the ruins eating weeds.

In Algiers several of us stayed one night in an ornate mansion, high on a hill overlooking the bay, which had been converted to army use. The architecture was Moorish and tiling in the rooms and passageways was of intricate and colorful designs. A row of rooms on the second floor had formerly been occupied by the owner's harem.

Below this mansion was the modern city and above it the old Moorish section, called the Casbah, crowded with people of all types. Its narrow alleys, lined with tenements, small workshops and stores in great variety, formed a maze in which a stranger might become lost. It was intriguing, nevertheless.

Once we were allowed transitory quarters in a schoolhouse room which we tried to improve for our use with additions such as boxes, hooks and temporary partitions. Lieutenant Barnsy acquired one side of a big packing case that would be useful if altered. He carried it out saying, "I'm taking it to a carpenter shop that I saw not far from here."

He had been gone about ten minutes when an excited young Arab appeared at our door and said, "Come! Your soldier passed out. He's bad off."

We followed him and found Barnsy lying on the ground as if in a stupor, his piece of packing case beside him. He was surrounded by a crowd of natives staring at him in amazement. We lifted him onto this large piece and carried him back. On the way he recovered to the extent that, when we arrived with our fallen soldier on the improvised stretcher, the others kidded him with "Like a true Spartan you came back on your shield."

Some of us were able to get rooms with French families for a short time in a village near our hospital in one of our locations. Chaplain Jennings and I got a room together on the upper floor of a well-built, clean home on the main street. There was a front balcony overlooking the shops and one above the back yard.

The front balcony was over the main street. From it I could watch the people in their varied activities and listen to the sounds as one sitting in a theater box watching the actors on a great stage as they appeared in costumes of infinite variety, some drab and some colorful. There were British soldiers wearing short trousers, men of the U.S. Army, civilians of all ages, mostly Arabs and French people and a few black Africans. Some people were well dressed; others were barefoot and covered with rough, loose garb the color of the soil. In addition to military caps I saw fezzes, burnooses, berets, turbans, straw hats and tropical helmets.

A large stork's nest on a nearby building could be seen from the rear balcony. I watched the great birds flying high with wide wingspread, feet back, circle beyond the village to return and alight with feet down and forward. Then they stood on a long, slender leg as if meditating over the population explosion.

"The nest keeps getting bigger," Madame Larousse, my genteel, eighty-year-old landlady said. "The storks add to it each year. The people, where they build, do not disturb them as their presence is said to bring good fortune."

Our food was that which the army supplied and consisted mostly of C-ration-type cans, powdered milk, powdered potatoes, powdered eggs and Spam. It was not the policy to obtain food locally. The people living there usually did not have enough for their own needs. Rarely we exchanged some of our supplies for fresh fruit. Once some pilots, for a special celebration, bought eggs from farmers in the area and paid one dollar each for them. "I'd give five dollars for a cold Coke right now," one of our young lieutenants said.

Madame Larousse invited several of us to have dinner with her one evening. The items that she could obtain were tastefully prepared and graciously served. The war "coffee," it seemed, had been made from a combination of grains, such as barley, that grew in the vicinity. The meal was a change for us.

After dinner Madame Larousse produced her Roman Catholic book of rituals and showed it to the chaplain. He compared it with that of the Episcopal Church and pointed out the many similarities. Sometime later he said to me, "I intend to run for Congress when I get back home."

I was on a mission with a few of our officers and when darkness came we were near a British field hospital. We asked if we could sleep there that night and the medical officers were hospitable. "You are welcome to eat with us," they said. We had roast beef for the first time since our arrival in North Africa.

"We have some vacant tents where you can sleep," an officer said. "One of the men will show you."

I put my bedding roll on the ground in one of them and was soon asleep. Early the next morning before I was awake, an orderly appeared in my tent with a pot of hot tea. This, apparently, was the custom with them, but it was the first time that I had ever been served tea in bed. To me it seemed ludicrous, lying there on the ground in a bare tent and propped on an elbow, sipping tea.

Food that we usually ate—the C-ration that came in small cans or the K-ration which was packed in water-proofed wax boxes, each package containing a meal—was high in food value. There was not much variety in our meals. A navy friend of Buchignani, Lieutenant Stark, invited several of us to their place for dinner one night.

"You will get something good to eat," Buck had promised. However, we were not prepared for the varied assortment of delicious foods that our naval friends put before us. We could appreciate chicken, beef and the many other items that did not come out of cans.

"We're on shore duty here at the port," Lieutenant Stark said. "We receive supplies for the area. This includes food and we get first crack at it so live very well." We could believe him.

Zaghouan in Tunisia was the nearest town to the last spot

where our hospital was placed in North Africa. The nearest large city was Tunis, the capital. As usual, when this hospital in tents was set up, some improvisation was necessary. This was especially true in respect to surgery. To avoid infections, efforts were made to keep dust and other contaminants out of the spaces where operations were performed by use of all means available.

Disinfecting or sterilizing materials and instruments was more of a problem than in permanent hospitals. Making provisions for securing an adequate water supply and lighting, for scrubbing, for maintaining asepsis, for patient protection and comfort and all of the other requirements for successful surgery and proper treatment under difficult circumstances called for ingenuity as well as work.

At first our water was hauled from an ancient well at the site of a Carthaginian or Roman community, of which little remained. Later we obtained water from a Roman aqueduct that was still in use. In the well we could see a mine. It had been installed by the enemy to explode when we, supposedly unsuspecting, would activate it, to our sorrow, by careless contact.

Yeatts, Barnett, Wolcott, Cave, Burk and I decided to try our hands at archaeology. At the first opportunity, we got some picks and shovels and selected an ancient dwelling, or what was left of it, not far from the well in which to dig. Parts of the walls still stood and within them was the dirt and blown sand that had accumulated through the centuries since they had been built.

We discovered some pieces of pottery in the lower levels but, being amateurs at this, were discouraged when, becoming weary after moving much earth, we found no whole pots. The most substantial object that we uncovered and that gave more satisfaction than anything else was what appeared to be a stone bathtub. Seeing this and small artifacts of another age that we unearthed rewarded us for our efforts.

We visited Tunis and the ruins of Carthage, one of the greatest cities of ancient times, as soon as we could. On the way we passed the surprisingly majestic remains of the long Roman aqueduct from Zaghuan to Carthage, still supported on its high stone arches.

The Carthage Amphitheater was filled with British army tents. Walking among the ruins, I thought of the period in history when, for centuries before its destruction, Carthage was famed for its size, commerce, wealth and the great empire it ruled. What would be the appearance of Washington, D.C., and our other great and important cities in two thousand years?

In Tunis I was looking at some curios in a store when an Arab boy came to my side and said, "I can show you a place where you can buy these things much cheaper."

"Can you tell me where it is?" I asked him.

"That would be difficult and you might not be able to find it, but I will go with you."

His command of English was very good and he could be helpful. After a little more conversation, I went with him. The way led through tortuous, narrow streets, crowded with picturesque people, the air laden with strange aromas and the little suks, or shops, filled with unusual items. The uneven pavement and debris on it in some spots took part of my attention, as did the craftsmen making a variety of articles. So I did not devote much attention to where we were going in the old town.

The Medina, or central city, was the primitive settlement of the native, walled town and several gates were still standing. It was quite different from the European part built in blocks and avenues, some of which were shaded with trees.

A U.S. military policeman confronted me and my Arab guide. "Sir, may I see your pass?" he said to me. A big crowd of Arabs quickly gathered around us to see what exciting thing was happening.

"I don't have one," I told the M. P.

"None of our military personnel is allowed in the Casbah without a permit. Both of you come with me." He conducted us to a jeep, where another M. P. waited to drive us outside the main gate and to headquarters. There the officer in charge advised me that, for their own safety, U.S. military people were permitted inside the Casbah only when authorized and in groups. "If you should want to go back another time, first come by here and get a pass. That Arab boy with you knew better. The French authorities will probably be tough with him."

I went back to the Casbah on another day but this time on a conducted tour with a group from the hospital, including Red Cross ladies. We saw the Palace of the Bey or ruler of Tunisia, the mosques and the other points of interest. But it was not quite as exciting as the first time.

Enemy forces had recently withdrawn from the Zaghuan area when we arrived, so we felt free to explore the neighboring

Atlas Mountains. We often saw knocked-out abandoned tanks and other military equipment, printed material, helmets with swastikas on them and a row of new graves with an iron cross at the head of each. A few times we saw one of our planes, disabled and smoking as it came down.

We walked up a mountain road looking at signs of the fighting there and, seeing some mounds of earth in line on a nearby knoll, went to them. They were crude, shallow graves and protruding from a few could be seen a leg or boot-covered foot.

Prisoners, either German or Italian, in compounds or being transported in trucks had become a familiar sight to us. An Italian was heard to say, "I am not a Fascist. Only our officers are." Mussolini's soldiers who had surrendered were not difficult to guard. One U.S. soldier in the rear of a big army truck could be seen guarding the truckload of prisoners crowded around him.

Doctors of our hospital were given temporary assignments with other military units in the area whenever we did not have enough patients to keep us busy. I took sick call each morning, for a short time, at a British field prison. Here, in a large enclosure, British soldiers were confined for various offenses. Those with injuries or complaints were conducted to the medical tent where I saw them, one at a time.

The soldier would advance to within a few paces. Then, if able, he would stand at attention until asked, "Fit or unfit?" in a military manner by the noncommissioned officer with a roster. The answer would be, "Unfit." I would ask for his complaint; get a brief history; examine and treat or prescribe for him; dress a wound, if needed, and make a recommendation. For "bad boys," they were very cooperative while I was with them.

Night duty included writing a report of an event when a record of it was indicated. The following is quoted from my recording of such an occurrence:

"On 16 January 1944, I was called to the enlisted men's mess in bivouac area of the Station Hospital to see Ernest F. Farmer, 34568476, identified by me by his identification tag, personal recognition and statement of his detachment commander. Examination revealed absence of pulse and respiration. Auscultation revealed no heart tones or breath sounds. The body was still warm. I pronounced him dead at approximately

0155 hours, 16 January 1944. In my opinion the deceased was not under the influence of alcohol at the time of his death."

Lieutenant Marc Erosco, Medical Administrative Corps, shared a tent with me. Two officers were assigned to each of the small, walled tents in the male officers' area. The nurses and Red Cross workers were quartered in tents on the other side of the supply, mess and administrative area, near the hospital tents.

Erosco had a problem about which he talked to me when bothered. He had met Amy Welles, was attracted, saw her a few times and became infatuated. Looking to the future, he worried as he thought of returning home without her.

"I don't want to give up my wife and our two children. One was born after I left. Maybe I could keep my family in one part of the city and Amy in another. Guess I'll talk to the chaplain sometime, but I've got a date with Amy tonight," he said one evening after mess while getting ready to go out as I prepared to write a letter.

A letter from Mildred had said, among other things, "Edwin's arm seems to be doing well, the doctor said." She wrote often but the mail did not come regularly or always in the order written. It was about a week before the letter came telling what was wrong with his arm. In the meantime I was puzzled. Not knowing the seriousness of his condition was worrisome. He or his arm could possibly be in danger.

The missing letter finally arrived with a few others. I read it quickly. It said, "Edwin tried to climb out of his crib while I was doing something on the other side of the room, fell and broke his arm. I saw that it was bent and took him to Dr. Lavender right away. He said it was a greenstick fracture, straightened it and put on a cast." Later letters assured me that the results were good.

Living close to nature as we did while trying to repair some of war's wounds, it was necessary to meet the challenges of nature as well as those of men. Changes in the weather to which we were subjected during our year in North Africa were felt more, no doubt, because we lived under unusual circumstances.

Our tents were erected carefully and special attention was given to the ropes and pegs to keep them from being blown down. Trenches were dug around them to carry rainwater away. The tautness of the ropes was adjusted for wet weather so that their pegs, pointed inward, would not be pulled out of the ground. We slept under mosquito nets in addition to taking anti-malarial pills, as we were in one of the world's major malarial regions. Nets to wear over our helmets were issued. As the pills made me ill, I relied on the mosquito bar when sleeping.

Toilets were outside and without the comforts of privies. Our latrines were essentially deep, open ditches located at some distance to the rear of our bivouac area. From time to time chemicals were added to the bottom and sides of a ditch and the accumulated material was covered with dirt. When filled, new ditches would be dug.

Helmets were found to be useful for many purposes in addition to protecting the head, such as for washing, shaving and washing clothes. Our underwear became rather dingy under this laundry system. In rare localities if we furnished the soap (a scarce item), women in a nearby village might be hired to wash clothes.

Siroccos—south winds, hot and dry from the Sahara Desert—darkened the sky with fine sand for days at a time and then there was a yellowish tint to the air for a while longer. The sand and dust sifted into just about everything that was not airtight—tents, bedding, clothes, food, equipment and hospital supplies. It even managed to get into foot lockers. Eyes and skin burned and throats felt parched, but the work had to go on. The possibility of contamination of sterile surgical supplies was a matter of concern.

At mess the tables and other things were covered with dust and when a plate was moved a dark ring was around where it had been. A girl who had not seen such as this before laughed hysterically and said, "It's so awful that it's funny."

Nearly everyone had diarrhea one night after a sirocco. It may have been a coincidence but Lieutenant Colonel Boyle, our new commanding officer, later said, "Our laboratory has not been able to find a cause for the illness that most of you had. The same kind of soap and water and method of washing were in use that day. It cannot be blamed on dirty utensils or spoiled food. Perhaps it was due to the large amounts of sand and dust we swallowed." The wind had blown down a few tents.

A cloudburst came after a long period of dryness. The rain was so heavy that it overflowed the trenches, covering the area where we slept. Water ran through our tents. We awoke to see everything floatable on the floor of the tent floating in the flood.

Temperatures varied greatly in Tunisia from summer to winter and a warm sunny day might be followed by a cold night. Instead of undressing when going to bed in wintry weather, one would be apt to add more covering to keep warm.

Erosco devised a contraption to heat our tent. He put an oil can on a stand and to its lower end connected a tube leading to a pan on the floor into which the fuel from the can dropped, regulated by a valve that he had difficulty in obtaining. Oil drained from our ambulances and other vehicles to be discarded was utilized as fuel and burned in the pan. I was skeptical at first and considered the possibility of an accident but it helped to keep us comfortable. It became the prototype of a similar device that was officially accepted for general use.

A world war, any big war, can be seen only as varied little pieces, one at a time, in a variety of places. These bits, when recorded, are put together by historians as a mosaic of the whole.

World War II was being fought on every continent and every ocean. An individual such as I could see, hear, smell, taste or touch only that taking place near enough to be perceived, although we had contacts with those of other units, especially the casualties. The action in any sector was not always as noisy or spectacular as one thinks of battles. I managed to read *The Outline of History* by H. G. Wells by utilizing spare moments while in Tunisia.

We read of happenings elsewhere in bulletins and in *Stars and Stripes*, the army newspaper which also carried pictures and cartoons of interest. I saw Bill Mauldin once when our paths crossed. He wrote "Up Front" and was considered to be the outstanding soldier cartoonist of the war. His popular characters "Joe" and "Willie," weary, unshaven soldiers in wrinkled, muddy uniforms, were rough but unselfish and were risking their lives.

Patients with wounds inflicted by the enemy were given Purple Heart awards. There were forms that we filled out for them and some soldiers received the award several different times. Sometimes when I asked for information needed on the form, a wounded soldier would say, "I don't want the award. I heard that they bring bad luck. If you get one you are apt to get another."

Captain Eddie Rickenbacker, the most famous American army aviator in France during World War I and the ace who brought down twenty-six enemy aircraft, came to our hospital to confer some special awards and decorations on a number of patients. During one of his tours during World War II, he and seven companions made a forced landing in the Pacific and drifted for twenty-four days in a lifeboat before they were rescued by a navy plane. After recovery, he completed his mission. He described this adventure in *Seven Came Through* and in his autobiography.

Captain Rickenbacker in World War I earned nineteen decorations for bravery in action. His experiences in that war are written in his book, *Fighting the Flying Circus*. Our patients who received the medals and ribbons felt especially honored in having them presented by this hero.

One of my patients described for me General Eisenhower's headquarters and its location. He had helped in its construction deep underground. "Layers of concrete and dirt over it are thick enough to keep it from being destroyed by bombs, or should be," he said.

Chaplain Matthews, a consecrated man who ministered especially to the spiritual needs of the hospital's personnel and patients, was later awarded the Silver Star for conspicuous bravery in action. Under enemy fire, he took a jeep, drove it onto a battlefield and collected wounded men for treatment and such solace as he could give.

Our doctors, nurses and administrative officers were by now able to work in their specialties or in positions for which they were best fitted by education and experience. The commanding and executive officers were physicians. One of our dentists had been rather gloomy but brightened remarkably when it was determined that he had malaria and was being transferred back to the states.

Erosco apparently had put home and the problem that he would have on his return there out of his mind for the time being. Girls, particularly Americans, were decidedly in the minority overseas so some of them enjoyed a popularity that they had never before experienced. They could perceive the aroma of orange blossoms.

Amy and Erosco, from all indications, enjoyed their evenings whenever it was possible for them to be together. They preferred to be alone, it seemed. One African night, filled with romance, they went forth for a stroll in the darkness of blackout conditions. Thinking only of themselves in their blissful state, they forgot where they were and stumbled into an open latrine, a revolting development in their heretofore exquisite relationship.

We wondered where our hospital would be sent after the fighting in North Africa stopped. According to most of the rumors, we would go to Italy, probably Bari.

When we rolled away from Zaghuan, strange as it may seem, there was a little sadness on looking back on the barren field for the last time where, for several months, we had known misery but had experienced such a wide range of incidents, sensations and emotions that a significant contribution had been made to our lives.

Bizerte, a port on the Mediterranean coast of Tunisia and the most northern city on the continent, was the next place we bivouacked. Here we were to wait until shipped to a location where our hospital would be established again. Axis forces occupied the city when we arrived in North Africa, but it had been captured by the United States 2nd Corps and allied troops.

Snow, the cold of early February and sickness were our main problems in the Bizerte camp. I had influenza with fever as did a number of others. Getting to the latrine, under the circumstances, made us more appreciative of indoor plumbing in the future.

Rome-Arno And Germany Campaigns

We had been in North Africa exactly a year the day we left for Corsica, the Mediterranean island to the north, just beyond Sardinia. It lies between the southeast coast of France and the northwest coast of Italy. I had not known much concerning it except that Napoleon was a Corsican, but I would live here eight months. On a hill among the olive trees, near the town of Cervione on the east coast, we raised our hospital tents.

Many of the olive trees were gnarled, had thick trunks and appeared to be very old. Local people said that some of them had been planted by the Romans centuries ago.

Deep trenches were dug for protection in case of attack. There was more danger from the air than from land or sea, or so we thought. Being hit by bombs was always a possibility.

Whenever we moved to a new place, particularly one taken from the enemy, a search of the area was made for explosives, land mines or booby traps that might be inadvertently detonated by weight pressure or by trip wire. Special trained squads sought these with detection instruments, then dismantled or destroyed them and designated spaces that were cleared.

Many British and American airfields, airplanes, airmen, and supporting troops for engineering, signaling, supply, maintenance, trucking, anti-aircraft and other requirements were on the island, as well as medical units. From these fields were flown missions to Italy, France, Germany and targets elsewhere to destroy factories, refineries, bridges, railroad yards and such that were aiding the enemy's war effort.

We did not get to hear a radio often, but there was one in a utility tent where some of us could occasionally listen at night.

An enemy propaganda program that we heard sometimes was that of "Axis Sally" broadcasting from Italy. One purpose of it seemed to be to make us homesick, worried over conditions back home, uncertain of our purpose overseas and to make us think that our efforts were futile.

"Axis Sally" would talk beguilingly, give some biased news and play some popular American tunes. One night she said, "That's a fine hospital you have set up over there in Corsica at Cervione. You will need it." At least her prediction was correct, as events to come proved.

Our troops had landed at Anzio, establishing a beachhead there. They were trying to break through the German defense lines. The fighting was heavy and, from the reports we heard, it appeared that our forces were having difficulty in holding onto the narrow strip they held. There was grave concern as to the outcome.

Some of our patients were from an army airfield about a mile south of the hospital at a lower level, nearer the shore. A few miles to the north of us was a British airfield with planes that were intended especially for night fighting.

American Indians from a nearby army security unit guarded our hospital for a while. Some of them had names such as Standing Bear, Running Wolf and Red Fox. A few I knew as patients. Indians were especially valuable in the Signal Corps. The enemy could not decode the tribal languages.

Our patients, in addition to ones with the usual surgical conditions such as appendicitis, hernia and hemorrhoids, were those suffering from injuries due to the war and its implements. Pilots, navigators and aircrew members flying at high altitudes, especially on bombers, wore electrically heated suits and gloves as protection against the intense cold. We had a number of them whose fingers were frozen when they had to remove their gloves for some reason.

A navy man explained to me how he lost his leg and received other injuries. "I was on the beach and saw something exciting happening near the water which was attracting attention. I walked down there to see what it was. A land mine had exploded, injuring one or more men. On the way I stepped on another one and it blew my leg off."

A soldier described the way he was injured and lost his hand. "I was fishing with hand grenades, would pull the pin, and throw the grenade in the water. It would explode, kill some fish and I would wade in and get them. The last time I tried it, I held it too long."

"We hitched up to a tank that the Germans left, to pull it away, and just as soon as we pulled on it the thing blew up," a patient with multiple wounds said. "You never can tell when that is going to happen."

Lieutenant Weems stopped the jeep we were in and jumped out to get a German helmet on a pile of rocks near the road but was warned in time, "Better watch out, it may be a booby trap!"

Each day I heard accounts of how injuries occurred, how vision was destroyed or impaired, how parts of the body or limbs were lost or damaged and faces disfigured. In some instances the patient was the only survivor of a group of men.

On Corsica, as in other sectors, when the patient load was not heavy enough to keep us busy, we might be given other duties temporarily. One month I was attached to the First Platoon, 15th Field Hospital, for duty. This hospital was smaller and more mobile than the station hospital and there was more informality.

The Field Hospital had to operate with less supplies and equipment than it normally would have on hand. Major Newton, the commanding officer of the platoon, spoke of this as we ate breakfast on a sunny morning with some of his men at a table in the open air outside the mess tent.

"We don't have much to work with because the ship bringing our hospital stuff to Corsica was sunk by a mine or a torpedo," Newton said. "I was on the same ship. It went down fast and I was in the water holding onto a piece of something that floated in reach until finally a British destroyer that came by picked me up. The worst part of it was staying in my wet clothes a long time before I could change. When I got back with the others of the Fifteenth I was a hero for about an hour."

One of our station hospital nurses had married a war correspondent and a few other couples were on the verge of matrimony, but the situation was different with the 15th Field Hospital. So many male officers and nurses of the unit had married that a special row of tents had been set apart for them, an unusual state of affairs for an overseas army hospital. The couples united in marriage could only hope that circumstances or orders would not separate them. They had not been disturbed at the time I returned to our hospital at Cervione.

Corsica, to a large extent, is mountainous and rocky with small plains along the sea and marshy lowlands on the central part of the east coast. I visited most of the important places of historical or scenic interest while on the island including Bastia, the largest city; Ile Rousse in the north; and Bonifacio on the southern coast.

At Calvi on the west coast we walked through the old fort. It was here that Admiral Lord Nelson, the British naval hero, in taking the city, received a wound in his right eye which resulted in the loss of sight.

In Ajaccio, the capital, we looked at the Bonaparte brothers' statue. Inside the house in the Place Letizia in which Napoleon Bonaparte was born, we saw reminders of the great military genius who became emperor of the French and brought glory to France when he dominated Europe. On a clear day, from a mountain on the east coast, we could see the island of Elba, where Napoleon lived in exile when his power waned.

Towns on the east coast were usually built on high ground, hills or mountainsides. From the sea a string of them could be seen, each with one or more Roman Catholic churches visible, generally the largest buildings. The inhabitants had found that they were healthier and safer at these elevations. They were less vulnerable to attacks from mosquitoes and belligerent men who came to this island to plunder from time to time.

Walking to Cervione was a pleasant diversion when hospital duties permitted, although some preferred to pitch horseshoes for recreation. The townspeople were more friendly than otherwise, often talked with us and sometimes would swap us a souvenir for something they wanted. In my travels I liked to save a few coins from each country visited, not for their monetary worth but for variety, artistic, historical and other values.

"What do you want to go into town for?" Barnett asked me once as I was leaving camp.

"For one thing, maybe I can get some coins for my collection. Want to come along?" I replied.

"I collect money, too," Major Groen interrupted.

"What kind do you collect?" I responded.

"Thousand dollar bills," he said with a smirk.

The road to Cervione wound up a steep hillside by olive groves, vineyards, orchards, vegetable gardens and grassy slopes where sheep grazed and past small old homes built of stone with chestnut trees, twisted oaks and flowering bushes around them.

By the side of the road was an irrigation trough with water from high above flowing through it. Some of the water was diverted to the side into each cultivated, terraced plot on the way down.

In town were the church, school, business houses, tradesmen's little shops and the activities of the people. I watched a man baking bread in a large oven, not in a building, a short distance from the center of town while others waited. The mound of dough would be put on a flat shovel with a handle about six feet long, placed in the back part of the oven and the shovel withdrawn. This was repeated with other mounds. When the hot oven had changed them into baked loaves of brown bread, the aroma of which filled the air, they were removed from the long oven.

Coming down a narrow street toward me was a long procession of people, those in front wearing priestly robes and many of their followers carrying bright banners. Some groups were bearing obviously heavy statues, such as usually seen only in churches. I got out of their way by standing in a ditch and watched as they passed in solemn but assured mien on this special holy day.

"The Fascists claimed that Corsica was Italian and they sent two divisions here," a Corsican said. "They got no support. We are French. Most of the Italians that live on the island are in the lowland towns. A German SS armored brigade came too and later there was a panzer division. The German soldiers were beautifully trained."

We learned that Free French units had landed at Ajaccio a few months before our arrival and, after the fighting, the Germans retreated to the mainland and the Italians to Sardinia. The Corsicans did not appear to be concerned regarding our presence on the island.

One warm day a few of us were out of place, it seemed. We took a little excursion by jeep and saw a lake that looked inviting. We decided to take a swim and removed our clothes except for shorts. We were enjoying the water when two M. P.'s appeared on the scene and one of them called to us, "The women from the village will be here to swim in a few minutes; you had better come out." Naturally we took his advice.

The army maintained a rest camp in a pine forest in the mountains near the center of the island. Our hospital doctors were assigned there, one at a time, for several days. It was a quiet spot of natural beauty which seemed far from the war.

The magnificent trees were tall and straight. It was said that from these forests the Romans got masts for their sailing ships.

Certain army hospitals were designated to treat particular diseases or injuries. To one, for example, were sent mental cases, to another those requiring brain surgery and to others patients in need of special treatment.

An Italian laborer employed by the U.S. Army to work on a construction job was injured by an object falling on his head, according to his medical tag. He had remained unconscious since the accident. I was volunteered to take him and a seriously wounded soldier to the 33rd General Hospital near Tunis by order of Colonel Harrison, our new commanding officer, who had replaced Lieutenant Colonel Boyle.

The pilot who appeared at the Borgo airstrip to fly us to Tunis was surprisingly youthful in appearance. I thought that he was the youngest officer that I had ever seen wearing the eagles of a colonel. A sergeant was with him. The unconscious man, on a stretcher, was placed on the floor to the rear of the little plane and I sat on the edge of the stretcher so I could watch him closely. My other patient was near, on the other side of me.

I was returning to North Africa sooner than anticipated. The flight was not smooth but in my position I could not see outside. After about the length of time expected to reach our destination the sergeant came back. Stooping, he shouted in my ear, trying to make himself heard over the engine noise, "The weather is too bad over North Africa to land. What shall we do?"

"Where can we land?" I asked.

"We could make a landing at Cagliari in Sardinia."

"Do we have a hospital there?"

"Yes; we could radio ahead and have them meet us with an ambulance. Maybe we can go on to Tunis tomorrow."

"We will land there if the hospital can take care of these patients properly."

An ambulance was waiting. The hospital was a large one and in a permanent building. It seemed to be well equipped and adequately staffed but on talking with the hospital's commanding officer I was advised of a complication. "You will not be able to take that Italian to Tunisia. The French would not allow it. They say that Italy stabbed France in the back and the feeling against Italians is very strong now."

"But my orders are to take him to Tunis. What can I do?"

301

I asked.

"You can talk to the commanding general for all of the Island of Sardinia if you wish, but I'm sure he will tell you the same thing."

I did talk with him. He was sympathetic with my position in the matter but unyielding. "We can't let you take that Italian to Tunis. It would create an international incident."

"Can this be settled with those in Corsica who ordered me to take him there?"

"I will write a letter to your commanding officer that will clear up the situation and get you off the hook. You can take your other patient to Tunis tomorrow if the weather permits."

This relieved me. I recalled that once when I was in Tunis it was reported that some French colonial troops the night before had been knocking heads of Italians against a wall. Our officers ordered all Americans to stay off the streets. "All" was underscored. I asked a young Frenchman if they would do to us what they had done to the Italians. He laughed and said, "No. The Americans would tear us apart."

Sardinia is the second largest island in the Mediterranean and is nearly all mountainous. Only Sicily is larger. During the war Sardinia became an important air and naval base for Fascist Italy, but in 1943 American fighter planes had smashed two convoys and destroyed many airfields. Italian ships lying in Sardinia's naval base were damaged by American Flying Fortress attacks.

Cagliari, the capital of the island, had a population of over a hundred thousand. One of my most vivid memories of this Italian island is of the donkey carts on the roads, standing or moving slowly. Brightly decorated in a variety of designs and hues, they were a colorful contrast to the background and our vehicles, which were drab or camouflaged.

The doctor in charge of the hospital assured me that there were specialists on the staff who were qualified to treat the patient that I was leaving with them and that they were prepared to give him every attention. I slept well in the hospital that night and the next day delivered safely the other patient to the 33rd General Hospital for further disposition. It would be a long time before he would be fit for duty, if ever, so he was probably returned to the United States. I returned to the hospital in Corsica, my station, at once.

A British engineer employed on a project near us mentioned his troubles when talking with me one day. "In England the army asked for an engineer to volunteer for an undertaking abroad to aid in the war effort. I volunteered and now all I'm doing is digging bloody ditches through these swamps."

The ditches were dug to drain off water that could be used by mosquitoes for breeding. Helping in this malaria prevention program was a Yugoslavian work company temporarily assigned to us. One day I went to see these men at work in the wooded lowland. When not working they would catch frogs, which were numerous there, and prepare them for eating over an open fire. Another measure employed by the army to control mosquitoes was the spraying of chemicals from airplanes flying low over the breeding grounds.

Doctors of our hospital were sent to a variety of places for temporary duty. One of these where I served was the Third Service Group Dispensary, relieving Dr. Cave. Here I treated some of the local people as emergencies. Several people injured in a car accident near us were brought in one night and I gave them attention, including minor surgery. They seemed to be grateful, were very emotional and, thinking that they could not express their gratitude otherwise, kissed my hands when the treatment was completed. A man that I treated in another instance brought me an egg the next morning, a token of thanks that was deeply appreciated.

Work in the hospital was not all strictly medical or surgical. For example, I received this order: "...in addition to his other duties, is appointed a Board of one officer in any case within the provisions of AW 105, and will likewise constitute the investigating officer and board of officers required by Army Regulations for the investigation of any accident involving death or personal injury. All investigations will be conducted in the manner and of scope and character provided by par 8 AR 25-20. Auth:...." That was the first time that I was a board all by myself, if not a one-man army.

Accidental wounds with firearms were common. Two officers who had arrested a man for rape stopped for the night on the way back to their station. While talking to us that evening an officer happened to point his pistol toward me and I said, "Point it in some other direction."

"It's not loaded," he tried to assure me.

"I've had many patients who were shot with unloaded guns," he was advised, getting my point.

303

The U.S.O. entertainers did not get to our hospital often but were appreciated when they came. We learned that they shared some of our problems. Even when performing for the relatively few who could attend a particular show, under the circumstances, they did it with as much effort and feeling as when playing before the capacity crowd of a large theater. An example of this was a singer from the show *Oklahoma.*

Jane Froman, whose back had been injured while on a tour, sang for us although she needed assistance to walk. I was near while she was singing and could see tears coursing down her cheeks. "You'll Never Walk Alone" was a popular song then.

Joe Louis, world's heavyweight boxing champion, visited our hospital to cheer the patients. They were glad to see the "champ" and joked with him. "Billy Conn will knock you out the next time you fight him," a poor predictor said.

We saw a movie once in a while, but usually it was shown by someone without previous experience as a projectionist. Often the reels were shown out of proper sequence so that the last part of the story might be seen first. Somehow a reel was occasionally started backward or upside down. A broken reel would sometimes cause a delay or the showing might be discontinued because of an air-raid warning. One of Bob Hope's movies was shown so many times that we came to expect it when there was an announcement that there would be a show.

A planeload of our patients was being sent to a sorting center, or "triage," as it was called, for disposition. Our forces now controlled Italy and the plane's destination was Naples. I was ordered to accompany these patients and with me were two or three other doctors. We were allowed a little extra time to accomplish the mission and return.

Ambulances met the plane and it did not take long to release our charges to the triage doctors and check the lists. After a short stop we went to Rome on the same plane. There we found Chaplain Jennings, who had been transferred to the transportation organization for Italy with headquarters in Rome. The commanding general was an old friend of the chaplain from his home state. We had dinner with them and saw what we could that evening and the next busy day.

The Colosseum, Pantheon, Arch of Constantine surrounded by protective sandbags, Arch of Titus, King Victor Emmanuel II Monument, Roman Forum remains, Tiber River and its fine bridges, Hadrian's Tomb, Piazza of Spain and the catacombs were a few of the many sights that we were pleased to see. Rome had been spared from attack, so war damage was not seen here.

Flying into Rome, the first thing that we recognized was the great dome of Saint Peter's, the largest church in the world. We visited it while in The Eternal City and were privileged to see Pope Pius XII and attend a service given for military people by the pope in several different languages, including English. Yeatts asked him to bless articles for some of his Catholic friends.

Our trip back to Naples was by jeep and through Anzio on the coast, where the beachhead had been established to start the campaign on Italian soil. After a quick look at Naples we returned to Corsica and our station hospital.

We heard muffled booming sounds to the north at irregular intervals, interspersed with bursts of gunfire that sounded like anti-aircraft fire, one night just before taps. "Hear that?" Jones said, and everyone in the tent listened.

"It sounds like bombs," Wolcott said. "I think that we're going to have a busy night."

Major Groen came in a few minutes later and said, "The British airfield up the road is being bombed. They will probably need help. Colonel Harrison said for us to fall out by the ambulances."

Four doctors were assigned to each ambulance sent to the airfield to treat the casualties there or bring them to our hospital according to what we found. "Blackout is still in effect so you will have to drive without lights," Major Groen said.

The road was not paved and our driver was not familiar with it. It became evident that we were likely to have an accident or get there too late to help some of the injured. Captain Jones sat by the driver.

"Turn on the lights or we'll never find our way," Jones said. "We might as well be attacked as wrecked."

We reached the airfield, located the senior medical officer there and offered our services. There was much hurried activity all over the place, with nearly everyone in motion. We were ready to bear some of their load.

The British officer paused long enough to say, "We can take care of our own. It will not be necessary for you to assist." Apparently their medical staff was sufficient for the emergency so we returned to our own hospital. The night was rather cold.

"They got caught napping," Captain Wolcott said. "Planes from that field were supposed to patrol every night and watch for enemy aircraft to prevent what happened."

It had been an exciting evening but nothing to compare with what was to come. After talking a while, we went to bed and had just gone to sleep when the noise of planes flying over the hospital aroused us. A moment later we heard the explosion of the first bomb dropped on the American airfield near us. This was followed by many more and, mingled with these tones of terror, were the almost continuous sharp reports of anti-aircraft guns and bursting shells and the roar of bombers flying menacingly low over us.

We did not crouch in the trenches that had been dug for situations such as this, at least I did not get in one. Feeling shivery in this cold, alarming hour before dawn, I decided to get as much rest as possible, before the casualties began to arrive, for the task that lay ahead. There would be little rest for us in the next few days.

Nearly all the patients in some ward tents were given intravenous fluids, saline, blood serum or whole blood. To meet the need, the laboratory personnel set up a tent to receive blood donations and a line formed in front of it. The blood type of each person was on the dog tags that everyone wore on a chain around the neck.

One of my patients who had manned an anti-aircraft gun said, "The planes bombing us were flying right over the hospital. If we had fired at them as they came in we would have been firing straight into your hospital." No doubt our gunners' concern for us had given the attackers an advantage so that they got more bombs on their target while technically refraining from attacking tents marked with the red cross.

Another patient said, "The Germans planned and carried out their raids very well. First they knocked out the British field and destroyed their night fighters and quickly followed it up with the attack on us. They made their bombing approaches over the hospital, dropped their bombs, then went out over the sea. The time that they were in range of our fire was short, not much chance for sighting, especially with explosions all around. That's why we got so many casualties."

The hospital received a citation for its action in response to the needs of this great number of casualties. We were awarded decorations to be worn on our uniforms signifying performance beyond the call of duty.

Every night after this disastrous one, at any hour from darkness until dawn, the drone of patrolling planes could be heard to give us some assurance that there would be no surprise attack that night.

Each morning we could see our bombers, usually in V-formation, flying northward. Once I noticed a large flock of geese in similar formation, in more nearly perfect alignment, flying near them as if to show the pilots how to do it. But one morning the flights were different in number from the usual and continued through the day.

That day a row of plane formations, flying toward France at uniform height, extended as far as we could see in both directions and they kept coming, wave after wave. No announcement had been made, but we were confident that the invasion of France had begun and this assumption was correct. Our work in Corsica was nearly over; France would be next.

The ship that took us from Corsica stood off the port of Marseille for three days—why, we did not know—and then landed at San Rafael. It was an LST (landing ship for tanks) type of vessel and was propelled toward the shore until the bottom rested on the beach at the bow end. The bow was opened, the ramp, or platform, was let down and we walked onto the sand. There were rows of massive concrete structures along the beach to stop tanks and some "pillboxes" built to protect anti-tank guns.

We were on the Riviera for two or three weeks before being given a location in which to establish our hospital again. We took advantage of an opportunity to spend a few days in Nice while waiting. I went with Groen, Burk, Yeatts, Barnett and Cave. We stopped in Cannes for a while and then continued on the scenic road following the Mediterranean coast to Nice. There we got rooms in the Negresco Hotel that the army was using for officers' quarters.

Going from bedding rolls in tents to a luxury hotel was a big change for us and we appreciated the brief recess. The regular hotel employees were still working there and the service was as usual but, because of the shortage of food in France, we had to provide our own rations. Canned goods and packages that we took with us were turned over to the dining room staff for them to serve after its preparation in the kitchen.

Cannes, we heard, was being used by the army as a rest area largely for enlisted men, while Nice was reserved primarily as a place for the convalescence and recuperation of officers. For those who could take advantage of the Riviera for a brief period during the war, it provided an attractive setting for quiet rest and recreation.

At dinner we sat at tables covered with white linen. China and silver service of character were still being used. Our dignified, distinguished waiter, in formal attire with swallow-tailed coat and with a long linen napkin over his arm, brought the dinner in a magnificent, covered silver tray. He proudly removed the cover at the table before us and "voila," there for our admiration were the items from our C-rations and K-rations that had been issued to us back at camp. We had never seen these served with such elegance.

After dinner we walked along the Promenade des Anglais following the curve of the waterfront, with the beach on one side and the long row of handsome hotels on the other. Most of us were impressed by the splendid view and commented accordingly.

"There must not be another quite like it," I said.

"Miami Beach is," Major Groen contradicted. "This is not my first time to be in Europe. I've traveled before."

The next day we noticed that the sand on the beach was not as fine and white as that usually found on the Atlantic beaches in the United States. Too, we discovered that the sea bottom was not as smooth, being more rocky. However, even with its faults, the scenery was wonderful and here was used the smallest amount of material ever seen in bathing suits. There must have been a shortage of cloth also in France.

At our last meal Major Groen said to our waiter, "We will take the rest of our rations with us."

"The rations that you gave me were used in the kitchen to prepare meals that I served to you," the waiter said with an expression of surprise.

"According to my calculation there should be some left over," said the major impatiently.

"I will see," said the waiter and shortly was seen with the chef. The head waiter was also approaching. The rest of us were not concerned as to the fate of the leftover C-rations and suggested that Groen forget about them, but he did not want to give up.

"You have to be firm with these frogs," he said to us and glared around. The Frenchmen were now talking excitedly together. Embarrassed by the unfavorable attention aroused, we left.

I recalled a little incident in North Africa when we were in a convoy. While we were stopped, an Arab boy brought to our truck some oranges that he wanted to sell. Lieutenant Weems haggled over the price with him for nearly half an hour and then bought some just as we were leaving. On the way we passed a number of storks standing in the tops of dead trees, in a row along the road, near their nests. Lieutenant Weems threw the oranges at them but his aim was poor as we bounced along and none was disturbed.

In France we moved from place to place toward Germany with the movements of the armies, by truck or by train. When by train, we would be sidetracked to let French civilian passenger trains speed by. A trip that normally took hours might take days and there were no provisions for sleeping.

While our train was stopped in one French town, some of us got off, found a lumber pile, returned with a few boards, pitched them in and got on the train as it was leaving. We laid these boards across the tops of the seat backs, put our bedding rolls on them and slept. Two missed the train but caught it at the next stop. The next morning the engineer let us have hot water from the engine in our helmets for shaving. On the ship to North Africa I had grown a mustache but did not like it and shaved it off.

Many of the railroad bridges in France had been destroyed and replaced with temporary wooden ones. Once our train, for some unknown reason, stopped on one of these that was unusually high and sat there for a long time. Looking down into the deep gorge and at the wooden supports, we wondered how strong the structure was. It held, of course.

"For the move tomorrow we are to have breakfast at 0400 and be on the trucks at 0500," we might hear the night before. This meant that we had to be up before four o'clock and the convoy which was supposed to roll out at five would probably leave about seven.

"Another snafu," someone on the truck would say after we had waited a while, meaning something like, "Situation normal, all fouled up." Lieutenant Lotti from New Orleans would take this as his cue to be the gang's morale booster and start singing a popular song. Everyone would join in and old and new songs would be sung, one right after another, to pass the time.

Some of the favorites were "Hail, Hail, the Gang's All Here"; "Oh, What A Beautiful Morning"; "It Ain't Gonna Rain"; "Happy Days Are Here Again"; "California, Here I Come"; "Sidewalks of New York"; "Carolina in the Morning"; "Loch Lomond"; "Oh, My Darling Clementine"; "She'll Be Comin' Round the Mountain"; "The Sweetheart of Sigma Chi"; "My Bonnie"; "When Irish Eyes Are Smiling"; "She Wore a Yellow Ribbon"; "Remember"; "I'll Get By"; and "Good Night, Ladies."

A few others that might be sung at such times were "Home On The Range"; "Don't Fence Me In"; "Moonlight Bay"; "Bye Bye, Blackbird"; "Swing Low, Sweet Chariot"; "I've Been Workin' on the Railroad"; "Hand Me Down My Walkin' Cane"; "There's a Long, Long Trail"; "Man on the Flying Trapeze"; "There's a Tavern in the Town"; "Old MacDonald Had a Farm"; "I've Got Sixpence"; the Australian favorite, "Waltzing Matilda," and a popular one of England, "The White Cliffs of Dover."

When we went through some of the little French towns by truck convoy, most of the population, men, women and children, would be on the sidewalks watching as the trucks rolled through the old, narrow streets. Many would give the "V" for victory sign and some would wave little flags and smile. Then, in other places, we saw young men sitting in sidewalk cafes sipping wine, apparently contented and perhaps pleased that they were not in uniform while the army of another country restored their freedom. We did not know their circumstances, however. Maybe some of them had worked in the underground.

Chalon-sur-Saone was the first location of our hospital in France. The other important towns in which I served were Dijon, Epinal and Chalons-sur-Marne. I was on temporary duty in several more places. Some of these were given names of cities in the United States such as "Philadelphia," a tented area as different from the "City of Brotherly Love" as could be imagined.

"Do Not Waste Food," "Take No More Than You Can Eat" and similar statements on large signs were posted in our messes. Checks of garbage cans were made to see how much food was being wasted. Food was being rationed in the United States and practically all we ate overseas had to be brought through submarine-infested waters. In our mess we had a choice of meals. As the sergeant said, "You can take it or leave it." Once we had "fresh" eggs instead of the powdered kind, which was regarded as extraordinary news. You could hear various ones saying, "I hear that we are having eggs for breakfast" and everyone got there early.

We did not realize how hungry some other people were. School buildings, barracks or similar buildings were usually utilized for our hospital in France and it was generally surrounded by a stone wall or a wire fence.

German prisoners were working at certain jobs around the hospital in our first location in France. After our first meal, when we started to the garbage and wash cans, these men rushed up to us to get the food left in our mess kits. Once when our train stopped, pieces of crackers and bits of food were thrown out the window. We saw prisoners picking crumbs out of the cinders by the train. In another location, well-dressed French people would line the wire fence near the mess with utensils for the leavings of individuals who did not eat all the food they had taken.

Our patients were now mostly land soldiers from the infantry and artillery. Often an injured man had many wounds instead of only one. Corporal Edgar Hargrove, for example, had seventeen in his body and extremities. He was on the operating table a long time but made a good recovery and remembered me. Mildred and I were on the main street of Jackson, Mississippi, after I left the army when we met Mr. and Mrs. Hargrove. He extended his hand and said, "I have you to thank." He informed our wives, "This is the doctor who took care of me when I got my seventeen scars. I'm fine now."

The number of patients we had at a time varied considerably. Soon after we arrived in one location in North Africa we were notified that we would receive five hundred patients the next day. Instead, we moved again on the next day. Thus was the uncertainty concerning what might happen. Sometimes neither the guards nor our patients were Americans.

"We are receiving five hundred Russian patients this afternoon," Colonel Harrison announced one morning. "They had been prisoners of the Germans and were hospitalized in a town that we took. Some of them have tuberculosis so the usual precautions should be observed. They are in charge of a Russian major. We will invite him to eat at our mess. You will be given a list of Russian words and phrases, with the English equivalents, that will be helpful."

Preparations were made for them and they were admitted with dispatch. Those known to have tuberculosis wore gauze face masks. Some of the men were weak and emaciated. A few of them had chain marks and sores on their wrists and ankles. They made us understand that at times, as punishment, they had to stand in a stooped position holding up one end of a log between the legs and, if they let go with their hands, the weight of it was borne on the wrist chains. We had only Russian patients while they were with us.

The Asiatic features of a large proportion of the Russians surprised me at first as I had always thought of Russia as a European country. Then I remembered that it is so large that the eastern part of it is in Asia and that it would be natural for the people in that region to have the appearance of orientals.

Russian girls in uniform, perhaps two dozen of them, were with the patients to give them aid and comfort. Some of them, admiring the things worn by the American girls, would pull the shirtsleeve of one of our nurses and by sign language indicate that they wanted such things issued to them. "I saw one of them in bed with a patient," the ward nurse informed me as a matter of fact.

The Russian major saw our officers' mess and thought that he was entitled to something better. Accordingly he was given his meals in a small room by himself. A clean bed sheet as a tablecloth and flowers that someone found were put on his table. Our C. O. felt that we should make every effort to appease and please the Russians. We learned that the commanding officer of the next hospital to which they went tolerated no nonsense from them. The disgruntled major had been captured early in the war and while he was held as a prisoner, his fellow Russian officers had advanced from grade to grade and were generals.

Our hospital was filled with German prisoners for a while. It was evident that they had lacked drugs and dressing materials. Their wounds were wrapped with paper, from beneath which ran thick, stinking pus. Military discipline was observed by these patients and the officer in charge of them, as it was by those Germans I had observed on work duty in the hospital elsewhere. Heels were clicked whenever I passed one of them.

"Achtung!" the officer would command my patients when I approached. Those able to stand would stand at attention until told to be at ease. At first I had an odd feeling when I was the only American in the far end of a long ward filled with enemy soldiers. I gave them the same treatment, however, that was given to our soldiers, even the new and precious antibiotics, as long as they were made available. Many of these young men had severe infections including osteomyelitis, infected broken bones. They showed concern for certain ones and would point to them when I came on the ward. Their injuries were healing and the stenches nearly all gone, with sterile gauze dressings covering all wounds, when they were transferred to another place.

We found that people of other nationalities preferred to be treated in our hospitals during the war when they had a chance. For one thing, we seemed to have more supplies than the others.

The many hundreds of United States soldiers with battle wounds that I treated included a number of American-born Japanese. The 100th Infantry Battalion, formerly a National Guard unit in Hawaii, composed of volunteer Americans of Japanese ancestry, was outstanding for the many decorations awarded its members for their conduct in combat. I asked a wounded patient, for whom I was filling in a form needed for an award, "What is the address of your parents?"

"They are in a concentration camp in Utah," he answered.

Pearl Harbor had aroused public opinion against all Japanese in the United States and a War Relocation Authority was created under which all American-born Japanese in the United States, as well as enemy aliens, had been moved away from factories and defense installations. The parents of my patient had thus been displaced from his and their home while, ironically, he served the land of his birth in such a way as to merit a decoration.

Buildings that had previously been occupied by the Germans were sometimes used for our hospital. The walls in one were adorned with excellent paintings, mostly comical, by some talented artist. I was reminded of them when, much later, I saw the walls in a venerable building formerly used as a prison for unruly students in Germany's oldest university, Heidelberg. The ceremony of raising our flag on the high pole in front of the hospital where the flag of the enemy had flown was a thrilling experience.

Repairing and dressing wounds occupied most of my time.

Usually a first-aid bandage had been applied on or near the battlefield. Occasionally the bleeding was profuse when this was removed. In one case, for example, blood gushed from an extensive, deep wound of the groin which involved the upper part of the thigh and lower abdomen. The hemorrhage could not be controlled by the accepted, standard methods. However, to be sure that nothing was left undone, I asked Major Groen, the chief surgeon, who happened to be in the room examining other casualties, to assist me, although he had never been helpful before. I learned that actually I could rely only on my own knowledge and skill as he was of no assistance. Groen, too, was only human, regardless of what he professed.

Surgical teams from our hospital were sometimes placed on temporary duty elsewhere. Captain Cave and Captain Lotti were sent to Dachau and Buchenwald, where many Jews had been gassed and cremated. On their return they mentioned the ovens and other gruesome features but did not seem inclined to elaborate on what they saw, although Captain Lotti did say, "It was horrible."

Captain Cave once found that he was behind the German lines, such were the movements of the armies. Another time he left his clothes in a village to be laundered. Enemy forces overran the area and he had to wait a few days before it was retaken by our troops and he could recover his laundry.

Minor incidents are often recalled long after momentous ones are forgotten. "Don't you salute, Captain?" an officer asked me as I passed him. I looked up and saw that it was a major wearing the insignia of the 101st Airborne Division with the screaming eagle shoulder patch. Maybe he did not expect much military courtesy from medical officers, but he had been given the duty of enforcing regulations in the town where this famous division was at the time. Other officer patients had said to me, "I hate that kind of duty, but someone has to do it or the army would get lax."

Our nurses were invited one day as a group to attend a dance to be given that night by the officers of a unit stationed near us at the time. It came as a request through the commanding officer. The nurses had been overworked because of an unusually large number of casualties, were near exhaustion and in no mood for dancing. In addition, they did not appreciate the way in which the invitation was extended. It seemed to be in the nature of a requisition.

"If ordered to go, we will wear our combat boots and fatigues," I heard Susanne Searron say. Ordinarily she was pleasant and agreeable. She and Warrant Officer Boddeau had been seeing each other, whenever there was a chance, for several months. Although there was not much enthusiasm for that dance, some of the nurses volunteered to go but not for very long.

"Susanne and I want to get married," Boddeau confided. "But there is a lot of red tape, ours and the French. We have to get it authorized, then have a license for a civil, also a church ceremony. To make it more complicated, I am a Protestant and Susanne is a Catholic. We are going to see a priest in town tomorrow. Would you like to come along?"

I waited outside while they talked with the priest. When they came out they did not appear unhappy but he wore a rather serious expression. "I will have to come back and receive instructions," he said. "Anyway, we've got things started."

We tried to see as much of France, Luxemburg, Germany and Belgium as circumstances permitted at various times. Riding in a jeep to Nancy, where Gen. George S. Patton had his headquarters, we were on a road along which the Germans had planted mines. Tape fastened to stakes on each side of the road marked the strip that had been cleared of land mines. Along the way were slogans on small, simple signs such as "Keep 'em rolling. Stay out of the ruts. Get the ammo to Blood and Guts." "His guts, our blood," was a soldier's quip.

Military policemen stopped us at one point and said, "You had better put on your ties and straighten up. You're in Patton territory now." We had heard that in one of the hospitals Patton had slapped a soldier suffering from battle neurosis that Patton regarded as cowardice. Gen. Dwight Eisenhower had him apologize for this act.

On one trip we ate a meal with some officers who had been on a boar hunt. The meat was a delicious variation from our usual fare. I wondered if it might be a cut from some farmer's hog that unwisely strayed into the woods too near our troops craving fresh pork.

Early in December, 1944, American armies hammered at the great Ruhr and Saar industrial regions of Western Germany in rain, fog and snow, while mighty Allied air fleets blasted the Reich railheads behind the bending German lines. The enemy was beginning to weaken, or so it seemed to us. Then came the

"Battle of the Bulge." The German armies struck on December 16 and the center of the attack bulged fourteen miles the first day.

Bastogne in southern Belgium was soon surrounded by the Germans and they pushed on. No one knew how far the push would extend, but it appeared that our hospital might be taken. Yeatts and several other doctors volunteered to remain with the patients and become prisoners should this occur. Our load was heavy at this time.

The defenders of Bastogne had been reinforced by airborne troops, but the city was under siege with no relief in sight. Within the heavy lines of enemy armor all around was the outnumbered 101st Airborne Division, commanded by Brig. Gen. Anthony C. McAuliffe. According to the *Stars and Stripes*, he received this message:

"To the U.S.A. commander in the encircled town of Bastogne. The fortune of war is changing. This time U.S. forces in and near Bastogne have been encircled by strong German armored units....There is only one possibility to save encircled U.S.A. troops from annihilation. That is, honorable surrender of the town. In order to think it over, a term of two hours will be granted, beginning with the presentation of this note.

"If the proposal is rejected, a German artillery corps and six heavy AA battalions are ready to annihilate U.S. forces in and near Bastogne. The order for firing will be given immediately after this two hour term." Signed, "The German Commander."

The German commander received the following reply: "To the German commander: N-U-T-S." Signed, "American Commander."

This one word used by General McAuliffe in his response, which was so meaningful to us and puzzling to the German commander at first, did much to boost our morale. We no longer felt that our hospital might be captured.

General Patton's Third Army, which in the autumn had taken Metz, the first time the city had been taken by assault in 1,500 years, drove north 150 miles in three days to relieve Bastogne and to beat back Marshal von Rundstedt's men. Germany's last major offensive collapsed.

A military cemetery was being established at Bastogne when I went there with a few other medical officers. "The bodies are being gathered from other places in this area and are brought here for burial," the graves registration officer said. "The worst thing to contend with is the odor." Gliders that had been used to bring relief by air were still lying in the fields around the city now quiet and calm.

Ground that had been lost in the German offensive was quickly regained and this was soon followed by rapid advances by the Allies on all fronts. The holding of Bastogne and turning of the tide, coming just before Christmas, was as a present to our country. It permitted us to observe the day in our hospital with a special dinner for patients and personnel. Our officers were privileged to serve the enlisted men on this occasion.

Back on the ward I asked a young infantry officer, whose battle wounds I was dressing, "What stopped the offensive; did they reach a natural barrier such as a river, or what?"

"It was the guts of the American soldiers," was his answer.

The most pleasant temporary duty to which I was ordered was in Paris, where I was assigned for a few days to assist with the investigations of a congressional fact-finding committee. I stayed near the Arc de Triomphe in a small hotel used by the army. A sign in the lobby announced when hot water would be available. Fuel was scarce. Blackout at night was still in effect, yet there was much to be seen in this remarkable city. It had been spared by the bombers.

The delegate from Hawaii, our island territory where over a third of the people were of Japanese ancestry, talked with me concerning my Japanese-American patients and their attitudes. He particularly referred to the relocation camps for citizens on the West Coast. To me it seemed that these soldiers, while not happy with the situation, were making a special effort to show evidence of their loyalty to the United States. More than one thousand Purple Hearts, forty-four Silver Stars, thirty-one Bronze Stars, nine Distinguished Service Crosses and three Legion of Merit medals had been awarded members of the 100th Infantry Battalion since it landed in Italy, according to figures I had seen in July. Fifteen battlefield commissions had been awarded to its enlisted men, all volunteer Americans of Japanese ancestry.

"We are meeting with General Eisenhower today," a committee member said to me. "I asked if you could come but was told that the meeting place was too small to admit any more, so you will be on your own." This gave me a chance to visit some of the places that interested me, including the Palace of Versailles

317

built by Louis XIV where, in the Hall of Mirrors, the treaty ending World War I was signed.

In the Louvre, the largest art gallery in the world, I found that most of their famous paintings, such as the Mona Lisa, and other art objects had been removed and hidden for safekeeping until the war ended. I did get to see this and other magnificent buildings and the Garden of the Tuileries. That night I saw the glittering Folies-Bergere, then had difficulty finding my way back to the hotel in the darkness.

A citizen pulled me out of a line in the Metro, or underground, where I was awaiting my turn to buy a ticket and said, "Go and get on the train. You don't have to pay. The Germans never did."

Some of the other things that I remember about my first visit to Paris were the wide Avenue des Champs-Elysees; the unknown soldier's grave and flame honoring him beneath the Arch of Triumph; Place de la Concorde, site of the guillotine where Louis XVI and Marie Antoinette lost their lives during the French Revolution; Cleopatra's Needle, an Egyptian obelisk; Place Vendome, a few blocks away; Les Invalides and the tomb of Napoleon; the majestic Gothic cathedral of Notre Dame with its twin towers; the Church of the Sacred Heart, high on Montmartre; the Eiffel Tower; the absence of skyscrapers; the presence of the Parisians; eating at the Ritz; and meeting our ambassador and congressmen from home in wartime.

Back in the barracks, Boddeau and I had another talk about his and Susanne's marriage-to-be. "For seven generations the men in my family have either been Episcopal ministers or had army careers. I'll be the first one to be different. Where I live, they think that if you are of the aristocracy it does not matter what you do, you are still an aristocrat. Maybe I'll be the black sheep," he said.

"Did you and Susanne get a license and all the approvals you need?"

"The priest wants to see me again. I have to learn some things and agree to bring up any children that we have as Catholics. I'm willing. We may get separated while we're in the army. I'll find out what the old man, the new C. O., has to say. Maybe we can be ordered back to the states at the same time when the fighting stops here or only one of us could be sent to the Pacific." I did not see Boddeau for several days after this.

Burk, Yeatts, Barnett, Cave and I were assigned to a duty

tour that included Luxemburg, then Liege and Brussels in Belgium, as well as Aachen, Germany. We entered Luxemburg by a bridge over a deep gorge, the heavy stone fortifications of which were built in the Middle Ages and were similar to the Morro Castle guarding the entrance to Havana harbor in Cuba. The city, which had recently been under German occupation, appeared undamaged, standing on a high, rocky promontory surrounded by steep cliffs. Extensive caverns that we were shown reminded me of the catacombs of Rome. They were said to be large enough to hold the entire population of the city in case of air attack and their use went back to the days of the Roman Empire, of which Luxemburg was a part.

The people of the duchy said that their language was "Luxemburg" but we found that it was based on German. The Grand Duchess had returned to the large palace, with its beautiful recessed windows and old towers, after the German army retreated. We asked to confer with her but the guard informed us that she was at dinner and could not be disturbed.

The sounds made by the wooden shoes of children running on village cobblestone-paved streets is one of my memories of Belgium. In Liege the medical officers of our hospital there spoke of a new kind of German bomb that had been falling in the city. It made a buzzing sound and the damage caused by it was not limited to the initial point of impact. They called it a buzz bomb and thought that it was one of the secret weapons to which Hitler referred near the end of the war in Europe.

Brussels, one of the first Belgian cities occupied by the Germans in World War II, showed no appreciable damage to the King's Palace or the old market square area, called the Grande Place, around which the merchants of the Middle Ages met to trade and talk. Some of the buildings were of unusual construction with carvings and fronts that shone like gold, parts of them having been built in the early thirteenth century. The old town hall, the Church of Sainte Gudule and the trade-guild houses attracted our attention more than the modern buildings.

Costumed women were making lace in a few shops facing on the old square. Our interest in their skillful handiwork seemed to please the ladies and I bought a lace butterfly for Mildred as a souvenir of Brussels.

Crossing the German border near Aachen, we read the huge billboard-type warning sign placed there by our army which, among other orders, stated: "Do Not Fraternize with the

Enemy." In some French towns we had been ordered to wear our steel helmets because of the danger of snipers. We heard stories of atrocities on both sides.

"Never trust Germans, collectively or individually," was one of General Bradley's special seven orders. This was in the back of our minds when, as we were lost on a back road in Germany, the sun descended, the shadows lengthened and darkness came. But we got back safely to our station hospital. We were impressed by the industry of the German people in cleaning up the rubble and repairing damages caused by the war.

"Boddeau has been drinking," Captain Cave said, looking out at the company street. "You can tell by the way he walks like on a straight line, not looking to the right or left, very sedate and dignified. He's a real officer and gentleman." I noted that he was rather stiff, his face flushed.

All the obstacles to his marriage with Susanne were eventually overcome, the day was set and we shared their happiness at the wedding impressively performed in the attractive local church. Fortunately for them, the war in Europe was almost over. Our participation in it had not started when Mildred and I had married back in Vermont.

A disturbed soldier, murmuring of hallucinations and wandering around, was one of the types that could be seen in overseas military hospitals, but I rarely saw such persons. War neurosis, shell shock and battle fatigue were some of the terms used to describe certain disorders without demonstrable lesions. Most of my patients were GI's with GSW's received in action on battlefields.

While serving in the 239th General Hospital, however, I had about thirty-five on a special ward whose gunshot wounds were different. They were self inflicted, either accidentally or intentionally. Determining which, in a particular case, was often difficult. If the wound resulted from an effort to avoid duties, the soldier was subject to court-martial and this procedure had been recommended, after investigation, in some instances. This did not interfere with their treatment.

The foot, generally the right one, was a common site of injury. Usually a rifle bullet had gone through the foot just back of and between the first or big toe and the second toe. Thus the wound was of the fore part of the foot between the bones, which was not very disabling.

In answer to the question, "How did it happen?" one

soldier said, "I rested the muzzle of my rifle on my foot and it was discharged accidentally."

Another said, "I didn't think it was loaded when the trigger was pulled. It was a big surprise to me."

"I was cleaning my rifle and it went off. The projectile happened to go through my foot," was the way one man explained his injury.

"While I was sitting in front of my tent, a bullet came from somewhere and hit me. I don't know where it came from. Somebody just shot, I guess, and it happened to hit me," was the explanation of one patient. "Just a freak accident, is all I can say."

The war would go on and on, it seemed. A year passed as we crossed Algeria and Tunisia toward Libya, most of the next year while in Corsica, and month after month on the bloody way through France to Germany. Then one day we heard, "Hitler is dead!" Apparently death had come to him and Eva Braun, both by suicide, on April 30, 1945, in the shelter of the Reich Chancellery, a day after their marriage.

Mussolini, the Italian dictator, and Clara Petacci had been apprehended by Italian underground troops and "tried and executed" two days before near Como. It was said that they were shot to death and their bodies taken to Milan and hung by their heels in front of a garage. Later they were buried. Surely the war would end soon.

Peace And Civilian Practice

"Germany has surrendered! We can all go home now!"
someone shouted one day a week after Hitler's death. Nearly
everyone seemed excited and happy over the news, but they
reacted in different ways. "That's too bad. I wanted to stay in
Europe a while," a disappointed individual said. Maybe he had
not been there as long as some of us had. Another said, "I suppose we'll be sent to the Pacific Theater next. The war is still
going on there."

All could not go home at once. I wondered when my turn
would come. It could not be too soon for me. Much remained
to be done, however, and months would pass before I could
return to our homeland and be with my family again. Anyway,
the sounds of artillery were heard no more.

General Alfred Jodl signed the unconditional surrender of
Germany in a red brick schoolhouse in Reims, where General
Eisenhower had his headquarters, early on May 7, 1945. Later,
several of us rode through quiet vineyard country, where the
white grapes for champagne are grown, to that small building
and went through all the rooms of the various allied officers.
The long table in the large room where the signing, a momentous historical event, took place was still in the same position.
Place cards indicated where each participant in the ceremony
had sat. That of General Jodl was of special interest. Weeks later
he was arrested, tried at Nurnberg as a war criminal and eventually hanged.

A huge military situation map was hanging on a headquarter's wall showing the positions of the many enemy units as
well as those of the Allied forces. I would see this remarkable

map again, as an exhibit, hanging in a great building on Constitution Avenue in Washington, D.C.

The magnificent Cathedral of Notre Dame in Reims, which was started in 1211, was still standing although damaged in two world wars. One tower showed results of the shelling in 1940 by the Germans, who occupied the city from then until 1944. Nearly all the French kings were crowned in this cathedral, which is one of the world's most beautiful examples of Gothic architecture. It towers high above the modest structures around it. One of the many statues of Joan of Arc in France stands near the cathedral.

At what time a soldier could be returned to the United States was determined by a rotation system based on points that were related to the individual's service and the length of time overseas or by disabilities that made one unfit for duty. Those who had been thrown together at Fort Rucker, Alabama, and had served together in so many places were now separated. A few were ordered to the Pacific islands. Some of us would keep in contact in civilian life.

Doctors that I had worked with overseas came from New Orleans, Vicksburg, Greenville, Memphis, Nashville, Savannah, Indianapolis, Chicago, Youngstown and a dozen other places. Certain ones I would see again.

The 119th Evacuation Hospital was the last one to which I was assigned overseas and with it I would return to the States. We spent our last days in France in a camp on a wooded hill above the port of Le Havre, from where we sailed for Southampton, England. As General Eisenhower said, we were glad that the British were on our side in this war.

We begrudgingly conceded, with all our complaining of the army way of doing things, that it was generally effective in providing essentials such as food, clothing, shelter, material, transportation and organization while fighting a war. The British brick barracks of a tank unit in the Downs of southern England sheltered us for a few weeks as we awaited our turn for the voyage home. In the meantime we kept busy seeing as much as possible from Bournemouth, a seaside, shivery resort on the Channel coast, to Edinburgh and Glasgow in Scotland, in this land where the inhabitants spoke a sort of English.

The fast train from London to Edinburgh was comfortably filled with passengers whose moods suggested that they were feeling relief from the long ordeal through which they had suffered. An engineer with whom I talked part of the way explained to me why British trains and locomotives were better than those in the U.S.A. "Your builders add too many frills at the expense of basics and efficiency," he said. This reminded me of an incident that occurred in North Africa when the train on which we were riding stopped at a station where a German hospital train standing on a siding aroused our interest and a few of our doctors boarded it. A German medical officer showed them the equipment, bunks for patients and provisions for treatment. One of our officers said, "Your hospital trains are very much like ours."

"You mean that yours are like ours," retorted the German. It was probably true that the Germans had some of these before we did.

On the way to Scotland I tried to see some of the English countryside from the train. There was so much to be seen—towns that were old but new to me, factories, homes, little farms, pastoral scenes. I was sitting next to the aisle, sharing a seat with a small, elderly gentleman. After a while he went to the rear and I slid over to the window. My enjoyment of the view was abruptly disturbed by "Sir! You are sitting in my seat," said imperiously. Looking up, I saw my traveling companion standing very erect and glaring at me, so, after making a quick estimate of the situation, I moved.

A man across the aisle, noting the behavior of his fellow countryman, appeared chagrined and offered me his magazine. "Would you like to look at this?" he asked. His gesture was appreciated and it was accepted with my thanks.

My walking tour of Edinburgh, Scotland's capital, included the large Sir Walter Scott monument in a garden and, beyond it on a high hill, Edinburgh Castle. Holyrood Castle, home of the Stuarts before they became kings of England, was a tranquil spot when I visited it. Next I was pleased to pay my respects to the university and its famous medical school, about which I had often heard. The Royal College of Surgeons, chartered in 1505, which occupied a classical building, was of special interest to me as a Fellow of the American College of Surgeons.

I rode a bus to Glasgow and got off in the business section of this city, which is the largest in Scotland and an important manufacturing center. Looking for a souvenir in a store, I saw berets for children and thought I would get one for Edwin, but they asked me for a war ration ticket. A Scotsman, seeing my predicament, gave me one of his tickets, an act of generosity which was disillusioning but not unusual, I discovered. Now I had a child's beret to take home with my sprig of heather.

The cathedral which dates from the 1100's, the University of Glasgow, endowed by Mary Queen of Scots and her son, King James I of England, and the City Museum were among the impressive things I saw. These, however, were not as moving as a boat ride on Loch Lomond, famed in tradition, song and story, among the hills about twenty miles northwest of the city. I found this to be a recreation area with structures and homes around it, but still a large, very long, beautiful lake with many islands in it and nearby mountains. Scotsmen's sentimental attachment to Loch Lomond was understandable.

At Clydebank, a suburb of Glasgow, one of the world's greatest shipbuilding centers, I saw where a great variety of vessels, from the small to the huge, were built. These included the giant liners, the *Queen Mary* and the *Queen Elizabeth*, which carried over a million soldiers across the Atlantic while serving as transports during World War II.

In London thousands of buildings had been demolished by the bombs of various kinds that fell on the city during long periods of the war. I saw block after block where nothing was left standing and numerous others in which buildings were completely destroyed, reduced mostly to rubble or damaged to some extent.

Buckingham Palace, St. James Palace, Westminster Abbey and the Houses of Parliament had been damaged but were standing. The damage to St. Paul's Cathedral was slight. Big Ben, although shaken by the bombs, was still ticking. Much of the debris had already been removed and the lights of London had been turned on again. The city seemed to be recovering from the most trying test in its long history. Most of its historic institutions stubbornly remained.

In the British Museum, I gazed upon the collections from the Greek, Roman, Egyptian and Assyrian civilizations; the Elgin Marbles; sculptures; mummies; and the famous Rosetta Stone. I visited the "Old Curiosity Shop" where a Charles Dickens character, Little Nell Trent, had lived. As I walked across the famous bridge over the Thames River, I thought of the song that we sang as children, "London Bridge Is Falling Down."

The Tower of London, an ancient structure with historical relics and related stories and strange costumes of the Yeomen of the Guard, or "Beefeaters," carried us back to the distant past. The Nelson Monument in Trafalgar Square; Piccadilly Circus; Scotland Yard, police headquarters; Number 10 Downing Street, residence of the Prime Minister; and Haymarket, the street in the center of the theater district, were points of interest to be remembered from my first sight of London. I saw a variety show that featured a Scottish bagpipe band. I also saw a moving picture that was, as might be guessed, a story of the war.

The Red Cross arranged trips to Oxford and to Stratford-on-Avon, both northwest of London. We went by bus and were on secondary, or country, roads part of the time. This allowed us to see a bit of rural England, including pastures, sheep, cottages with thatched roofs, orchards, gardens and villages with the composed look of maturity.

Our guide at Oxford University was the daughter of one of the eminent professors. She rode her bicycle from one college to another, waiting at each stop to give information concerning what we saw. The attractive, gray buildings were usually around a quadrangular, green, well-tended lawn. At the center of the building on the lower floor was the dignified dining hall, hallowed with tradition, with oak panels, exposed beams and old portraits honoring the teachers of previous generations. Faculty tables were on a higher level than those of the students.

Our guide could not give the exact date when the university was founded, but its history goes back more than eight hundred years. University, Balliol, Merton, Exeter, Oriel, Queens, New, Lincoln, All Souls, Magdalen, Brasenose, Corpus Christi and Christ Church were some of the older colleges to which our guide directed us. At Christ Church she showed a room that had been occupied by John Wesley, who was a student and later a tutor at Oxford. She also guided us to a chapel with a pulpit that was used by Wesley, founder of the Methodist Church.

In Stratford-on-Avon, we went first to the house where William Shakespeare was born. Then we walked through the fields to a thatched-roof cottage in a garden of roses, the home of Anne Hathaway, who became Shakespeare's wife. I went to the home of their first child, Susanna, who married John Hall, a physician of reputation. It was a sunny day and there were many small boats on the Avon as I walked on a path in the beautiful area through which the river flowed.

The Shakespeare Memorial, which includes a theater, is on

the river bank above the Holy Trinity Church. Inside the church I saw where the great poet and playwright and his wife are buried in the chancel. I had to rush back to the bus, but hoped to return to Stratford some day and perhaps see a play written by the man who made this quiet English town world famous.

Stonehenge, an ancient monument eight miles north of Salisbury, appeared to be a jumble of huge rocks when first seen from a distance. Approaching it, I saw that the stones had been arranged as circles within circles, although many were missing or fallen. What remained had the appearance of a ruined temple. The stones were rough-cut but accurately placed. The thirty originally in the outer circle seemed to be about twenty feet high and enclosed an area one hundred feet wide. Smaller blocks had been placed transversely on top of these to form a complete circle.

Scientists have estimated that Stonehenge was built approximately four thousand years ago. Near its center is a flat block of sandstone, fifteen feet long, which was probably an altar. A nearby stone marker, eighty yards east of the altar, was said to cast a shadow on it at dawn on June 24. Some think that Stonehenge was related to sun worship. Why it was built is unknown, but it was supposed to be connected with the Druids.

I rode the last part of the way to Stonehenge in a U.S. Army truck with several soldiers. They were laughing at the driver because of his tendency to drive on the wrong side of the road, because in England the custom was to go to the left. "It is the first time that he has driven in this country," they explained. On the way back I rode in a truck with some British soldiers and they, too, were kidding the driver. "Why?" I asked. "He never drove before today," one of them informed me.

Finally the day for leaving England came and we were taken to the ship on which we would sail home. It was a very large one, over a thousand feet long—the largest I had ever seen. Then we saw the name. It was the *Queen Mary*. We would have plenty of company. A whole infantry division and many other units were on board, comprising over thirty thousand people altogether, we were told. There were about a dozen decks on this great ship and at night nearly all available space was filled with sleeping soldiers.

The *Queen Mary*, not in a convoy, got us to New York in five days. Two weeks had been required for us to cross the Atlantic in the other direction nearly three years before victory in Europe. Japan's surrender had been accepted on August 14, 1945, Washington, D.C., time. The great war was over. We looked forward to all that peace had been promising as a new era began.

The greatest war in history had ended and from it I had returned, with battle stars but no visible scars, as a medical officer of the 119th Evacuation Hospital. The Statue of Liberty and the skyline of New York "never looked so good" and fresh milk served with doughnuts at the Red Cross canteen on the wharf "never tasted so good" to us. Some soldiers joyously patted the ground of their native land. Large banners and the music of a noted band welcoming us were the icing on my cake that unforgettable day when, by telephone, I got to talk with Mildred for the first time in nearly three years.

Our reunion was in Atlanta, where she was waiting for me with Edwin when I arrived from Camp Kilmer, from which I had departed for duty overseas and to which the army had returned me. Those returned for demobilization were sent from Kilmer to processing centers near their homes. At Fort McPherson, Georgia, my active army duty ended, I became a civilian again and was reintroduced to my young son. "Edwin, this is your daddy," his mother said. "Will you buy me a BB gun?" he asked me. Thus began the renewal of normal relationships in our little family. He referred to me as "That Man" for a while.

We went to Albertville, saw old friends and on Sunday attended church service at which, it so happened, someone in the audience was being welcomed home by the preacher. I wondered who the local hero was but was not very attentive to the tribute being paid this individual who had returned after serving his country in the war. As Reverend Wilkins talked, I was aware of the presence of many who were members of the congregation in years gone by. I relaxed while reminiscing, but hearing my name called snapped me to attention and the realities of the moment. It was such a surprise that I was not sure what was expected until Mildred nudged me and whispered, "You are supposed to go up and shake hands with him."

An army hospital of five hundred beds in Jackson, Mississippi, was being converted into a Veterans Administration hospital and I was offered the opportunity of organizing the Surgical Service and serving as its first chief. It would be larger than the others that I had inaugurated and the chief medical officer was to be Dr. Boykin, with whom I had worked in Memphis. I decided to accept the position instead of returning to the well-established hospital in Montgomery.

Our quarters in Jackson consisted of a wartime barracks building on the reservation that was previously occupied by thirty members of the Women's Army Corps (WAC) on duty at the hospital. It was furnished by the quartermaster. The toilet facilities were left as they were. We had two shower rooms with several heads in each, six commodes and a row of washbasins. In the kitchen was a big range of the type used in army messes. Our temporary home was not elegant but there was an abundance of the necessities and the rent was modest. We had access to a gymnasium and swimming pool.

Dr. Boykin and I swapped stories of our experiences after leaving Memphis. His war service had been in the Pacific. "I did not want to spend the rest of my life explaining why I was not in it," he said. "When war was declared I went to the recruiting office for doctors in Washington and was told that if I would volunteer I would be commissioned as a major and in six months would be promoted to lieutenant colonel and that was the way it happened. Later I was promoted to full colonel and came out of it as a chicken colonel but I'm through with the army now.

"All the doctors in veterans hospitals were put into army uniforms and given ranks comparable to their professional positions in the civil service, so if I had not volunteered I would have been a colonel anyhow and would have stayed at home but, of course, I did not know that at the time. They already had you and didn't have to offer you any inducements to serve, as they did me."

A group of young doctors was assigned to the hospital for training in various specialties following their internships. In addition to the usual work as chief of the Surgical Service, it was my duty to institute a training program for those aspiring to be surgeons. The administrative functions of my office became more burdensome as I looked to the future. Administrators in the top positions of the V.A. generally had little contact with the patients.

Dr. Rosenkranz, who was at Memphis while I was there, was transferred to the new hospital in Jackson when it opened and was on the medical staff. He and Mrs. Rosenkranz lived in one of the hospital buildings. He specialized in the treatment of metabolic diseases, particularly diabetes, and his hobby was numismatics. We had the pleasure of examining his collection of rare coins after a dinner together.

Ann Brooks, Chief Surgical Nurse, was happy to be back in her home state. She was in charge of the operating rooms, the same position she had held in Montgomery before volunteering for war duty as an army nurse. The hospital in which she had served overseas was located in England. We were pleased to be with her again but were saddened by something she had to tell us. "Jeff, Dr. Pafford's son, was killed at the end of the war in the Battle of the Bulge."

Dr. Yeatts was still in the army on the medical service of a hospital on a remote island in the South Pacific. He wrote, "The native boys working in our mess are becoming more civilized. They wear loin cloths now."

We seemed at first to be a curiosity, living as we did, to the people of Jackson. On Sunday afternoons they would drive slowly by our quarters and look us over. I was on duty every day and subject to call for emergency problems at night so there was little time for visiting. However, we made friends in this progressive capital city and enjoyed their hospitality. The area offered many advantages, but Mildred and I had decided to make our home closer to New England, from where she came, and also convenient to most of my family.

"Dr. Bright is dead," Boykin said as we talked of those who were with us in Memphis. "We were at a party one night when he got an urgent call from the hospital. He hurried to get there; his car skidded into a telephone pole and he was unconscious when the police arrived. They wrongly guessed that it was from drinking and took him to the station. I learned what happened, got him into a hospital and found that he was bleeding from a fracture of the skull. An operation was done but did not save him."

John, our second son, was born in the Baptist Hospital about ten months after our arrival in Jackson. The pediatrician advised us to take him home before the usual time for discharge and prescribed baby-food meat as part of his diet, a new measure at that time. He tolerated it well and progressed satisfactorily, almost uneventfully. One day while he was sleeping, I looked to see if everything was all right and found him covered with ants, a stream of which had entered the room by climbing a pipe near his crib. Fortunately they had not hurt him.

The practical nurse that we employed for a short time was

very helpful. She was well trained, efficient and pleasant. "After I started nursing, I heard that it would be better for me in Chicago," she related to us. "I went to work but did not like the people or living there and did not stay very long." She enjoyed her neat white frame home surrounded by a yard almost filled with fragrant flowers in all colors.

For many years government hospitals had provided me with the means to practice surgery with office, nurses, equipment, consultants, a steady flow of patients and without financial worries. However, this was as a unit in an organization and I was often unable to make choices that would have been available to me otherwise. Working conditions were generally satisfactory; there were Civil Service benefits; and those with whom I was associated were, as a rule, likable, honorable people. However, after consideration, I concluded that private practice offered certain attractions and more independence, in some respects. So I gave notice of my intention to resign after the end of the year.

Edwin had been enjoying the year we lived on the hospital reservation, which was enclosed by a high wire fence. There were children of other families to play with, including Tommy Boykin, his best friend, and always with him was our faithful dog, Snowball. Mildred could tell where the children were by seeing the dog, which somehow would manage to stay in sight of them and the house, too.

Snowball showed a special interest in John from the first time she sniffed and peeked at him. She might have been called a mongrel by some, but she was a pretty dog with black spots on her long white hair. We did not have room in our small car to take her with us when we left or a suitable place for her where we were going. Therefore, one sad day we reluctantly returned Snowball to the kind man who had given her to us.

Edwin had enjoyed an only-child status for five years when John arrived and some adjustments had to be made. He wanted a baby sister. When I informed him, "You have a little brother," he made no comment, so I asked, "What do you think?" His reaction seemed important.

"I don't like it," he said, with emphasis on the "don't." But in time he did like it and took great pride in his little brother.

After years of a demanding private practice in Washington, D.C., I served as an advisor on scientific matters for an agency there. This enabled us to enjoy many vacation trips. Mildred and I found that we could do this without always being extravagant and that indiscretion is not necessary for pleasure.

"See America First" seemed to be a good slogan. We visited, by auto, all the states and most of their capitals before going to Europe. We drove over this great country from Key West, Florida, to Fairbanks, Alaska, and from Acapulco, Mexico, to St. John's, Newfoundland. We took one or both of our boys with us whenever possible. While fully appreciating the opportunity for more home life now, we also anticipate traveling throughout the world.

A doctor sees many new medicines and treatment methods introduced and then replaced, after a period of time and trials, by newer ones that may be better. Too, he observes numerous changes in other spheres all around him and, with hope, looks forward to tomorrow.